LETTERS OF THE
WRIGHT
BROTHERS

LETTERS OF THE WRIGHT BROTHERS

LETTERS OF WILBUR, ORVILLE AND KATHARINE WRIGHT
IN THE ROYAL AERONAUTICAL SOCIETY LIBRARY

EDITED BY
BRIAN RIDDLE AND COLIN SINNOTT

TEMPUS

Frontispiece: 1. Orville, Katharine and Wilbur Wright.

First published 2003

PUBLISHED IN THE UNITED KINGDOM BY:
Tempus Publishing Ltd
The Mill, Brimscombe Port
Stroud, Gloucestershire GL5 2QG

PUBLISHED IN THE UNITED STATES OF AMERICA BY:
Tempus Publishing Inc.
2 Cumberland Street
Charleston, SC 29401

British Library Cataloguing in Publication Data.
A catalogue record for this book is available from the British Library.

ISBN 0 7524 2584 6

Typesetting and origination by Tempus Publishing.
Printed in Great Britain by Midway Colour Print, Wiltshire.

CONTENTS

2. Orville and Wilbur Wright.

PREFACE

Since its formation in 1866 the Royal Aeronautical Society (and under its earlier title as the Aeronautical Society of Great Britain) has been recording developments in aeronautics, aviation and aircraft/aerospace technology through its meetings, lectures and publications. From its foundation the Society has been acquiring material for its Library, which now has one of the world's major collections of material on the evolution of man's attempts to conquer the dream of flight. Spanning from ancient to modern times, there are books, pamphlets, journals, reports, letters, photographs, lithographs, posters, paintings and other material reflecting the wide-ranging aeronautical interests of the Society. The Society's website (www.aerosociety.com) gives a detailed description of the Society's holdings in its 'Library' section pages.

Many of the early members of the Society and their descendants had the foresight to leave for posterity their books and papers to the Society. Amongst those of other aviation pioneers, the Society's Library holds extensive files of original correspondence (letters, cablegrams, patent applications, etc.) between Wilbur, Orville and Katharine Wright and early members of the Society and their associates. Much of this material was presented to the Society by these early members and their relations, in particular by Griffith Brewer (the Society's President 1940–42). Through his work as the Wrights' patents agent, Brewer became a close friend of the Wright brothers and in particular of their sister Katharine, as did Alec Ogilvie, an early pilot of Wright gliders and powered aircraft.

9

Wilbur Wright's first technical paper, entitled 'Angle of Incidence', was published by the Society in *The Aeronautical Journal*, Vol.5, July 1901, and Octave Chanute and others kept the Society's members informed of the Wrights' aeronautical experiments. In his Presidential Address delivered to the Society on 4 December 1902 (published in *The Aeronautical Journal*, Vol.7, January 1903), Major B.F.S. Baden-Powell observed, 'In America, Mr Wilbur Wright and his brother have been making wonderful progress with gliding machines...' The first detailed account by the Society of the Wrights' maiden powered flight was published in *The Aeronautical Journal*, Vol.8, April 1904. It was based upon 'a true and authentic account of these experiments which had been communicated to the Society by Orville Wright'.

In total there are over 110 original letters from the Wrights in the Society's Library collections, with a large number of associated cablegrams. Together they form a unique record of the growing appreciation of the brothers' achievement, their relations with other early aviation pioneers and also an insight into relations within the Wright family.

On 17 December 1903 the Wright brothers achieved the world's first manned, sustained, controlled, powered flight in a heavier-than-air machine, with Orville Wright at the controls of the Wright Flyer. In 1953, on the fiftieth anniversary of the Wright brothers' flight, the Royal Aeronautical Society devoted a whole issue of its journal to the Wright brothers – 'The Wright Brothers and the Royal Aeronautical Society: a Survey and a Tribute'. This was published in the *Journal of the Royal Aeronautical Society*, Vol.57, December 1953; it included extracts from a selection of the letters in an article by J.L. Pritchard.

The year 2003 is the hundredth anniversary of the Wright brothers' first flight. Some years ago I believed it would be appropriate for the Royal Aeronautical Society – the oldest aeronautical society in the world – to contribute to the centenary celebrations by publishing the texts of the Library's Wright letters in full. This would add to existing knowledge about the Wrights, for much of this material has never been published before.

The Wright correspondence consists of letters, postcards and cablegrams, some of it typed, but much in handwriting which sometimes needed to be deciphered. The correspondence is arranged chronologically in this volume. Explanatory notes are added to clarify and describe the people, events and publications referred to in the letters.

The texts are illustrated by a selection of photographs, mostly taken from the extensive photographic collections in the care of the Library. The source of other reproduced photographs is acknowledged in the List of Illustrations.

In the preparation of this volume for publication the valued assistance of Dr Colin Sinnott, CEng., FRAeS in editing the letters and my explanatory notes is gratefully acknowledged, as are the services of Jean Wright and Shumi Syed of the Royal Aeronautical Society, who transcribed all the letters (including the Wrights' occasional variant spellings) onto an electronic database.

A number of others have kindly contributed with their comments and suggestions. The assistance of Ken Harman, Brian Elliott, Bill Croydon and Captain John Cox, DFC, FRAeS is acknowledged. Steve van Dulken of the British Library and Gill Jackson of the Royal Society Library were of particular help in identifying references to patents and scientific publications not held in the Royal Aeronautical Society Library.

The Royal Aeronautical Society has obtained approval for publication from the trustees of the Wright Family Fund (www.wrightbrothers2003.com), and the support of the US Centennial of Flight Commission (www.centennialofflight.gov) and the USAF's Airforce History and Museums Program's Centennial of Flight Office (www.centennialofflight.af.mil). Their support is gratefully acknowledged.

Brian Riddle
Librarian, Royal Aeronautical Society

I

THE POWER OF FLIGHT
AND ITS DEMONSTRATION:
JANUARY 1904–MAY 1912

3. The world's first manned, sustained, controlled, powered flight in a heavier-than-air machine with Orville Wright at the controls of the Wright Flyer, Wilbur Wright standing to the right.

On 17 December 1903, the Wright brothers — Wilbur (1867–1912) and Orville (1871–1948) — achieved the world's first manned, sustained, controlled, powered flight in a heavier-than-air machine, with Orville Wright at the controls of the Wright Flyer. Their achievement was founded on years of wind-tunnel experiments on wing surfaces of various configurations, and with their own kite and glider designs. These they flew from the four hills of Kill Devil, near the village of Kitty Hawk, North Carolina, selected by the Wrights for its favourable winds. From 1900 to 1903 they would travel there from their home in Dayton, Ohio.

A few weeks after the momentous first flight, Wilbur Wright wrote the following letter to Lawrence Hargrave. Born in Britain, Hargrave (1850–1915) had emigrated to Australia in 1865, and corresponded with many of those who were seriously pursuing the science of aeronautics. Hargrave's invention of the box-kite structure in 1893 (later reflected in the early Voisin aircraft designs) was a highlight of his aeronautical experiments with various kite shapes over a number of years.

Dayton, Ohio.
January 28, 1904.

Mr Lawrence Hargrave

Dear Sir:

Your letter of some months ago came while my brother and I were in camp at Kitty Hawk, which is nearly a thousand miles from here. We were there from the latter part of September till almost Christmas time. We continued our experiments with our 1902 gliding machine, giving special attention to attempts at soaring on the face of the Kill Devil hill in winds of 20 to 30 miles an hour. We frequently stood almost still for a half minute at a time, but as it was necessary at times to move forward a little in maneuvering we would after a time pass out of the rising current. As we did not feel it safe to allow the machine to float back again, we were of course compelled to land. The longest flight was one minute and twelve seconds.

Most of our time was taken up with the construction of a machine of 510 sq. ft on which we mounted a gasoline motor. The total weight of the apparatus was about 600lbs, and including the operator, 745lbs. The machine was finished so late in the year that we made only such trials as were necessary to determine whether the machine possessed the power of flight, and a capacity of control such as would make it reasonably safe in operation. As imaginative newspapermen have sent out some very incorrect statements regarding these trials, I take pleasure in sending you a statement which we have ourselves given out. When the warm weather returns we shall try to obtain further practice, and make longer flights.

I presume that this time of year is much more favorable for experimenting on your side of the earth than on this and that we may soon hope to hear of your further progress.

With kindest regards, in which my brother joins me, I am,

Yours Truly

Wilbur Wright

4. Lawrence Hargrave and James Swaine experimenting with four man-lifting kites, based on Hargrave's invention of the box-kite structure.

Within a month of undertaking their first flights on the North Carolina dunes, the Wright brothers began construction of a new, larger, more powerful Flyer in January 1904. Its flight trials were made at a new site much closer to their home: Huffman Prairie, located eight miles outside the city of Dayton, Ohio.

An early member of the Aeronautical Society of Great Britain, Sidney H. Hollands, corresponded with Hargrave and other early experimenters, and was put in contact with the Wright brothers by Octave Chanute. Chanute (1832–1910), who had made his reputation as a civil engineer, was an early designer of man-carrying gliders. The Wrights first contacted Chanute in 1900, after they had read his book, Progress in Flying Machines *(New York, 1894). This was a compilation of articles on the growing science of aeronautics that Chanute had published in* The Railroad and Engineering Journal *from October 1891 onwards. It was to become a key work in the development of early aviation.*

Wright Cycle Company
1127 West Third Street
Dayton, Ohio
May 31, 1904

Mr Sidney H. Hollands,
London

Dear Sir,

Your letter to us, sent through Mr Chanute, was received some time ago, and would have been promptly answered but for the fact that we were expecting almost daily to be able to send you some account of more trials of our flyer. However, we have already been so long delayed that we shall not wait longer in answering.

We expect to be able to make a trial of our new flyer within the next ten days. It is almost an exact copy of the one we used at Kitty Hawk, NC, last December, but is so constructed that it can be more easily torn down for shipment. We have also slightly changed the shape of the surfaces for the purpose of higher efficiency at high speeds. This, of course, will somewhat increase the difficulties in getting started, on account of the higher initial velocity required; but we do not anticipate any serious trouble on this account.

Your letter of last year, of which you write, asking for photographs, was not received. We are not yet ready to make public the details of our flyer, and so have been compelled to refuse all requests for photographs; but we will be pleased to furnish you information, from time to time, of our progress. Thanking you for your most welcome letter, we remain,

Respectfully yours

W. & O. Wright

Octave Chanute helped to organise the aeronautical competition that was part of the 1904 St Louis Universal Exposition. In the following letter, Wilbur Wright refers to the October 1904 demonstration flights by William Avery of a new variant of Chanute's 1896 biplane glider, and to John J. Montgomery's tandem-wing glider. He also makes the first of many references to Samuel Pierpont Langley (1834–1906). Langley's tandem monoplane Aerodrome *crashed into the Potomac River south-east of Washington for the second time on 8 December 1903, a few days before the Wright brothers' first successful flight. At the time Langley was the Secretary of the Smithsonian Institution, and the Institution had funded his aeronautical researches. After Langley's death, the Smithsonian promoted Langley's aeronautical achievements over those of the Wright brothers. This was to be a source of contention for many years to come.*

5. Langley *Aerodrome* on the houseboat in the Potomac prior to being launched unsuccessfully, 7 October 1903.

Wright Cycle Company
Dayton, Ohio
July 16 1905

Mr Sidney H. Hollands

Dear Sir

We have received your letter with much pleasure. Our experiments were continued during a considerable part of the summer and autumn of last year with quite favorable results. It is not our desire, however, that too much interest in our work should be publicly aroused at present, and accordingly can not make any extended reports until the experimental period is past. In 1904 we succeeded for the first time in making a complete circle and landing at the starting point. On two different occasions the flight extended over nearly four rounds of the field, a distance of nearly three miles. The duration of the flight was five minutes and four seconds in one case, and four minutes and fifty seconds in the other. The speed was about 35 miles an hour. The new problems previously unsuspected, which are met at almost every step, consume much time in developing a machine for practical use, but the critical points have been passed, and within a reasonable time we expect to have the machine ready to present to the world for some serviceable purpose.

The articles in 'Flying' were read at the time with interest, and it would please us to see some experiments along that line to see whether it would offer any advantage over gliding as a method of practice.

We hear from Mr Chanute, now and then, and at last report he was well, though he had a troublesome attack of the influenza last winter. You have probably seen some account of the experiment which Mr Avery made with a Chanute glider at St Louis last summer. We have no recent word regarding Prof. Langley, but think he has abandoned the effort to fly his machine. It was evidently too frail to be of real value for experimental purposes. There is much more interest taken in aviation than for some years past, but except the experiments of Mr Montgomery, little of the work is of much value.

Yours truly
Wilbur Wright

Major Baden Fletcher Smyth Baden-Powell (1860–1937) was an early enthusiast of the military potential of aeronautics. In 1897 he founded The Aeronautical Journal, *the technical journal of the Aeronautical Society of Great Britain, of which he was in turn Honorary Secretary and then President.*

After 1905, the Wrights did not fly again until May 1908, concentrating their efforts on improving the aircraft engine's performance and in selling their invention to interested parties, but their achievements with the 1905 Wright Flyer III inspired aircraft development in Europe. The Brazilian pioneer of European aviation, Alberto Santos-Dumont (1873–1932), after some years of experimenting with free-flight balloons, built the first of his fourteen airships in 1898. On 19 October 1901 he became the first man to circle the Eiffel Tower in his No.6 airship, and was to continue his airship numbering sequence when, inspired by the Wright brothers, he moved into aircraft construction. In his No.14-bis design Santos-Dumont made the first aeroplane flight in Europe on 23 October 1906 at Bagatelle, Bois de Boulogne, Paris.

Wright Cycle Company
Dayton, Ohio
January 12th, 1906

Major Baden-Powell,
London

Dear Sir,

Your letter of December 18th has been received. We thank you for the kind expressions of felicitation.

Our first motor flyer, that of 1903, was in many respects like our later gliders, but of quite different construction in details as is required in a motor machine in order to withstand the shocks of landing. The landings of the glider were rarely at speeds of more than ten or fifteen miles, while those of the motor machine are often forty to fifty miles. We have also changed somewhat the construction and shape of the surfaces in order to secure a higher efficiency. We had not experimented long with the power flyer when we began meeting with difficulties that we had never encountered in gliding flight, so that we soon saw that our means of control were not sufficient. The machine has been passing through one change after another, and it was not until the latter part of September that we had all of the dangerous features overcome. From that on progress was rapid, and it is now only a matter of perfecting the mechanical details to produce a flyer that will travel hundreds of miles in a single flight.

In looking over our records of our experiments of the last three years, we find that we have made 160 attempts to put the machine into flight. A number of these were failures in getting sufficient initial speed to support the machine when it left the track. But we find that we have averaged just one mile for every attempt, nevertheless. Our last flight of 1905 covered a distance equal to that of all the flights of 1904 combined, which were 105 in number.

We are sorry that we are not able to give a more detailed description of our machine, but business considerations forbid. We have already closed a contract for governmental use in one country and have inquiries from several other countries.

Very respectfully yours,

Orville Wright

Wright Cycle Company
Dayton Ohio
October 16, 1906

Major B. Baden-Powell,
London

Dear Sir:

Your very nice letter of June 23rd was duly received. We do not contemplate making any further experimental flights, as we do not think it necessary. Our time in the last year has been occupied in experiments with our motor, which we have greatly improved. Through our lack of experience in building gasoline engines, our first motors did not develop more than half of what they should have developed. But our work of the past year has been devoted more especially to the development of a reliable motor, one that can be depended upon to run continuously for long flights. Our new motors will enable us to carry two men and supplies of fuel for flights of several hundred miles

We have noticed considerable discussion of aviation in the English automobile papers, and that a number of persons are busily engaged in experiments. We presume that Santos Dumont will soon be ready for another trial of his machine.

Trusting that we will soon have the pleasure of hearing more of your experiments, we are,

Very truly yours

Wright Brothers

6. Santos-Dumont 14-*bis* at Bagatelle, the first aeroplane flight in Europe, 23 October 1906.

Note that the letterhead is no longer that of the Wright Cycle Company.

WRIGHT BROTHERS
1127 West Third Street
Dayton Ohio
January 31, 1907

Mr Sidney H. Hollands,
Sheffield, England.

Dear Sir:

Your letter of November 24th was duly received. We were pleased to hear from you again.

We have made no further out-door experiments since October 1905, and consequently have nothing very interesting to report at the present time. We have been devoting all of our time to the building of new machines and to business matters.

7. Wilbur Wright – from a series of caricature postcards of early aviation pioneers by César Giris, produced by A. Noyer of Paris, c.1909.

The propellers we have been using give us such good results that it is not probable that it would pay us to look for anything better. What we most need now is a perfectly reliable motor that is able to run continuously for hours at a time. We think that our new motors will give much better results than the one we used in our last flights. Our new engine weighs 160lbs not including water, tanks or any of the other necessary equipment. Complete with water, etc., it will weigh about 250lbs. It will produce from 25 to 30 horse power. This is only about two-thirds the weight per horse power of our old motors. If we find that we can make it more reliable by building it heavier, we shall not hesitate to do so; for reliability is of a great deal more importance that lightness.

Very truly yours

Wright Brothers

In May 1908 Wilbur Wright travelled to France. His demonstrations of the flight control of the Wright A at the Hunaudières racecourse, near Le Mans, and then at nearby Auvours, and later at Pau, revolutionised the development of European aviation.

8. Griffith Brewer and Wilbur Wright after their flight at Camp d'Auvours, 8 October 1908. Later that day Wilbur took Hon. C.S. Rolls, Frank Hedges Butler and Major B.F.S. Baden-Powell on flights in the Wright A. Baden-Powell immediately wrote to Colonel Fullerton of the Aeronautical Society of Great Britain – 'We have all been flying!'. His postcard showed Wilbur Wright flying at Camp d'Auvours.

An amateur balloonist, Griffith Brewer (1867–1948), was among a group of members of the Aeronautical Society of Great Britain who travelled to Le Mans to see the Wright machine. He became closely acquainted with Wilbur Wright and later with the Wright family. On 8 October 1908 Brewer became the first Englishman to fly as a passenger in a Wright aircraft. He became the Wrights' British patent agent the following year.

The silver stop-watch mentioned by Wilbur Wright, and used on his European demonstration flights, is now in the care of the Royal Aeronautical Society.

Le Mans
26 Sept. 1908

My dear Mr Brewer,

I have your very nice letter of this 18th September inst., and also the watch by the hand of Mr Butler. I scarcely know which I appreciate the more.

My brother and I have often said to each other that regardless of any other recompense for our work the fact that it had been the means of bringing us the friendship of several exceptionally congenial spirits was alone worth the effort. I am sure that when my brother comes to know you he will feel the same attraction that I have felt.

I thank you most sincerely for your kindness.

Yours truly

Wilbur Wright

The following letter was written on the headed paper of Hart O. Berg, an American sales representative of Flint and Company in England, France and Russia, to whom the Wrights had assigned the management of their foreign business.

9. Wilbur Wright flying the Wright A at Pau, January 1909. This photograph was presented to Griffith Brewer, signed by Wilbur and Orville Wright.

HART O. BERG
32 avenue des Champs-Elysées
Paris
2nd November 1908

Major F.S. Baden Powell
32 Princes Gate
London S.W.

Dear Major Baden-Powell,

I have your letters of last month, and also the book which you were so kind to send me. I find it contains much information, which I sometimes find it difficult to obtain when away from home.

I am not certain as to when I can get over to England, still I certainly hope to be able to stop there for a few days before I return to America.

Very faithfully yours
Wilbur Wright

At a meeting of the Council of the Aeronautical Society of Great Britain held on 9 November 1908, it was decided to award the Society's first Gold Medal to the Wright Brothers – 'In recognition of their distinguished services to aeronautical science'.

Le Mans
3 Dec., 1908
[To Major Baden-Powell]

Dear Sir

I have your letter of November 21 and beg to request that you will convey to the Aeronautical Society my most sincere thanks for the honors, which it has accorded to my brother and myself.

It would give one great pleasure to be present at your meeting next week if it were practicable to do so, but my engagements make it very difficult to be in London at that time.

I am hoping that I will be able to persuade my brother to spend a few months in Europe in the near future, and that we may have the pleasure of making a visit to England together before the winter is over.

Yours very truly
Wilbur Wright

10. Wilbur Wright flying the Wright A at Camp d'Auvours, 18 December 1908.

Le Mans
21, Dec. 1908
[To Major Baden-Powell,]

Dear Sir

I have your letter of Dec. 12 1908 and would reply that whatever course you prefer as to the delivery of the medal would be satisfactory to me.

I may say that I am expecting my brother to arrive in Europe soon after the beginning of the New Year and that we will make a visit to England together before our return to America about the first of April.

It would suit me very well if you should hold the medal till that time.

Yours very truly
Wilbur Wright

The following letter was written to Alec Ogilvie. Alexander (Alec) Ogilvie (1882–1962) first met Wilbur Wright in December 1908 at Le Mans. He had travelled there 'to learn as much as possible about the design and construction of an aeroplane before setting off to build one of my own' ('*Some Aspects of Aeronautical Research*', The Aeronautical Journal, *October 1922).*

Le Mans
22 Dec. 1908

Dear Sir

I have your letter of the 18th Dec.

Arrangements are not yet completed for the manufacture of our flyers in England, but we expect to be able to have some machines ready before the summer season comes.

I will probably be in England in a month or two and will be pleased to see you.

Yours Truly
Wilbur Wright

In December 1908 a group of members of the Aero Club of the United Kingdom, led by Lord Royston, travelled to Camp d'Auvours, near Le Mans, with the aim of securing the British patent rights to the Wrights' invention.

Hotel du Dauphin
Place de la République
Le Mans
4 January 1909

My dear Mr Brewer,

I received your letter of 23 Dec. some days ago but have been unable to find opportunity to answer till now. I have finished my season at Le Mans and today brought the machine into town purposely to dismantle it.

As to the proposition of Lord Royston and his friends I do not feel able to give a definite answer immediately. My brother is just leaving for Europe and I wish to have a general consultation with him before taking up the English Mission. It is probable that we will wish to come over to England to personally look over the site selection, before committing ourselves to any particular place. I will write you further when I have seen my brother.

My best regards to Mrs Brewer and family
Yours truly
Wilbur Wright

11. At Camp d'Auvours – Wilbur Wright examining the engine of the Delage which won the *Coupe des Voiturettes* at Dieppe, 1908.

On 14 January 1909 Wilbur Wright moved to the warmer region of Pau in the south of France, and was soon joined by Orville and their sister Katharine who had recently arrived from the United States.

Grand Hôtel Gassion,
Pau
14 Jan. 1909

My dear Mr Brewer

I received your letter a few days ago and was very sorry to hear that you were not well. However I must confess that this thought that it may be the means of bringing about a visit from you at Pau, somewhat alleviates my sorrow.

I sincerely hope that your recovery may be rapid and that I may have the pleasure of seeing Mrs Brewer and yourself soon.

Yours very truly
Wilbur Wright

12. The Wright A at Pau, showing the starting pylon, 1909.

Colonel John Davidson Fullerton (1853–1927) was Hon. Secretary of the Aeronautical Society of Great Britain from 1907–09.

Orville refers to F.W. Lanchester's paper 'The Wright and Voisin Types of Flying Machine: a Comparison' which was originally read before the Society on 8 December 1908 and published in The Aeronautical Journal, *January 1909.*

Grand Hôtel Gassion
Pau
Feb. 9th 1909

Colonel J.W. Fullerton
53 Victoria Street
London S.W.

Dear Sir:

Your letter of February 4th is received, for which we thank you. You may direct the Journal to our address at 7 Hawthorn St., Dayton, Ohio, USA. The January number sent to us at Le Mans has not yet been received.

As to the Lanchester paper on the Wright and Voisin types of Flying Machines, I do not think a discussion with him in this subject would be of any

13. The Hon. C.S. Rolls and Cecil S. Grace on their Short-Wright biplanes at Eastchurch on the Isle of Sheppey, 28 March 1910.

use, since there would be no agreement as to facts on which to base a discussion. He discredits our assertions as to our own machine. The performance of machines themselves will give the best answer to his paper.

Thank you for your very kind offer of an opportunity to reply, I beg to remain,

Very truly yours,

Orville Wright.

Your letter was addressed to my brother Wilbur, but he has asked me to answer, since his work keeps him away from facilities for attending to his correspondence. OW.

The flying demonstrations of the Wright A in France resulted in a number of enquiries for replicas of the Wright aircraft. On Brewer's recommendation, the firm of Short Brothers was approached in January 1909 to construct the first six aircraft orders on behalf of the Wrights. After years of experience in the manufacture of balloons, the new partnership of Short Brothers was registered at Battersea in November 1908, with its initial capital subscribed in equal shares by the three brothers – Horace Leonard (1872–1917), Albert Eustace (1875–1932) and Hugh Oswald (1883–1969). Again on Brewer's intervention, Shorts bought a tract of marshland between Leysdown and

Shellness on the Isle of Sheppey in Kent, and erected a factory to build the Wright aircraft.

The production order for the first six Short-Wright biplanes was distributed as follows, all the gentlemen concerned being members of the Aero Club of the United Kingdom and of the the Aeronautical Society of Great Britain (with the exception of Egerton):

Short-Wright No.1 – Hon. C.S. Rolls;
No.2 – Alec Ogilvie;
No.3 – Francis K. McClean;
No.4 – Hon. Maurice Egerton;
No.5 – Percy R. Grace (and flown by Cecil S. Grace);
No.6 – Hon. C.S. Rolls; this aircraft was later purchased by Ogilvie from the executors of Rolls' estate.

The construction of the Short-Wright biplanes was based upon a series of detailed sketches of the Wright A at Pau in February 1909. These were made on graph-lined paper by Horace Short, and are in a notebook which is in the care of the Royal Aeronautical Society Library.

Pau
20 Feb. 1909
[To Alec Ogilvie]

Dear Sir,

Your letter of 30 Jan. received but I have been so busy that correspondence has been much neglected.

My brother and I after discussing the English business have reached the conclusion that it would not be satisfactory to us to have machines built on a royalty basis unless the number of machines guaranteed was very much greater than we could expect any one to be willing to guarantee. We would prefer to sell the business outright or to run it ourselves. Such an arrangement as you suggest would make it difficult to make permanent plans on a large scale.

With kind regards.
Yours truly
Wilbur Wright

14. The Wright A at Pau. Wilbur Wright made a flight of twenty-eight minutes in the Wright A in the presence of King Alphonso of Spain on 20 February 1909.

Hôtel Meyerbeer
rond–point des Champs–Elysées
Paris
18th Mar. 1909

Dear Mr Brewer:

I am sending inclosed a check for £200, for which I will be very much obliged to you if you will send it to Messrs Short Brothers. I can not find their address, having mislaid their card.

In regard to the machine for Mr McLean, the first and second machines are already taken, but we should like to enter his order for one of the other six now under construction

Very truly yours
Orville Wright

P.S. – I will be in Paris for a week or ten days. Wilbur will be here also next week.

George Crosland Taylor, an experimenter in aeronautics, was one of Lawrence Hargrave's most frequent correspondents.

Wilbur Wright refers to the accident to Orville in the Wright A on 17 September 1908 during the US Army's Signal Corps trials at Fort Meyer, just outside Washington. Lt Thomas E. Selfridge was killed while flying as a passenger.

In April 1909 Wilbur began a series of demonstration and training flights at Centocelle, near Rome, at the request of Italian military officials.

Paris
27 March 1909

Mr G. Crossland Taylor

Dear Sir

On my arrival in Paris last night I found your letter of 23 March forwarded from Pau. I am leaving Paris myself today so I presume we shall miss each other. My brother is here however and may be in the city for several days yet. He is recovering nicely from his accident but is not entirely well yet. He is at the Hotel Meyerbeer on Rond-Point, Champs Elysées.

I expect to return from Rome in about one month.

Yours very truly

Wilbur Wright

Comte Charles de Lambert (1865–1944), a French nobleman of Russian nationality, was a student pilot trained by the Wrights. He held the Aero Club de France's Brevet No. 8. Lord Montagu of Beaulieu was an early advocate of the military potential of aeroplanes and airships and was later to sit on the Parliamentary Aerial Defence Committee.

This letter also mentions the automatic stability device which the Wrights applied to patent in 1908; it was granted in 1913.

Paris
March 31 1909

Dear Mr Brewer:

Your letter of the 24th has been received. Many thanks for your trouble in forwarding the check to Messrs Short Bros.

We have made arrangements to have Mr Rolls taught by Count de Lambert (I believe he is number 6 on the list) but I am afraid it will be some months before he can receive the training, as Count de Lambert is now severely hand-icapped in having only one machine with which to do all his training. The weather at Pau is now so bad that no training is being done.

We will make the price in England correspond with the price set by the French Company, which is 25,000 frs (£5,000) for machine, training extra.

We lately received an order for the third machine. As this was already reserved for Mr McLean we are reserving #4 for this gentleman, if he wants it, #5 is therefore the best we can now promise to Lord Montagu, though there is a possibility he could have #4.

We received the reply of the British Patent office on automatic from Mr Thierry some days ago, and are now going over the cases cited.

Wilbur left for Rome day before yesterday; Katharine and I expect to follow him some time next week.

Thanking you for the trouble you have taken in our English business, I remain,

Very truly yours

Orville Wright

15. The presentation of the first Gold Medal of the Aeronautical Society of Great Britain to Wilbur and Orville Wright at the Institution of Civil Engineers, London, 3 May 1909.

In May 1909 Wilbur, Orville and Katharine Wright travelled to England. On 3 May 1909 Wilbur and Orville were presented with the first Gold Medal of the Aeronautical Society of Great Britain at a meeting of the Society held at the Institution of Civil Engineers, Great George Street, London. The presentation was preceded by a banquet at the Ritz Hotel given privately by the Society's Council in honour of Wilbur, Orville and Katharine. The following day the Wrights visited the Isle of Sheppey to inspect the Short Brothers factory at Shellbeach, and later had lunch at nearby Mussel Manor, close to the flying ground of the Aero Club of the United Kingdom. That evening the Aero Club hosted another banquet at the Ritz Hotel in honour of Wilbur and Orville, who had already been presented in France with the Aero Club's first Gold Medal.

The following cablegram is Katharine Wright's acceptance of her invitation to the banquet at the Ritz Hotel given by the Society's Council. The Wrights were to stay at Long's Hotel as guests of Brewer.

Paris, 2nd May 1909
To Council of Aeronautical Society London

Accept with many thanks, Longs Hotel New Bond Street
  Katharine Wright

Wright Brothers
1127 West Third Street
Dayton, Ohio
May 26, 1909

Dear Mr Brewer:

Your cable asking permission to contradict the report that we demand twelve thousand pounds from Tussard, for a machine, came yesterday. Our experience is that if we begin to contradict reports we will have more and more of them to contradict. We do not see that this report will do us any particular harm. It looks to us like an attempt to get some free advertising and, if we enter into controversy, it will only further that purpose. However, if you think the matter demands attention, let us hear from you.

Your letters of May 15th were received today. Thank you for the blue prints which you have had made for us. In regard to the Pearson machine, we have never been keen to take this order, as a delay in delivery would affect the value of the machine to them. We do not wish to be bothered with such orders. Moreover, Mr Pearson himself has never seemed much interested in placing a

16. The visit of Orville and Wilbur Wright to inspect the Short Brothers factory at Shellbeach, 4 May 1909. Horace Short, Oswald Short and Griffith Brewer are shown in the background.

machine. The only letter we ever received, signed by him, was one in which he asked to have the matter dropped.

We hope you and Mrs Brewer did not find the voyage back to England too disagreeable. Our passage home was delightful and we found all well. With kindest regards to you and Mrs Brewer, in which Katharine joins,

Very truly yours,

Wright Brothers.

In August 1909 Orville and Katharine Wright travelled from Dayton to Berlin. Orville undertook a series of demonstration flights at the Tempelhof parade ground sponsored by the Berlin newspaper Lokal-Anzeiger. *Earlier in the year, on 13 May 1909, the Wrights had established the Flugmaschine Wright-Gesellschaft company to manufacture the Wright aircraft design in Germany.*

17. The Wright Brothers outside Mussel Manor at Shellbeach, 4 May 1909. Back row, left to right: T.D.F. Andrews, Oswald Short, Horace Short, Eustace Short, Francis McClean, Griffith Brewer, Frank Butler, Dr. W.J.S. Lockyer, Warwick Wright. Front row, left to right: J.T.C. Moore-Brabazon, Wilbur Wright, Orvillle Wright, Hon. C.S. Rolls. Orville Wright refers to this photograph in his letter to Brewer of 20 November 1934.

Berlin
Sept. 17th 1909

Dear Mr Ogilvie:

I received your letter a few days ago just as I was leaving the hotel and had only the opportunity to glance over it at the time. Since I have not been able to find the letter.

If I fail to answer any questions contained in it you may repeat them, if you please. I may yet find the letter.

I think your machine will be ready now in a few weeks. The first motor was delivered just a few days ago, which is to go on Mr Rolls' machine. Yours will be the next. I hope to be able to let you know in the course of the next week when the second motor can be delivered.

I am glad to learn that you have progressed so well with gliding, and think you will have no trouble in teaching yourself to operate the machine. In learning, always be cautious. Begin in very light winds. Do not attempt high flights until you have had many hours of practice. Before you attempt flights with the

power machine I wish to send you some further instructions as to speed of propellers, etc.,

    Yours truly

    Orville Wright

*Orville Wright refers to Léon Bollée, who had allowed Wilbur Wright the use of his
automobile factory at Le Mans for assembling the Wright A aircraft in France, and was
subsequently awarded a contract to manufacture Wright engines. All six Short-Wright
biplanes were due to be installed with Bollée engines, but only two were finally delivered.
A firm of precision engineers, Bariquand & Marre of Paris, supplied the remainder.*

Berlin

Sep. 29, 1909

Dear Mr Ogilvie:

    I have your letter of the 24th, from the photographs enclosed you seem to
be making good progress with the glider. As I understand from your letter, the
levers are arranged as they were on the power machine which you saw at Pau.

18. The Wright A, which Orville Wright flew in Berlin in 1909, exhibited at the German Air
Exhibition, Berlin, 1932.

There are several ways in which turns can be made, but the way which I would recommend would be this: To make a turn to the left, for instance, shove the lever forward, in amount according to the quickness with which you wish to turn. As this would tend to cause the machine to 'skid' to the right, you should push the lever a little to the left to cause it to take the proper inclination from side to side. You will find, however, that in a second or two the machine is banking on the turn too much, and you will be compelled to draw the lever to the right until it maintains the angle you desire. You should keep the lever forward as originally set until you wish to bring it back straight again. I think the dimensions of your glider are all right. The front vane is quite sufficient; it must not be too large.

I have not yet heard from Mr Bollee about your engine, but I am expecting word every day.

I will be in England a few days on my way home to America and I will be glad to assist you in any way that I can.

Very truly yours

Orville Wright

Berlin

Oct. 8th. 1909

Dear Mr Ogilvie:

I have received word from Mr Bollee that your motor was shipped to Short Brothers several days ago, and word from Shorts that the machine is ready for the motor. I have written Messrs Short that this second machine is for you.

You had better communicate with Short Brothers directly as to when the machine will be ready for delivery, and when you receive your machine you can hand to them your check for the balance of £800.

I will be in England the end of this month, I hope, and if there is any advice you need in learning to operate, I shall be glad to give it to you.

Very sincerely yours

Orville Wright

Wilbur Wright had been contracted for the sum of $15,000 to undertake a flight of at least ten miles in length, or of one hour in duration, as part of the Hudson-Fulton Celebration held in the area of New York Harbor. On 29 September 1909 Wilbur Wright circled the Statue of Liberty and a few days later, on 4 October, undertook a twenty-one-mile round trip from Governors Island to Grant's Tomb.

New York
26 Oct 1909

Mr Alex Ogilvie

Dear Sir

I received your letter just before leaving home and have been too busy to attend to correspondence since. I think you did very well with the gliding. The tail is apparently large enough but I do not see any <u>vertical vanes</u> in the front rudder. These are very necessary and should be put in if you wish good results. I hope that ere this you have received your machine from Messrs Short Bros. as they promised to have it ready long ago. It is difficult to make things move rapidly from a distance.

I am here to make a few flights at the Hudson Fulton celebration, and then go to Washington to train a few men to operate the US Government machine.

I hope to hear of your further success soon.

Yours truly

Wilbur Wright

19. Secretary Charles D. Walcott, Wilbur Wright, Dr Alexander Graham Bell and Orville Wright leaving the Smithsonian Institution following the award of the first Langley Medal to the Wrights on 10 February 1910.

In February 1910 the Smithsonian Institution awarded the first Langley Medal to the Wrights for achievement in aerodynamics investigation and its application to aviation. The award followed a suggestion from Dr Alexander Graham Bell in a letter dated 5 December 1908. He said, 'The Wright brothers are being deservedly honored in Europe. Can not America do anything for them?...' (C.G. Abbot, 'The Relations between the Smithsonian Institution and the Wright Brothers', Smithsonian Miscellaneous Collections, *Vol.81 (5), 1928).*

Smithsonian Institution
Washington D.C., USA

The Editor
Aeronautical Journal
53 Victoria Street, Westminster
London, England.
February 14, 1910

Dear Sir:

I am authorized by the Secretary to enclose herewith an account of the presentation of the Langley Medal to Messrs Wilbur and Orville Wright, at the meeting of the Board of Regents of the Institution on February 10, 1910.

There are also enclosed excerpts from the minutes of the Board meetings of December 15, 1908, and February 10, 1909, describing, respectively, the establishment and the awarding of the Medal.

Very respectfully yours,

H.W. Worsey

Chief Clerk.

On 12 July 1910 the Hon. Charles Stewart Rolls (1877–1910) died while flying at the Bournemouth International Aviation Meeting. The tailplane of his French-built Wright aircraft broke up in mid-air. Rolls was a founding member of of the Aero Club of the United Kingdom and in 1904 together with F.H. Royce formed the partnership that was to evolve into the Rolls-Royce company.

Cablegram. 'Infallible London' was the cablegram address of Griffith Brewer.

20. The Hon. C.S. Rolls at the controls of his Wright biplane.

12th July 1910
To Infallible Ldn

Please convey our most heartfelt sympathy to Mr Rolls' family.
    Wilbur & Orville Wright

Wright Brothers
1127 W. Third Street
Dayton, Ohio
22 August 1910

Major B. Baden-Powell
London

My dear Major Baden-Powell,
    Please accept our thanks for your letter containing particulars of the accident
to poor Mr Rolls. It is exceedingly difficult to fix the cause of such an accident.

It may have been caused by some fault of construction or assembling. A part may have been left unfastened or may have worked loose. I am, however, rather inclined to think that the catastrophe was due to an attempt to descend through a rising wind just in front of the grand stand into the horizontal wind just beyond it. So that the wind caught the machine on top and slammed it into the ground before it could be straightened up. We have had similar experiences when gliding off of a steep ridge. But whatever the cause it is most sad and a great loss to English aviation.

Please accept kind regards not only from myself but also from my brother and my sister and remember us all to your sister & believe me,

Yours truly

Wilbur Wright.

On 22 November 1909 the Wright Company was incorporated to manufacture and sell Wright aircraft in the United States. Cornelius Vanderbilt, a leading investor, was on its Board of Directors.

Walter Brookins ('Brookie'), Arch Hoxsey, Ralph Johnstone and Frank Coffyn were among the first pilots to be selected and then trained by Orville Wright to support the work of the Wright Company. On 29 October 1910 Brookins crashed in the Wright Model R during a trial flight for the annual international Gordon Bennett Cup Race, held that year as part of the International Aviation Tournament at Belmont Park Race Track, Long Island, New York. Ogilvie (who competed in a Wright biplane), James Radley and Claude Grahame-White were members of the British contingent of pilots; Hubert Latham a member of the French team. The American John B. Moisant was to be eventually disqualified for starting late in the Thomas Fortune Ryan prize of $10,000 for a round-trip race to the Statue of Liberty, although his time was slightly faster than Claude Grahame-White's.

The Baron de Forest prize for the longest flight from Britain into France by a British pilot in a British built machine was won by T.O.M. Sopwith in a Howard Wright biplane. Howard Wright was no relation to Wilbur and Orville; he built his own machines based upon Henry Farman's designs. Cecil Grace, flying a Short pusher biplane, disappeared while over the English Channel in his attempt to surpass Sopwith's achievement.

On 15 November 1910 Orville sailed for Germany aboard the Kronprinzessin Cecile *to try and resolve the business problems of the failing German Flugmaschine Wright-Gesellschaft company.*

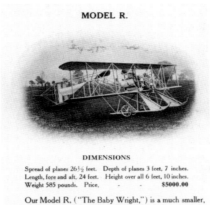

MODEL R.

DIMENSIONS

Spread of planes 26½ feet.   Depth of planes 3 feet, 7 inches.
Length, fore and aft, 24 feet.   Height over all 6 feet, 10 inches.
Weight 585 pounds.   Price,   -   -   **$5000.00**

Our Model R, ("The Baby Wright,") is a much smaller,
lighter type designed especially for speed and altitude work.
This is by far the fastest climbing aeroplane ever built.   It carries only the operator and is equipped with our standard motor
and control.   This model was used in making the world's
altitude record of 9714 feet at the recent International Meet.

For information concerning deliveries, etc., address
THE WRIGHT COMPANY, Sales Department
DAYTON, OHIO

21. Description of the Wright Model R in the Wright Co.'s brochure
'The Wright Flyer' (Dayton, The Wright Co., 1911).

Cablegram
Dayton, Ohio
5 Sep. 1910
To Infallible, London

Will furnish Ogilvie Racer
    Wright

This letter from Katharine Wright (1874–1929) to Alec Ogilvie is the first of many to him, and to Griffith Brewer, as the Wright family's friendship with them developed.

7 Hawthorn Street
Dayton, Ohio
Nov. 17, 1910

My dear Mr Ogilvie,

I'm a 'widow' now so it's lucky for you that you escaped when you did! Orville went to New York Sunday evening to sail last Tuesday for Germany on the Kronprinzessin Cecelie. Wilbur has been in New York all the time since

45

you went away, except for two days at home. So the little white house on Hawthorn Street is rather a forlorn place, though today we are trying to stir up a little gaiety in honour of Father's eighty-second birthday. A birthday cake with eighty-two candles is no ordinary affair.

But I commenced this letter to tell you that I had to come home and rest for a week before I really began to enjoy the coffee cups. After we left you on the boat we went over to see Walter and I suddenly discovered that I was <u>dead</u>! I managed to get back to my room where I dropped down and stayed the rest of the day, catching catnaps between telephone calls. Wilbur and Orville went to Belmont Park for various errands. Orville took Cornelius Vanderbilt for his first ride. That evening I pulled myself together to go with Will and Orv to dine at Mr Collier's. There Will discovered that he was more dead than alive. I was really alarmed about him. To top it off, he had to go to Baltimore on the midnight train. However, he survived and looked hearty enough when he came home several days later.

Orv and I came home Wednesday, bringing Brookie with us. He was much improved and spoke of having received your message Tuesday night. I saw in the paper this morning that he flew at Denver yesterday with Hoxsey and Johnstone. I think the winter on the Pacific coast will be good for him. He isn't as strong as the men who are a little more mature. He gets a good deal of advice from me — I can't <u>bear</u> to see him spoiled by such men as Coffyn.

But as I was trying to say before, I was too tired for several days before and many days after we came home to realize how much I liked my lovely cups and how much I appreciated your wanting to give them to me. The china is <u>so</u> exquisite and I do love fine things much more than my precious brothers do though they are tremendously proud if I happen to show a little good taste once in a while. They are ridiculously indulgent as far as money goes. It was my own fault that I came back without buying anything but common dishes for everyday use. I didn't see <u>just</u> what I wanted and I knew I could go to New York any time I liked and do my shopping when I was not so mortally weary. Because I am so specially fond of china I can't buy anything without a lot of thought and care. I wish you could know how much I like the lovely red and gold cups and that I like even more everything connected with the giving of them.

You will be seeing Orville before long. He is going to Germany first and from there will run over to see if he can help you whenever you want him. We are all tremendously interested in your winning the de Forest prize. I have been getting sicker and sicker over your old spark plug. At the time I was so glad to hear that you were safe that I didn't realize how disappointing it was to you to

22. The first German factory for Wright aircraft at Reinickendorf. From an original Flugmaschine Wright-Gesellschaft company brochure, 'Wright-Aeroplan', c.1910.

have 'Old Reliability' go back on you. It was really heart breaking. We were so pleased with the way you flew that <u>we</u> didn't mind so much. Orville's address in Berlin will be Esplanade Hotel. We were afraid you were caught in the storm that wrecked everything at Baltimore. Did you have a bad passage?

 Kindest regards and best wishes from all, including the Russells.

 Sincerely

 Katharine Wright

We have heard nothing of any decision in your case against Moisant. Latham & Radley are going to California. K.W.

Hotel Esplanade

Berlin W.,

Bellevuestrasse 18

Nov. 24th 1910

Dear Mr Brewer

 The German Company was so urgent in its demands for our presence here in Germany that I thought it inadvisable to stop over in England until after attending to matters here. I am sorry that you were put to the inconvenience of meeting the boat train. I had thought that I was slipping out of America without any body finding it out and consequently was much surprised to find that you and Comte de Lambert were both expecting me. Comte de Lambert met me at the boat at Bremerhaven.

As I may be some time in Germany, it is my intention to run over to England for a day or two soon, if I can be of any assistance to Mr Ogilvie in his preparations for competing for prizes. I think I will be able to come within the next two weeks. I will then take up the matter of license.

With kindest regards to Mrs Brewer and yourself.

Very truly yours

Orville Wright

Hotel Esplanade
Berlin W.,
Bellevuestrasse 18
Nov. 24th 1910

Dear Mr Ogilvie

I have just arrived in Berlin, and have not yet learned the condition of our affairs here, so that I do not know how long my stay here will be. If you are preparing to go after any of the prizes, of which you spoke when in America, and you think I can be of any service to you I will try to run over to England for a few days as soon as business here will permit. After your departure from America we looked up the rules of the International Federation but were not able to find anything that prevented a contestant in the Gordon Bennett from flying after sun down, but according to certain rules we believe that the protest on account of the absence of officials at the pylons would disqualify Moisant.

I hope you are getting along well, and would be greatly pleased to hear from you of your progress.

Very truly yours

Orville Wright

The 1910–11 Michelin Cup was awarded to the aviator who accomplished the longest distance in an all-British machine.

Hotel Esplanade
Berlin W.,
Bellevuestrasse 18
Dec. 1st 1910.

Dear Mr Ogilvie:

I do not know the exact conditions of the British Michelin prize, but if it be allowed to fly for a longer time with a slow machine, I believe your chances of success would be greater than with an attempt to change your machine in so short time. You could not expect to make your present machine more than five miles faster than it now is. Therefore I would think provision to stay in the air a longer time would be easier and more certain.

Your old machine will be some faster and will operate better, if the cloth is sewed to the ribs on the upper side of the surface. I would not advise cutting off the rear ends of the ribs. It would take too much time. A better plan would be to reduce the area of wing tips. You could cut four or five feet off each end much easier. What is the speed of your present machine with the new motor? If you have 40 h.p. or more you should have a speed of 43 or 44 miles an hour.

23. Wilbur and Orville Wright with their student pilots Walter Brookins, Frank T. Coffyn and Roy Knabenshue, Dayton, 1911.

I am now hoping to leave Berlin the early part of next week for England. I will have to return here to complete my work. I will telegraph you when I start.

Very truly yours

Orville Wright

P.S. Please do not delay any of your work in the expectation of my coming. I may be disappointed in being able to start next week.

17 November 1910 was the eighty-second birthday of Bishop Milton Wright (1828–1917), the father of the Wright family. On that day Ralph Johnstone died when he failed to pull out of a spiralling dive at an air show in Denver, witnessed by Walter Brookins and Arch Hoxsey. Phil O. Parmalee and Clifford Turpin were other student pilots of the Wrights.

Katharine Wright refers to Frank Russell who had been appointed manager of the Wright Company's factory at Dayton. The Russells (no relation) were local friends, and Lorin was one of Katharine's four brothers.

7 Hawthorn Street

Dayton Ohio.

Dec. 5 1910

Dear Mr Ogilvie,

Your letter came the day after I had written to you. I am very glad indeed that you had a good passage. We have a letter from Orville today saying that they had fine weather all the way over. He landed at Bremen and found Comte de Lambert at the boat to meet him.

Most of my brilliant thoughts are 'after-thoughts'. I racked my brain trying to think of things that were nice to have on the boat but couldn't get an idea of any sort. You were no more than out of sight when <u>dozens</u> of things occurred to me. I must confess that I was so tired the last few days in New York than I wasn't far short of imbecility!

The evening of Father's birthday – which I remember now was the day I wrote to you – just as the Russells and Wrights were arriving for the birthday party, I got the message that Johnstone had been killed. I didn't tell anyone at first but a little later I thought I must tell Mr Russell and Lorin because Wilbur was in New York and I thought there might be things to be done. So I got them aside on some pretext and told them what Brooky's telegram had said. The rest of the party knew nothing about it and so Grandpa and the children and Mrs Russell and Netta had a happy time. Mrs Russell made a cake, on which were burning <u>eighty-two</u> candles.

The stories about Johnstone's accident are so confused and confusing that we don't know what to think. Brooky told Will that when he first noticed Johnstone – Brooky had finished and was getting ready to leave – he saw that there was something the matter with the one wing. It was somewhat out of shape – not crumpled. He says that the machine was coming down in a big spiral – rather steeply but not dangerously so. I understand Will to say that he (Brooky) did not regard Johnstone's situation as very serious until right at the end. Brooky did not see when the machine dashed into the ground. There were trees between them. He said that four or five reliable people told him that Johnstone climbed out of the seat right at the end.

Now Eichstadt, who was Johnstone's mechanicien (how <u>do</u> you spell that word?), says that Brooky, Hoxsey and Johnstone agreed that they would not do stunts. When Johnstone came down after a good, sensible flight and got no applause and learned that Brooky and Hoxsey had, because they <u>had</u> done some fancy stunts, he said, 'Well, if that is what the crowd want, I'll show them a few tricks.' Then Eichstadt says Johnstone went up and tilted the machine almost ninety degrees and that the machine turned clear over, throwing Johnstone out

MODEL B.

DIMENSIONS

Spread of planes 39 feet. Depth 6 feet 3 inches. Length fore and aft 29 feet. Height over all 8 feet.
Length of propellors 8½ feet. Weight 800 pounds.   **Price $5000.00**

THE wonderful range of control of The Wright Flyer in both lateral and fore and aft balance is obtained by the simplest and most direct application of the principles invented by the Wright Brothers. The entire machine is governed by two levers; the first of which, when moved forward or backward, warps the wings and at the same time turns the rear vertical rudders permitting the operator to maintain his balance without changing his course, regardless of the direction of the wind. The vertical rudders can also be operated independently to turn to the right or left by simply twisting the end of the lever with a wrist motion. The second lever controls the rear horizontal rudder by which the direction of flight upwards and downwards may be governed. The speed of the engine is controlled by a foot pedal and the power can be shut off instantly at any time by pulling a cord within easy reach. The controlling power is transmitted entirely by steel cables with nickel steel chain sections wherever they pass through pulleys. The entire mechanism is exposed so that even a casual inspection suffices to ascertain the condition of all working parts.

The bi-plane type permits of double trussing throughout, offering a strength obtainable in no other design and the efficiency of the planes and propellers is so high that there is no need to sacrifice strength for lightness.

All machines are equipped with shock absorbing wheels for starting and landing. Our Model B is designed to offer the greatest maximum of safety and reliability. This aeroplane carries two persons comfortably and the levers are duplicated so either person can operate the machine. It is a refined type of The Wright Flyer used this year by our Exhibition Department.

24. Description of the Wright Model B in the company brochure 'The Wright Flyer' (Dayton, The Wright Co., 1911).

of the seat. After that, it righted and came down fairly well, though Johnstone could not get to the levers again. The wing that was out of shape may have been warped that way while Johnstone had hold of the levers. We can't understand how the stories could be so different. Brooky ought to have seen if Johnstone was out of the seat. Still <u>every report</u> said that the machine did turn over and that Johnstone was thrown out of the seat. Whatever happened, it was bad enough and it seems to me I can't endure any more of this exhibition business.

Parmalee, Coffyn, and Turpin are here. They have been working on an arrangement to change the spark by a movement of the foot. All the boys hate to let go of the lever to reach under for the spark control. Orv always says that there is plenty of time but I must say that I sympathize with the boys. Parmalee will go west to join Brooky and Hoxsey in California.

25. Close-up view of the engine on the Wright Model B, taken from the brochure 'The Wright Flying School' (New York: Wright Flying Field Inc., 1916).

The Russells are well and thriving and would want to send remembrances if they knew I was writing. We all wish you the greatest success – especially in the de Forest business – but we hope most of all that you will be careful even if it means losing the prize. Father sends regards. I hope this will reach you in time to let me say 'Merry Christmas' to you! Believe me, as always.

Sincerely

Katharine Wright

Wilbur is away again. He was home again for a few days after Johnstone's funeral. KW

On 28 December 1910 Ogilvie had remained in the air for 3 hours 55 minutes while competing for the Michelin Cup.

On 31 December 1910, Arch Hoxsey died after the Wright Model B that he was flying plunged into the ground at a very steep angle at an aviation meeting in Los Angeles.

7 Hawthorn Street

Dayton, Ohio

Feb. 7, 1911

Dear Mr Ogilvie,

Things have gone rather badly with me since Christmas and I haven't been in any mood to write a decent letter. Now I've decided to <u>forget</u> all about tonsilitis and rheumatism and a lot of other ills which have been plaguing me.

Your last letter was especially welcome because it came the day after Orville arrived home and I was flat on my back, while Wilbur and Orville were down town talking as fast as they could and I was missing some of the news! I did need something to sustain me under such trying circumstances. The news of your 'dandy' (Mr Brewer thinks this is a horrible perversion of English) Michelin flight had come just two days before and Orville was full of news about you. We were all <u>so</u> pleased over your splendid record and <u>so</u> anxious to have you win – especially when we read in your letter that you were particularly 'keen' on that prize. Not having anything to do but lie and think, my nerves were getting pretty much on edge by New Year's Eve, when the boys came in and said that insufferable <u>Englishman</u> had beaten you. If the boys had let me know about Hoxsey, that night, I shouldn't have spent so much energy worrying about your disappointment.

Altogether, New Year's Day was a night-mare to us all. After I heard about poor Hoxsey, your not getting the Cup seemed a trifling trouble. I am so sick of this exhibition business. It is so absolutely wrong. Neither the aviators nor the public have the right attitude. I must say that sometimes I am exasperated almost beyond endurance that Wilbur and Orville should have to scramble with a lot of Showmen – or else let their machine lose out. They are so patient and calm about it. I'm not.

We were sorry that you could not have the satisfaction of winning the Michelin prize but, honestly, wouldn't you rather lose every prize than be in Cody's boots? It was nothing but a bit of bad luck that that last day should have been such an ideal one and that you could not take advantage of it. As for the de Forest, I was so glad that you did not undertake it. The fame, if you won, might be worth more to you than the risk you would take, but I doubt if it would be to your family. You couldn't have been ready for it. It was wonderful that you accomplished what you did, getting back to England so late. Anyhow, I can tell you one thing, you have nothing to worry about when it comes to your standing with the Wright family!

The new house seems to be well on the way finally. We have quite unexpectedly agreed perfectly on our style of exterior. The interior is 'up to me'. We won't be in it when you come the next time, if you come, as we hope you will, this summer, but if you will stay long enough, you may initiate the guest chamber, which is going to be as pretty and comfortable as I know how to make it. Better come!

I wish I could tell you the kind of news you care most about but I only hear enough now to worry me without really understanding what is going on. I saw your machine in the shop the other day. It is a trim looking affair. Orville said this noon that he had found out why Brooky's four cylinders dropped out, in the Gordon-Bennett. Something broke – but like the flour in the pie making – I don't know just what! Some pump was out of commission. That reminds me to tell you that our dear Brooky has become quite impossible. He isn't being properly appreciated. He is very young yet – very young.

It was painful to hear that I just missed getting a real English plum-pudding! Orville did have such a good time at your house. He told us all about everything. He likes Mr Seawright, too. I asked about 'Dan'l and Sam' and Orville says they were always pumping when he saw them!

The Russells help to keep your memory green. Mr Russell let us see your letters to him. Wilbur found a splendid picture of you at New York and we bought five. I had one framed for Mr Russell for Xmas. They have it in the liv-

26. Lazare Weiller (in the checked cap) and Wilbur Wright at Camp d'Auvours, Le Mans, 1908. Weiller was a leading member of the French syndicate La Compagnie Générale de Navigation Aérienne (CGNA), and eventually owned the Wright A aircraft which Wilbur flew in France.

ing-room upstairs. Mrs Russell hasn't been quite well but none of us have. The weather has been <u>abominable</u>.

Kindest remembrances from us all.

Sincerely

Katharine Wright

In March 1911 Wilbur Wright travelled to Paris, at the request of Henry Peartree, Flint and Company's legal representative in France, to deal with various lawsuits brought against a number of French aviators and aircraft manufacturers accused of infringing the Wright patents. The Wrights' French patents had been assigned to a syndicate, La Compagnie Générale de Navigation Aérienne (CGNA), in which Wilbur and Orville were shareholders. Eventually in May 1911 the Tribunal of the Seine found in favour of the CGNA (and therefore the Wrights) in eleven of the twelve lawsuits. The exception was that against Alberto Santos-Dumont, whom it was decided had built his aircraft for pleasure not profit. Whilst the Tribunal was considering its judgement, Wilbur travelled to Berlin to oversee developments at the Flugmaschine Wright-Gesellschaft company.

[Lettercard]

Hotel Meyerbeer
Rond-Point des Champs-Elysées
Paris
22 March, 1911

My dear Mr Ogilvie
  I am in Europe for a few weeks and hope before returning to America to run over to England for five or ten minutes before returning to America. I expect be in France about ten days, and then go to Berlin for a few days before coming to England if I follow my present plans.
  The folks at Dayton all were well and wished to be remembered to you.
  With best regards
  Yours truly
  Wilbur Wright

[Lettercard]

Hotel Meyerbeer
Rond-Point des Champs-Elysées
Paris
Mar. 22, [1911]

My dear Mr Brewer
  I reached Paris yesterday after a very pleasant voyage – pleasant in the sense that I left a great volume of 'regrets' behind me as I came. But really it was not so bad for March voyages.
  I expect to spend a week or ten days in France; a similar time in Berlin; and then run over to England, before sailing for home.
  I hope I shall have courage to venture the channel though Orville's report of his last crossing was most alarming.
  Every one in Dayton is well and sending regards to you, Mrs Brewer and also the younger members of the family.
  Yours truly,
  Wilbur Wright

[Postcard of the Siegesallee in Berlin, posted in Berlin 14 April 1911]

Dear Mr Ogilvie

I am still expecting to have a few moments left for a visit to England but it will probably be a week or ten days later than I first thought.

Yours truly

Wilbur Wright

[Postcard]

Hotel Esplanade,
Bellevuestrasse 18
Berlin
Apr. 18. 1911

Dear Mr Ogilvie

I think I forgot to give you my Berlin address which you will find above. I am spending a little more time here than I at first intended, but hope to get to England before the first of May.

Wilbur Wright.

Katharine Wright refers to Lieutenant John Rodgers of the US Navy and Lieutenant Benjamin Foulois of the US Army Signal Corps. They were student pilots of the Wrights. 'Buster' was the Wrights' nephew.

7 Hawthorn Street
Dayton, Ohio
April 23 1911

Dear Mr Ogilvie,

It has been a long, long time since your letter came. Wilbur was just starting to Europe and it seems <u>months</u> since he went away. As a matter of fact, it was exactly six weeks ago today.

I knew there was no use 'boring' the precious brothers for answers to your questions because Wilbur would be over to see you so soon. However, we did not know that he would stay so long in Paris. So his visit to you has evidently been delayed. At least we have not heard of it yet.

Indeed the grunting is all over and we have all been as lively as crickets until two weeks ago when Father went to a little town ten miles away to spend

Sunday and took a very bad cold. It has been almost too much for him but he has managed to be out of bed every day, part of the time, at least. We thought he was better but last night was very cold for this season and he was chilled while he slept. We hope he will soon be quite well, again. Orville took a heavy cold, which settled in his throat, while out flying early the past week. It is such fun to see him go out and 'sniff' at the way the boys keep their machines. 'Everything is out of adjustment', 'Flying is no fun on such a trap', etc. etc. When we reached the Camp on Tuesday afternoon, Clifford came running out to say how glad he was that Orville had come because the engine wasn't giving enough power to keep two men off the ground. Orv got in, took Clifford with him, went out and did all kinds of stunts just to show poor, humble Clifford that he didn't know what he was talking about! Lieut. Rodgers, who was Clifford's pupil that day, looked a while and then said, 'Oh well, he knows what he is doing!' Lieut. Rodgers is a Navy man who went through very clever and difficult manuevers (how do you spell it?) to keep from being sent as a pupil to Curtiss. He looks rather stupid and slow but is about the wittiest person we have run across. Two Army lieutenants have been ordered here to learn to fly

Coffyn is down with Lieut. Foulois in Texas. Parmalee had to go to Denver and some other places in the West, so Coffyn was sent down to help with the government machine. Brooky is also in the West, but we have all lost interest in him. He turns out to be anything but nice in a great many ways, and to top it all off is so ridiculously conceited that his days of usefulness are about over. He was Orv's special pet and Orv staid by him long after all the others were thoroughly disgusted. Now even Orv can't endure him. Mr Russell told him that Orville had said that he was surprised that the 'boys' didn't have some suggestions to make about the machine. Brooky said he had, but he wasn't paid for ideas! Just what he had been paid for so very liberally (twice the contract price) no one seems now to know!

Parmalee is proving to be the best all-round man in the lot. He is loyal and faithful and very efficient.

The Russells are as usual. Mrs Russell is just as sweet and just as irresistible when she tells the story of Epaminondas, as ever. I am very fond of her. The children are very attractive. Little Frank is going to be a 'dead game sport' all right. I went by the house the other day and saw Frank standing on a narrow ledge outside the second story window! Needless to say his mother was out calling.

Buster spends his evenings studying catalogues, trying to decide whether he would rather buy an incubator, a gun or a tent! Of course, he hasn't any money to buy any one of them but he's having just as much fun as if he had.

The preliminary sketch of the house has just come from the architect. On the outside it says 'Residence for Miss Katharine Wright.' Orv says, 'It's no use. We can't fool anybody. Everyone knows who will own the house.' I really think we are going to have a pretty house and I am getting impatient now to have it materialize. Your room is all provided for! We hope you can come soon. Best wishes and kindest remembrance

Sincerely

Katharine Wright

We are glad you were elected in the Aero Club committee. K.W

Hotel Esplanade
Bellevuestrasse 18
Berlin
23 April 1911

Dear Mr Ogilvie,

I have finished translating yours of 20th Apr. Rather quick work, I think.

Your little acrobatic 'stunt' has both its serious and its amusing sides, and I am heartily glad it turned out so well, or perhaps I should say, 'turned over so well'.

It is always a serious matter to land <u>with the wind</u>, on any machine in which the center of gravity is high, as the numerous somersaults of the Bleriot Farman, etc. etc., have shown. In our old machine we purposely brought the machine as near the ground as possible to prevent this. I am not sure that your misadventure would have been less serious if you had used longer skids. The cause of the overturning was the higher center of gravity and higher speed. Brookins also turned a 'hand spring' at Belmont Park with our front skid not broken and the other only slightly injured. I have serious doubts whether longer skids would be safer, but only experience can determine the point.

It is always a serious thing to land with a strong wind on the back, because as soon as the speed is as little or less than that of the wind, the pressure on the tail tends to turn the machine over instead of preventing it.

Therefore I would strongly advise, with the better machine, that you always keep sufficient height when going with the wind so that you can turn and land facing it. Young birds often get rolled head over heels by making the mistake of landing with the wind. Old birds never attempt it. It will be well for us to follow their example as far as possible.

In practice I think it would be wise to fit an extra set of wheels at the front of the skids like we put on for Brookins at Belmont, but they should be fastened more securely. They almost saved him.

I had a letter from my sister yesterday (upon whom I depend like you for American news) in which she gives Parmalee's story of his adventures on the Mexican border. They were flying over a country where for a hundred miles there was no landing place except the Rio Grande River. The cut off cord got wet and shrunk so that it pulled the cut off handle till one cylinder stopped exploding, so they gradually began to sink toward the river. Parmalee tried to make Lt Foulois understand what the trouble was but could not succeed till too late. Finally just as they were touching the water Foulois 'caught on' and pushed the lever back, but the effect was to turn the machine downward a little and make it dive for the bottom of the river. The next thing Parmalee knew he was sitting on the rocks in the bottom of the river with eighteen inches of water over his head. He lost no time in seeking higher atmosphere. Foulois' head soon appeared above water also but as the Lt is only 5ft 1in tall and the water was four feet deep there was a margin of only about an inch under his chin. The banks were so steep that they had to wade down stream a quarter of a mile before going ashore. The machine was not much injured, and is all right again.

It was a foolish trip undertaken without proper precautions; and while the cause of the accident was ridiculously trifling, the results might have been very serious.

I hope to be over to England about the close of this week.

Yours truly

Wilbur Wright

[Postcard]

Hotel Esplanade,
Bellevuestrasse 18
Berlin
26 Apr. 1911

Dear Ogilvie,

I find I will not get over to England till some time next week, but by using stop watch will be able to utilize $\frac{1}{10}$" of seconds.

Wilbur Wright.

[Postcard]

Hotel Esplanade,
Bellevuestrasse 18
Berlin
2 May 1911

Dear Mr Brewer,

I have been kept in Berlin much longer than I expected, but think now I shall leave in a couple of days. I will stop a day or two in Paris, and then for England while 'May is there'. I hope the weather will be as nice as my sister found it in 1909. My own impression of English weather is not so good.
Yours truly
Wilbur Wright.

Robert Esnault-Pelterie was one of a number of French aircraft manufacturers charged by La Compagnie Générale de Navigation Aérienne (CGNA) of infringing the Wrights' wing-warping patents.

Hotel Esplanade,
Bellevuestrasse 18
Berlin
Saturday [received by Brewer & Son, London, 10 May 1911]

Dear Mr Brewer,

Matters have become so interesting in Berlin that I have been unable to get away. I even find that it will be necessary to be here a week or so hence.

So I have about concluded to go to Paris on Monday and after a visit to England come back again to Berlin to see whether the criminal laws of Germany are such as to put the most powerful business man in Germany into jail for an attempt to commit what would be a criminal offense even in the attempt in America and I think in England also. So you see that matters are really very interesting here and that I am depriving myself of the pleasure of your company in England not without good reason.

I enclose a copy of a letter written by Esnault-Pelterie to his French business associates. Such a letter is most laughable when one thinks of the quite different tone in which they spoke of our patent suit in France when I first reached France in March. It reminds me of a cartoon I saw in a German paper some weeks ago when the French papers were protesting against including Berlin in the aeroplane race Paris–Brussels–Berlin–London–Paris. The first picture showed French soldiers of 1870 marching off to the war to the cry of 'a Berlin', the second showed the French of 1911 grabbing the flying machines by the tails and shouting 'pas a Berlin'.

In February the French were so bold that they were crying 'On to Berlin' to attack the Wright German patents. Now they are even more earnestly crying 'Keep away from Berlin'. The French are really very amusing sometimes.

Please do not kill the fatted calf in anticipation of my arrival in England. It might spoil before I get there. But laying aside all jokes, I really am unable to fix definitely my arrival and if the telegraphic notice which I shall send in any event finds you gone to Switzerland or Scotland, I will run down and spend a few weeks with Mr Ogilvie, while are you getting back. I have cried 'wolf' so often that I fully expect to find you gone about other business when I really do come.

With best regard to Mrs Brewer & yourself.

Yours truly

Wilbur Wright.

Paris

19 May [1911]

Dear Mr Ogilvie,

Affairs in Germany and France have been so interesting that I have been much longer in getting over to England than I expected. I thought I would wait till I was done with other affairs and then take my vacation with you with nothing else to bother me.

But I see no hope of such a thing now so I think it may be better to make you shorter visits in between times than to spend a long time on one single visit. I might be able to slip over for a day or two toward the end of next week if you are still in 'camp'.

Would this suit you? and if so would it be better to come direct to Rye instead of going up to London first? I will let the visit to the Brewers go to another time, as it will apparently be impossible to stay more than a day or two just now.

Unless it would specially suit you to have me over as soon as convenient I would really prefer to leave my visit go over a week longer; but it may be that you have been holding things back waiting for me, and would prefer the earlier time.

Things are going very well with us in France and will make things much easier in other countries.

Yours truly

Wilbur Wright.

Wilbur Wright refers to the Société Zodiac. Originally formed by Maurice Mallet to manufacture airships, with comte Henri de la Vaulx as its technical director, in 1910 the Société Zodiac moved into the field of aircraft production.

Paris

19 May [1911]

Dear Mr Brewer,

I still 'fight shy' of England. The fact is that I am in secret negotiation with some of the French infringers for the settlement of the patent fight out of court. This of course is not to go beyond yourself for the present.

The judgement of the 3rd tribunal on the 29 April was so strong that the French have almost lost hope of escaping final judgement against them and are not at all averse to talking settlement. So I cannot well leave France for a few days or possibly weeks, though I may find time to run over to England for a few short visits in between times.

However as I said in my last letter, please ignore my existence so far as your own plans are concerned for a few weeks ahead. I certainly will arrange to make you a visit before returning to America after giving you notice.

I learn that the 'Zodiac' Company of which De La Vaulx and Mallet are principal figures has decided yesterday to acknowledge the Wright patent and take a licence. I have no doubt many others will follow suit.

Unless Orville should send for me, it is possible that I may take a position as muse to you on your transatlantic voyage and stay in Europe until then.

Yours truly

Wilbur Wright.

In June 1911 Wilbur Wright visited Ogilvie to assist with his 'Baby' Wright racer at the Royal Aero Club's flying ground at Eastchurch on the Isle of Sheppey. The 1911 Gordon Bennett Cup contest was to be held there in July, Claude Grahame-White's victory the previous year having brought the contest to England. Ogilvie was flying the aircraft which he had flown in the 1910 contest at Belmont Park, New York, but with a more powerful engine manufactured by the New Engine Company (NEC).

27. Alec Ogilvie, Wilbur Wright and F.G.T. Dawson at Eastchurch on the Isle of Sheppey, June 1911. Loaned by Mrs M.G. Varvill.

Wilbur refers to Captain Richard von Kehler, managing director of the Motor Luftschiff-Studien Gesellschaft airship group, who was formative in the establishment of the Flugmaschine Wright-Gesellschaft company. Captain Paul Engelhardt was a retired German naval officer being trained as a pilot for the German company.

Hotel Esplanade,
Bellevuestrasse 18
Berlin
27 June 1911

Dear Mr Brewer

'It is better to be born lucky than to be born rich' when it is a matter of crossing the Channel comfortably. Does the rule about 'eight to one' apply to the English Channel as well as to English weather? I have been across six times now and each crossing was like the last before it, simply fine.

I reached Berlin this morning and expect to have a talk with Captain Engelhard and Capt. Von Kehler this afternoon. So far as I have heard, nothing was done at the directors' meeting last week of such serious consequence as to make me regret that I stuck to Eastchurch instead of coming over here at that time. It was a rather risky thing to do, but I did not like to leave till I had seen the nature of the injury the 'baby' suffered, and its proper repair.

From a telegram just received from Mr Ogilvie I see that the machine is about a mile and a half faster than with the 4 cyl. American motor. This accords with our calculations based on the standing tests of the speed of the propeller indoors.

I will let you know as soon as possible what my plans will be.

Very truly

Wilbur Wright.

Wilbur Wright refers to the aircraft engines produced by the German company Neue Automobil Gesellschaft (NAG). The German National Circuit race, sponsored by Zietung am Mittag of Berlin, took place from 15 June–7 July 1911. Wilbur refers to the German pilots Theodor Schauenburg and Robert Thelen who took part in the contest flying Wright biplanes.

Hotel Esplanade,
Bellevuestrasse 18
Berlin
28 June 1911

Dear Alec:

I reached Berlin all right Tuesday morning, after a very nice crossing and found your telegram awaiting me. I make your speed with the wind 65.5 m. per hour and against the wind 49.3 m. per hr, an average of 57.4 m. per hr. If the wind was not straight up the course an allowance would have to be made for it which would slightly raise the figures for the average speed.

Orville at Dayton in a light side wind made the kilometre in 39 sec and 41 sec. which figures an average speed of 55.8. That machine had only one set of posts in the wings; the gasoline tank was behind the man; and radiator gave less resistance, as also the motor. The propellers were probably 2 per cent better. The skids were lighter and thinner. So the motor is evidently giving a little more power than the American motor, probably between 5 and 10 per cent more.

Captain Engelhard tells me that he recently turned the French screws 460 turns per min, with the NAG motor 118x100 mm. (34x11) gear. He is about to make the acceptance trials of a new motor NAG and will get its speeds on our flat fans.

I find the directors of our company did no serious business at the recent meeting, so my staying in England an extra ten days did no serious harm. It will be necessary however to start some suits at law to protect ourselves. So I do not know just when I can leave Germany.

The German circuit, Berlin, Magdeburg, Hamburg, Kiel, Hanover, Munster, Cologne has been going on regardless of the English and French newspapers. The Munster–Cologne stage is set for today. Schaumberg in a Wright, and Thelen on a modified Wright are third and fourth respectively.

With Best regards

Yours truly

Wilbur Wright

Hotel Esplanade,
Bellevuestrasse 18
Berlin
4 July 1911

Dear Mr Brewer:

I think it will not be necessary to book passage for me on the Olympic. Please give my love to the friends in America and tell them that I am staying for the purpose of making it as hot over here as it is in America. Of course I am sorry not to be able to see you through your troubles on the trip, but if you depend on luck instead of science you will probably get through all right.

The Gordon Bennett seems to have been run off with less serious accidents than I expected. I always feel better after such things are over if I have friends in them. Unless the power of the motor is limited and the size of the required circuit reduced I fear it will be worse next year.

According to the newspapers Mr Ogilvie seems to have handled his machine very well, although I judge that the wind must have been pretty bad. The various continental papers tell different stories on this point, but the fact that Mr Ogilive's speed was less than last year, although he had a machine a little faster than before, would seem to indicate that the wind was pretty bad. It was bad enough at Belmont Park during the last year's race.

As I shall not get back to England before you sail, I will send a few requests regarding the stuff I left with you. If you could arrange to take the photograph with you it would oblige me very much. The pillow case please send to my sister by registered mail and let them settle any questions as to whether any duty is due at that end.

Wishing you much pleasure and good luck.

Yours truly

Wilbur Wright

The Nieuport was a two-cylinder horizontally-opposed air-cooled engine manufactured in France during 1911. It was installed in the small tractor Nieuport monoplane.

Hotel Esplanade,
Bellevuestrasse 18
Berlin
5 July 1911

Dear Alec:

Your scrawl of Sunday received and guessed at! I had seen from the newspapers that you had finished the course and escaped without any smash up. These were the only things I really cared about in the race. A matter of a few miles speed more or less was not a serious matter. Your troubles would be amusing if they were not so heart-breaking while they are going on.

You are quite right in thinking that at high speeds the head resistance becomes very important but I see that you are fooled on several points. If you stop to figure up you will find that 80 miles an hour is the speed a falling body attains after a fall of 256 feet. While 40 miles an hour is attained in less than 60ft. So that a Nieuport cut off at 50 miles and landing at 40 has used up the equivalent of 200ft in addition to its actual drop. It ought therefore to go 6 x 230 = 1380ft before landing if cut off at 30ft height, your speed the day your motor stuck with you was probably not more than 45 miles so you had no surplus energy. A machine with 2 propellers naturally does not glide as far as with a single propeller.

Comte de Lambert tells us that the Nieuport motor is 135 x 145 and revs 1400.

Now $\dfrac{135^2 \times 2 \times 145}{111^2 \times 4 \times 101}$ is in the proportion $\dfrac{528}{497}$ so that it is a sixteenth larger than our 4 cyl. motor.

The speed of the Nieuport with 100 h.p. motor was about what Brookins had with not over 70 h.p. last year. We built that machine to prove that the talk about the speed advantages of the monoplane and the fore and aft arrangement was largely rot. It was faster than any of the 100 h.p. monoplanes of its time.

I have written a letter to the N.Y. Herald proposing that in 1912 no motor having a total piston area of more than 665 sq. centimetres and 8000 cubic centimetres displacement be allowed in the Gordon Bennett. This is the size of the 50 h.p. Gnome. If the proposition is accepted we will show them whether this biplane is slower than the monoplane. If they insist on motors of any size the

race will not interest us, as we do not care to fly over 100 miles an hour ourselves, or put our men on such a job.

I find I will be kept here several weeks, just what my plans will be beyond
that I do not know.

With best regards

Yours

Wilbur Wright

P.S. When I came to settle accounts with Mr Brewer I found several disputed
accounts in one of which he claims you were the only person interested. I claim
that if an old hat increases in value in proportion to the number of holes put
into it, that I have a right to see if there is any possible chance of getting in one
or two more before trashing it off!

*Wilbur Wright refers to Betty, the daughter of Griffith Brewer, who was later to marry
the airship pilot Captain George Meager, A.F.C. It is unclear whether in using the word
'Dutch', Wilbur was meaning the German word 'Deutsch'.*

Hotel Esplanade,
Bellevuestrasse 18
Berlin
9 July 1911

Dear Mr Brewer,

I would go with you – but it seems that it is impossible. A pleasant voyage
to you!

Today I took a stroll down to Tempelhofen field where Orville did his flying
in Berlin. I was rather surprised to find three or four games of cricket going on
in different parts of the field. You will wonder what cricket looks like and sounds
like in Dutch, but as I have never really seen a game in England I do not know
how to compare it with the genuine article. While you are in America have
Orville take you to see a base ball game. The conduct of the crowd will interest
you immensely whether the game does or not. A base ball game at a school for
deaf mutes would be noisy compared with this German crowd at a cricket game.

Tell Bettie that I saw a whole lot of lions and tigers and bears and elephants,
and nice little ponies and some monkeys but I couldn't find any fairies, I think
may be they do not grow in Berlin. If I find one I will catch it and ask it to go
over to England with me the next time I go there.

I hope the temperature will stay below a hundred and five Fahrenheit while you are in America. I can not quite forget the day you made the trip around the Gordon-Bennett course. I think the temperature was up to about sixty-five or sixty-six that day. My recollection is that the ice was melted in Ogilvie's bath tub.

Wishing you a good trip to America and a pleasant time while there.

Yours truly

Wilbur Wright

Hotel Esplanade,

Bellevuestrasse 18

Berlin

23 July 1911

Dear Alec,

I have a cable from Orville asking me to come home soon as possible so it is probable that I will sail about the end of this week if I can get passage.

I am hoping to get things here in satisfactory shape before going, but I see no chance of stopping in England on my way. If I do not get a chance to see you in person please accept my thanks for the nice time I had at Eastchurch, and remember that there are at least three people and probably from 20 to 100 who would be glad to see you in America soon.

With best regards

Yours truly

Wilbur Wright.

Postcard to Mr A. Ogilvie, 2 August 1911

Better come over to America when the weather is cooler.

W. Wright

In September 1911 Ogilvie visited the Wrights in America. From 16 October 1911 he participated in test flights of a new Wright biplane glider at Kill Devil Hill, near Kitty Hawk. This glider had been designed to test the Wrights' automatic stability flight control system.

Henry A. Toulmin had from 1904 been the Wrights' patent attorney. He had arranged for the Wrights' basic patent to be duplicated in every major European country.

On 18 August 1909 the Wrights sued the Herring-Curtiss Company for infringement of their patented system of flight control. On 3 January 1910 Judge John R. Hazel

28. Alec Ogilvie soaring at Kitty Hawk, 1911.

granted the Wright Company a temporary injunction preventing the Herring-Curtiss Company and Glenn H. Curtiss from manufacturing aircraft or making exhibition flights for profit. Curtiss appealed and the case dragged on.

7 Hawthorn Street
Dayton, Ohio
Nov. 8, 1911

Dear Mr Brewer,

I was away when your letter came and only received it the day before Orv and Mr Ogilive came hence. Then Mr Ogilvie left for England so soon that I knew you would hear all about the Kitty Hawk experiences from him as soon as I could reach you or before – and that it would be much more satisfactory to get the report that way.

We always enjoy having Mr Ogilvie visit us. Orv found him a most delightful camping companion. I was wishing you could be with them.

Mr Russell has gone and Orv is re-organizing the shop – in dead earnest. Will is up to his neck in lawsuits. He is trying to force a hearing of the Curtiss case before Spring, but he has our own lawyer to deal with – as well as the Curtiss outfit. Mr Toulmin is not finding the case as profitable as he had hoped and he does all he can to drag out the litigation.

Orv hopes to make a good many improvements in the machine for next year. He is very busy with the drawing board and seems very well and vigorous since his return from Kitty Hawk. He has some of the fire and enthusiasm of the years before his accident.

Father has not been so well for about a month. He is troubled some with rheumatism and is not quite so lively as he was. He did enjoy your visit so much. He has often spoken of you both. He is sitting by me as I am writing and asks me to thank you for the seal, which came intact this time. It was very kind of you to take the trouble to send it.

It's nearly time now for you and Beatrice to begin planning for your next trip to America. Hush!!! <u>Maybe</u> we'll have an automobile and <u>maybe</u> – but not likely – we'll have our building site selected! I think Will and Orv are very glad we did not go ahead on the original lot. Many things are making that neighbourhood rather undesirable.

Love to Beatrice and Betty and Cyril if he is within hailing distance.

Best remembrances from us all. As always

Sincerely yours

Katharine Wright

29. Orville Wright gliding from the hills of Kill Devil facing the Atlantic Ocean, with the Wrights' shed visible in the distance. From Griffith Brewer's 'Kill Devil Camp' photograph album.

30. The shed showing the rudder and wing of the 1908 Wright machine. From Griffith Brewer's 'Kill Devil Camp' photograph album.

The Wrights were a family of four brothers and a sister — Wilbur, Orville, Katharine, and their elder brothers Reuchlin and Lorin. 'Buster' was the nickname of Lorin's son Horace Wright. Ivonette was a name shared by Lorin's wife ('Netta') and daughter.

Van Ness Harwood worked for the New York Herald. *Charles Taylor was the Wrights' mechanic who had worked on the engine for the original Wright Flyer.*

Wright Brothers
Dayton, Ohio
December 11, 1911

Dear Alec,

I have often thought that that was a remarkable shot you made when you hit the gull on the wing, but after reading your letter from the boat, telling of the soaring of the gulls 'steady as a rook and calm as a cucumber' (I must stop here to correct your American slang: 'Cool as a cucumber'), I have come to the conclusion that maybe it didn't take so much skill, after all, to bring that poor bird down. I wonder what one of those birds would do if it got its tail in one of the under and its head in the upper current on the Kill Devil Hill, like the one when I rolled over backward. By the way, Harwood has just sent me a bunch of his pictures, and as there is a letter from him to you which I am forwarding, I suppose you will have them also. One of his pictures completes the series of the different stages of the turn over. We had already seen pictures of you starting for the machine as it began to turn, me in a rather strained and uneasy position on the machine, and Lorin in an attitude of serene composure, with his hand in his pockets, enjoying the situation. The next shows you in full speed, with arms outstretched for something (don't know what, the machine is still a long way off). Lorin beginning to get a little uneasy, gently takes hold of an upright, and I just rising from the seat. This last picture shows you hanging on to the tail, Lorin tugging at an upright, and me hanging to an upright and the front spar of the lower surface!

Since our return from Carolina I have put in most of my time at the shop in experiments with motors and the automatic control. We have one of the water-cooled cylinder head motors running. We have attached a silencer, but find that the power of the motor is materially reduced. This can no doubt be greatly improved with experiment. We have also one motor with one cylinder with a rotary valve. This has not been tried far enough to test its practicability. The only thing that encouraged me to undertake it at all was our experience with oil in the gasoline on the motor boat at Kitty Hawk. I thought this would be

31. Horace ('Buster'), Orville and Lorin Wright. From Griffith Brewer's 'Kill Devil Camp' photograph album.

a good way to lubricate the valve, which I had understood was a difficult matter in most rotary valve motors. So far the tests have been very satisfactory, yet from all the trouble rotary valves give, I will not take much stock in it until it has been thoroughly tried.

I have made test of gasoline with and without oil mixed in it, as on the motor boat, and have found that the gasoline with oil always gives as good results and in most cases better results than the plain gasoline, in our motors.

The test of your motor was not as high as it should have been at the highest speed, although it was all right with the two inch fan. We consider 1050 good with this fan. One of our old motors which I have been testing since our return from the South shows a speed of 1580 continuously. We do not pass any motor till it makes at least 1525 with the 1½" fan.

I suspect you think we have given up all hope of teaching Buster to spell after the experience at Kitty Hawk, but not so. We have discovered that the way to make him do things is to insult him by saying that he couldn't do them if he wanted to. One day when he didn't even know his multiplication tables up to ten, at least couldn't tell how much 4 times 9, and other such easy numbers, I happened to mention the fact in a sort of pitying way to some of his acquaintances, when he was present. You could see his eyes flash with indignation, and he suddenly was able to make any multiplication we gave him. I don't think he ever got a 100% in spelling before, but lately he has been getting 100% over half the time. This is because his Uncle Will proposed to give him a penny for every time he got a 100% and to assess him a penny for every time he failed. Buster objected to going into such a deal, as he said 'that is too risky'. But as Uncle Will advanced a couple of pennies as advance payments, the bargain was sealed, and Buster didn't know how to get out of it! Consequently Buster has been compelled to stop and think a little, and so far is ahead a couple of pennies!

Buster has unfortunately learned that there is no Santa Claus, which puts him in about as embarrassing a situation as when you offered him your gun. He has been in the habit of writing to Santa, a few weeks in advance of Christmas, giving a list of the things he wanted. He says he wants things as much this year as ever, but he thinks it too cheeky to ask for them when he knows that his father and mother or his uncles and aunts would have to buy them for him. Of course Santa always just has these things and didn't cost him anything!

The license papers which Mr Brewer sent over have been lying about the office waiting for Wilbur's signature – that is, I thought they were waiting for his signature – but I discovered to-day that he at some time or other has signed them without my knowing it. I will forward them at once.

Wilbur has been in New York practically all of the time since my return. Curtiss was on the stand some time ago, and was confronted with his affidavits in which he swore to exactly contrary things. I think the first time was while you were over here. Well, things looked so bad that he thought they ought to be patched up some way; so he went on the stand again to explain about these affidavits. After an explanation, in which he didn't help his case any, was through, Mr Toulmin simply stated that he reserved the right to cross-question this witness in open court. Curtiss' confussion [sic] had been enough before, but when Mr Toulmin said this, he fairly had a fit. He pulled a bit of paper out of his pocket and wrote something on it, then tore it up, and stepped off the stand to speak to Wilbur. He wanted to know whether there wasn't some way in which this case could be taken out of court. He said he didn't like these personalities.

Since you were here some more of his affidavits have come to light. In our case against him he has been making affidavits that regardless of what theory might indicate, there was absolutely no difference in the resistance of the ailerons on his machine when turned to different angles. Some time ago he applied for a patent on equalizing device to turn the ailerons always to equal angles, one above and the other below the line of flight. In his affidavit he said that in all machines in which his new device was not used, there was a difference in the resistance of the ailerons, which turned the machine from its course. The lawyer that is fighting his case for him drew up this affidavit for him to sign! Curtiss is not altogether responsible for these affidavits because he was advised by his attorney to sign them.

Taylor has been having a very sad time since he left for California. Mrs Taylor, before Charles reached California, was taken sick and sent to a hospital where she was operated on. It was thought for a while that she wouldn't live, but she is now out of the hospital, though her mind is much affected. Her brother here told us that she scarcely recognized the members of her own family. Charlie's letters to us do not indicate that it is as bad as that, but he seems to be afraid that she may not recover her mind.

With wishes for a Merry Christmas and a Happy New Year!

Sincerely yours

Orv

7 Hawthorn Street
Dayton, Ohio
Dec. 27, 1911

Dear Mr Ogilvie

Your Christmas gifts to 'the family at Dayton' would have been <u>absolutely</u> perfect if you could have come along with them to help us enjoy it all and to join in the merriment. As it was, I read your letter just before Emma brought the pudding in, blazing with the sprig of holly stuck gaily on the top.

I wish you could have seen the children! It was such a huge delight to them to have something from you and from far off England. Buster was right next to me and it was worth a dollar to see his eyes. I didn't notice any of that 'lazy blinking' that Grandpa Wright complains of.

The children voted me a perfectly impartial carver. Will you believe it, that I always struck a coin whenever I came to one of them? The older folks said it was scandalous the way I manipulated things but, from the expressions on their faces, I judge that they did not wholly disapprove. I wouldn't have had one of those little folks miss getting a coin from you for any amount of vituperation that might have been hurled at me. I <u>was</u> impartial as to what coin fell to the various ones. I couldn't manage that, anyway. But little sister got the gold piece, Ivonette the shilling, Buster a half-shilling and, by mistake, Netta got the other half-shilling. I meant that Milton should have that. The pudding was <u>good</u> too, and I think I might have had some trouble in saving Orville from over-eating if he had not already consumed a great deal of turkey, another rather 'filling' food. It was great fun for all of us to have a genuine English plum-pudding for our Christmas dinner and for the children it was a real event in their simple lives.

The fruit cake was a grand success too. I'd love to have the recipe for that and the pudding if your house-keeper will let me have them. I gave almost half of the cake to Netta and have given a small piece to people who never have any of these nice things happen to them. The rest is being rapidly consumed – most eagerly by the 'Bishop' and O.W., Will and I like it but we can't eat so much at a time.

The books of photographs arrived on Christmas morning. Buster's mother was <u>so</u> delighted to have the pictures of him especially. She is so very devoted to Buster – which accounts partly for some defects in his training. Her heart gets the best of the head. All the pictures were interesting. I think Orv must have been his old self down there – from the way he acted up for his pictures.

He had such a good time with you and he is so well and lively since he came back. He has been making things buzz – and has been full of new ideas and designs. As things turned out towards the last, he would not have gone if you had not come over. I can't tell you how grateful we are to you for coming. We have shouted over those pictures of you prancing so frantically to get hold of the machine when Orv was in trouble. Every line in your whole figure shows such wild concern. Orv doesn't often see such lively action expressed in one fraction of a second.

I am glad you liked Col Carter. I think that is one of our most exquisite American stories. 'Marse Chan' and 'Meb lady' give really faithful expression of the southern life in wartimes. The southern people were much more unlike us than now, I imagine.

I hope you and Mr Brewer and Mr McClean will have a nice outing in Switzerland as I have no doubt you will. I had a nice letter from Mrs Brewer which came in the same mail with yours, Saturday before Christmas. She speaks of your proposed balloon trip and asks me if I do not consider it 'maddish'? She does but she says her husband is a 'cautious piece of goods, if he is anything' so she subsides, hoping that it will be all right.

Oh, I must not forget about the house. The boys have come to my way of thinking, as they always do if I just have patience enough to rely on the sun instead of the wind to produce the desired state of mind. But it's not the place of which we spoke when you were here, but just across the road on the high hill. There are 17½ acres to be had there and we can have a lovely place if one or two matters can be arranged – a village water tower is one of the drawbacks.

The entire family sends thanks and affectionate remembrances.

Sincerely

Katharine Wright

P.S. I wish I could have a recipe for the sauce for the plum pudding. Orv says you had some that was <u>very</u> good when he was there.

Matthew Piers Watt Boulton's 1868 patent 'Improvements in Propulsion and in Aerial Locomotion and in Apparatus connected therewith, parts of which are applicable to Projectiles and to Boilers' and Richard Harte's 1870 patent 'Improvements in Means and Apparatus for effecting Aerial Locomotion' are referred to. These early aeronautical patents proposed the use of a form of ailerons for flight control.

THE WRIGHT MOTOR

Dimensions, four-cylinders, 4⅜ inch bore x 4-inch stroke, 30-35 h. p., weight 180 pounds.

THE Wright Motor, like the aeroplane and propellors is a development of years of experimentation by the Wright Brothers, while the rest of the world was busy with a motor for automobiles. Here again no effort has been made to reduce weight at the expense of safety. Extreme simplicity offers the greatest reliability. There probably has never been built a practical four-cylinder motor with fewer parts. The body is cast in aluminum and the cylinders are cast individually in gray iron. The nickel steel crank shaft is cut from the block, as is also the cam shaft, which operates the exhaust valves. The intake valves are automatic. Ample lubrication of bearings and cylinders is obtained by a positively operated pump. The cylinders are water jacketed with aluminum and a centrifugal pump furnishes effective circulation. As this motor must operate in constantly varying altitudes, the gasoline is supplied directly to a mixing chamber without a carburetor, by means of a gear pump and injector which controls the amount of gasoline supplied to each cylinder in direct ratio with the speed of the engine. Ignition is provided by the Mea high tension magneto, offering an exceedingly wide range of control.

The power is transmitted to the twin propellors by means of nickel steel roller chains and the propellor shafts are of chrome nickel steel. Hess-Bright ball bearings are used.

32. Description of the Wright Motor in the company brochure 'The Wright Flyer' (Dayton, The Wright Co., 1911).

Wright Brothers
Dayton, Ohio
Jan. 3 1912

Messrs Brewer & Sons
London

Gentlemen:

Will you kindly forward us at once three copies each of the following patents;

Boulton # 392 dated 1868

Harte # 1469 dated 1870

Your prompt compliance will greatly oblige us as we are needing them in our litigation here.

Yours truly

Wright Brothers

Orville Wright refers to the War Office's Military Aeroplane Competition for the selection of British military aircraft. Trials of the aircraft entered for competition were conducted during August 1912 on Salisbury Plain in Wiltshire.

Wright Brothers
Dayton, Ohio
February 28 1912

Dear Alec:

Your letter in regard to the British Military competition is received. I find that the conditions imposed by the English War Office are similar to those imposed by the American Department. We have a contract for three machines from the American War Office, in which the requirements are almost the same as your British specifications, excepting that a speed of 45 miles an hour is required instead of 55 miles. We are required to carry 400 pounds, rise 2000 feet in ten minutes and make a speed of 45 miles an hour; or carry a load of 600 pounds, and rise at the rate of 150 feet a minute. We are building three machines with six cylinder motors, having cylinders 4⅜ bore by 4½-inch stroke. This ought to give us a little over 1½ times the power of our present motor.

The climbing tests are rather severe. I understand that in the French competition, no one succeeded in making 150 feet with a 600-pound load. While the motors used were just about double the power of the motor we propose to use.

I am afraid you will fall short of your calculation in one or two particulars.

If you made 60 miles an hour with a certain area and a certain load, you ought to be able to make the same speed with a machine twice the area and twice the load, provided the design is changed to keep the efficiency of the machine equal to that of the first mentioned. But when you double the load on your original propellers, their efficiency will be decreased. I do not know how much power you used to make a speed of 60 miles an hour. Recent tests made by the Automobile Club of America showed that the power of our motor, running at 1640 turns per minute, was only 39 horse power. This is less than we had been estimating. The Navy Department made a break test in which the power was shown to be only 32 horse power at a speed of 1300 revolutions. With a pair of 8½-feet propellers and a speed of 60 miles per hour, the loss due to the slip of the propellers on a 900-pound machine, would be about 12% of the total amount of power, while the loss in a machine of double the weight with the same size propellers, and travelling at the same speed, would be about 22% of the total amount of power. You could not count on a speed of more than 54 miles in the second case.

It seems to me that the weights are excessive in your calculations. The engine and radiator should not weight more than 350 pounds, the fuel and tanks not over 275 pounds, and the transmission not over 125 pounds.

I think you would do better to keep the aspect ratio of your surfaces as low as 1 to 6, as the strength of the structure will be increased by doing so, and the efficiency will not be materially decreased. If you wish to use a large surface in proportion to the weight, I would suggest a curvature of 1 in 25. For the plans for a speed machine, that must meet the conditions imposed by the War Office, the curvature of 1 in 25 is better than 1 in 20, which we have used on most of our machines.

Your climbing speed in the heavy machine will be reduced far below that of a light machine, on account of the greater load that must be carried by the propellers.

Some time ago I made sketches for a design of a fast machine, in which the seat of the operator is located in the tail framing, and the motor just in front of the main surfaces, about as shown in your sketch. I located the seat well back, so that the surfaces would not interfere with the operator's vision in landing. The planes are attached to an enclosed fuselage frame, the lower members of which are 3x3 'I-beams' which extend from the rear rudder to about 8 feet in front of the planes, where they meet the skid, which consists of a single runner of large section. The radiator is located at the forward end of this frame. I have no copy of this sketch that I can send you, but will probably have one made in a short time.

We are making quite a number of changes in our new models. Instead of the solid rear spar, we are using one of 'I-beam' section, 1¾ inch thick by 2 inches broad. We fasten the rib tips into this 'I-beam' which makes the ribs flush with the top and bottom sides of the spar. With the same area of cross-section we get double the strength in our new spar. The method of attaching the rear rudder framing is also much improved.

We have no very accurate tests of the gliding angle of our power machines, but our calculations indicate that the angle should be about 1 in 7, if the propellers did not interfere. The angle should still be about 1 in 6, with the propellers.

Our field has not been in condition so that we could do any flying for several months.

We have been experimenting with an automatic device for lateral control, similar to that described in our patent. We have improved it to the condition where it now balances the machine very well on our indoor training machine, which you probably remember. This is much more difficult than balancing the machine in actual flight. We have also built one of the fore and aft automatic devices, like the one we took south, for the power machine, but have not as yet had an opportunity to test it.

33. Wilbur Wright inspecting the engine of his Wright A biplane.

As soon as we have our drawing for our American Military machine completed, I will send you a blue print, showing it general features.

Sincerely yours

Orville Wright.

On 30 May 1912 Wilbur Wright died after contracting a form of typhoid fever. Brewer's obituary of Wilbur was published in The Aeronautical Journal *of July 1912.*

The following cables were addressed to Griffith Brewer's company.

21 May 1912

from Dayton Ohio

No change since Saturday critical not hopeless.

Attached contemporary newspaper clipping: 'A message from Dayton, Ohio, reports that Mr Wilbur Wright, who is ill with typhoid, is sinking'.

23 May 1912

Slightly worse extremely critical.

24 May 1912

Slight improvement.

28 May 1912
   Wilbur gradually sinking – tell Ogilvie.

30 May 1912
   Wilbur died this morning.
   Orville

2

Business Concerns
and Patent Disputes
July 1912–August 1919

Following his brother's death, Orville Wright was elected to fill his place as president of The Wright Company. The other directors were Andrew Freeman, August Belmont, Cornelius Vanderbilt, Russell A. Alger, Theodore P. Schonts, Morton F. Plant, Edward J. Berwind, P.W. Williamson, Henry S. Hooker and A.F. Barnes.

In the following letter, Orville Wright refers to the Wrights' British patent for a steerable rudder ('Improvements in Mechanism for actuating the Rudders or Controlling Planes of Aeronautical Machines') that could be applied to the front horizontal rudder described in their original patent specification 'Improvements in Aeronautical Machines' [1904 No.6732].

WRIGHT BROTHERS
Dayton, Ohio
July 23, 1912.

Dear Mr Brewer:

Your letter of June 13th in regard to the British Patent No. 16068/09, dated 15th July 1908, was received. I do not think that we have kept up the tax on this patent for several years, as it was not broad enough to make it worth while to keep it up.

We are hoping to have the pleasure of having you and Mrs Brewer with us again this year. We also hope that Mr Ogilvie can take a rest long enough to come over for a little while.

Sincerely yours,
Orville Wright

WRIGHT BROTHERS
Dayton, Ohio
August 31, 1912.

Dear Mr Brewer:

Your letter of August 10th enclosing the copy of the Aeronautical Journal arrived the day that Katharine and I and Lorin's two girls were leaving for a week's trip through the East, so that I did not have a chance to acknowledge its receipt until now.

We were all very much pleased with your article in the Journal. It is so different from most articles of this kind, because every incidence mentioned had some real foundation, and most of them are exactly as I remember them. Father and Katharine were especially pleased, and thought it the nicest article they had seen concerning Wilbur.

I wish also to acknowledge receipt of your two letters of some months back, the first of which came during Wilbur's illness. I quite approve of what you did in regard to the Short account. As to the publication of the tables and other scientific data which Wilbur and I collected in the early years of experimenting, I do not think it would be good policy for us to publish them until after we secure a patent adjudication. At the present time it is the possession of this information that keeps our Company at the head of aeronautical work in America, and it is the only advantage it possesses over our competitors until we are able to enjoin others from the infringement of our patent by law. I would be glad if you would explain this matter to the member of the Aeronautical Society that wrote to Wilbur and me about the same time as your letter. I have not been able to locate these two letters, so that I could answer him directly.

We are all hoping, however, that you can find the time to pay us a little visit this Fall anyway.

Sincerely yours,
Orville Wright

Attached to the above letter is a typescript copy of the following letter.

THE AERONAUTICAL SOCIETY OF GREAT BRITAIN
11 Adam Street,
Adelphi, W.C.

[16 May 1912]
Messrs. Wright Brothers,
1127, West Third Street,
Dayton, Ohio,
USA

Dear Sirs,

The Council of the Aeronautical Society have learnt that prior to your building the first mechanical flyer, you invented an apparatus and carried out tests which you tabulated, and on which tables you have been working ever since. They understand also that it is your intention to give this valuable information which you thus derived to the world, by publishing the results of your experiments.

The Council, however, fear that your lives are too busy to permit you to give the time which would be necessary in order to carry out this work, and they venture to suggest that the publication of such matter would be better if it came from a scientific society, than if it were published in book form in the first instance by yourselves.

It is in these circumstances that the Council wish to remind you that the Aeronautical Society of Great Britain besides being the oldest Society on this subject in the world, has been revived by the introduction of new blood and is now probably the most energetic Aeronautical Society in existence also, and in their desire to maintain this lead they are anxious to do their utmost to make the Society most useful in the cause of aerial science. They feel that if they could persuade you to allow them to be the means of publishing your original experiments and the tables which you use now as the result of your experimental work, they would do a signal service in the interests of aerial science.

The Council recognises that even the collection of the data of your experiments would entail some considerable work on your part, and they are anxious to put every facility in your way for the collection of such data. They would, therefore, be glad to send a delegate to Dayton, Ohio, where copies of your work could be made and photographs of apparatus could be taken, and in this way you could be relieved of a great portion of the trouble to which you would otherwise be put. I would say that Mr Griffith Brewer has volunteered to act as delegate on behalf of the Society, should you regard this suggestion favourably, and he would probably be able to come over during the month of September next.

Yours very truly,
R.M. Ruck,
Major General.
Chairman of Council.

WRIGHT BROTHERS
Dayton, Ohio
October 17, 1912.

My dear Mr Brewer:

We are very much disappointed on receiving word that you would not be able to make the proposed visit to America this Fall. This has happened to be an unusually pleasant Fall, on account of the weather and the greenness of the fields and woods. Our Summer was not quite as hot as usual, so that the grass and trees have not their usual parched appearance.

We are just beginning the building of a new home in Oakwood, a suburb of Dayton. The next time you and Mrs Brewer come we will be able to make it more pleasant for you.

I hope Mr Rogers is getting along all right
Sincerely yours,
Orville Wright

The following is a copy of a letter from Brewer to Alex Ogilvie, written whilst Brewer was staying with the Wright family. He refers to A.E. Berriman, who was Technical Editor of the British weekly journal Flight.

7 Hawthorn Street
Dayton. Ohio
26th November 1912

My dear Ogilvie,

Orville met me at the dock at New York and we came through here together. He was full of interest as usual and one matter which prompts me to write to you at once is a question of safety in flying.

Orville has been going into the cause of a number of accidents, where for some unexplained cause the machine has suddenly pointed downwards and has not been corrected before coming into contact with the ground. This type of accident has occurred in several cases after gliding down from a considerable height and after being straightened out at perhaps 50 feet from the ground, the machine is seen to turn downward and to continue to turn down until it strikes the ground.

In some instances, such accidents have been attributed to the fouling of the control wires, but in an inquest held by the American authorities on the wreck of an army machine, the control wires were found to be intact.

The conclusion that Orville has come to, is that these accidents are caused by the stalling of the machine and he has been making experiments in the air in order to test the effect of stalling in actual practice. He went to a height of 300 feet and stalled the machine, and as he had expected the machine turned slowly downward and for a period of at least 5 or 6 seconds after first stalling, the elevator tail was useless and the moving of the lever had no effect on the inclination of the machine whatever. The machine pointed downward at a very steep angle, possibly 60 degrees before it had gathered sufficient speed to bring it under control. Instead of dropping fifty or sixty feet in this recovery, however, he dropped about 200ft before he could straighten her out, and he says that he did not stall her to the worst position possible, and he would not be surprised if it would be necessary in some instances to have 300ft clear below, to enable the stalling to be corrected in time to save a smash. I will show this letter to Orville before posting it to you so that should you think this experiment of value for the general safety of flyers in England, you are free to give the information to Berriman for use in Flight.

I have not sufficient paper to tell you of all the nice things I have heard about you so will not attempt to do so, but you'll just have to come over here as soon as I get back if it's only to carry a pair of ski's from myself to Buster and to give him a few preliminary lessons. I mention this so that you shan't crib my idea.

Yours sincerely,

Griffith Brewer

In February 1913 Orville and Katharine Wright travelled to Europe, where they became involved in various issues relating to the Wright business. On 21 February 1913 the British Wright Company was formed in London with Orville Wright as its Chairman. Brewer together with a number of those who originally ordered the Short-Wright biplanes – Ogilvie, Francis K. McClean, Hon. Maurice Egerton and Percy R. Grace – formed the Company with £6,000 capital, of which £3,000 in shares was handed to Orville in exchange for his British patents.

On 26 February 1913 the Supreme Court of Leipzig ruled against the Wrights' German patent [Patentschrift Nr.173378 'Mit wagerechtem Kopfruder und senkrechtem Schwanzruder versehener Gleitflieger. Patentiert im Deutschen Reiche vom 24.März 1904 ab.] so far as it concerned the system of wing-warping.

On 27 February 1913 the United States Supreme Court found in favour of the Wright patent ['Flying-Machine'. 1906 No.821,393].

Ch. Thierry was a Patent Agent based in Paris.

The Wright Company
Dayton, Ohio
January 31 1913

Dear Mr Brewer:

Your letter enclosing the patent specifications, and also the later one enclosing the papers for the formation of the British Wright Company, have been received. On receipt of the latter, I cabled you 'Approved'.

Katharine and I will be passing through England about the middle of next month on our way to Germany. We are expecting to sail on the Mauretania, leaving New York on the 12th, I will bring the Company papers with me when I come. There are several things in the patent claims that I would like to talk over with you before filing.

Our German patent lawyers have asked me to be present at the trial at Leipzig, February 26th. They are fearful that the German Court is going to hold that the early published descriptions of our machine were a disclosure of the invention. Germany did not come into the International Agreement until about five weeks after the filling of our German patent, and it is this five weeks that seems to be making the trouble.

A few days ago I sent a letter to Messrs Short Brothers, asking them to either make a remittance to me at Dayton of the 140 Pounds still due on account, or to turn over that sum to you.

Some months ago I received a notice from Thierry that the taxes would be due February 10th in the Automatic Case for Great Britain. As I had made up my mind to let most of the patents expire in Europe, excepting the original patent, I did not have this paid. If the Company desires this continued, the payment of the tax should be attended to at once.

Sincerely yours.
Orville Wright

Postcard from Berlin of the Lustgarten Altes Museum.

To Mr Alex Ogilvie,
Ride's House,
Warden,
Sheppey,
England.
February 27, 1913

Dear Mr Ogilvie

We got decidedly the best of the lawsuit. The Court gave its decision within ½ of an hour after the hearing was over. They allow the patent on combination, saying it is patentable and that 'we(!)' were the first etc. etc. Refused broad claim of warping alone because of Will's and Chanute's disclosure. Orville is well pleased but still very tired.

Best remembrances
Katharine Wright.

In February 1912 Wilbur and Orville Wright had purchased a 17-acre site in the Dayton suburb of Oakwood on which to build a new family home – Hawthorn Hill – into which Orville, Katharine and their father moved in April 1914.

Katharine Wright refers to Lord Northcliffe, the British press baron, who was an influential promoter of aviation in its pioneering years and had witnessed Wilbur Wright's demonstration flights at Pau in February 1909.

7 Hawthorn Street
Dayton, Ohio
March 24 1913

Dear Mr Ogilvie,

Buster needed only a little encouragement and a bit of moral support to write a letter to you last night. As a matter of fact he was awfully pleased to have you remember him and, of course, his great interest in the book itself – though, as he very conscientiously tells you, he hasn't 'read much of it yet'. He thought it was not quite honest to say he liked the book as if he had read it – without making some qualification.

While you were gone, Lorin sold his house in Second Street and bought a place in Dayton View. It is rather a large place for them to keep up but Lorin bought it at a very good price and can dispose of it, at a profit, if they find it too much for them. There is a fine big yard for Buster to roam around in — though that doesn't suit us so well for we wanted our place to be especially attractive to him!

We found Father just fairly well. He had had a severe cold and was just recovering from that. He had taken advantage of our absence to organize a family party to attend the eighty-seventh celebration of his sister-in-law's birthday! He persuaded Lorin and Ivonette to go with him. The sister-in-law lives in Indiana, near 'the farm'.

The house is coming on slowly. The weather has been the limit. It is raining this minute. One might almost fancy she was in England! That's not fair, though, considering how good the weather was the whole time we were there.

Orville received your telegram of congratulation in the German decision (or was it the American?). They all came so closely together. We heard from the French case, by wireless, on our way home. We would be awfully well pleased if these decisions should do some good in England and give your little bunch of good friends there some satisfaction. I enjoyed your brother and his wife and Mr Seawright very much indeed. We saw Lord Northcliffe in Paris and he said 'Tell Mr Brewer to call on me if I can be of any assistance.'

I have just received the letter you forwarded. Thank you very much. You will be interested to know that Judge Hazel allowed claim 3, which is the broad claim on warping alone, as well as the claims on the combination. Curtiss wants to compromise but he won't get any chance of that. But remembrances from us all.

Sincerely

Katharine Wright

I forgot to repeat my advice to give 'Votes for Women' to stop the racket! KW

Over the Easter weekend of March 1913, torrential rain resulted in a major flood around the city of Dayton.

The Wright Company

Dayton, Ohio

April 22, 1913

My dear Mr Brewer:

Your letters of March 14th and 25th were received, but both of which were very late in arriving on account of the recent flood.

The water covered over half the City. At our Third Street office the water was about ten to twelve feet deep in the street, but did not quite reach the second floor. On Hawthorne Street it was about eight or nine feet deep and stood six feet on the first floor. Most of the things downstairs were ruined. We saved a few of our books and several small pieces of furniture. We might have saved almost everything had we had more notice, but Katherine and I over-slept that morning and had to be out of the house within one half-hour of the time we were up. The water in leaving deposited several inches of a slimy mud over everything. The gutters of the streets of Dayton for hundreds of miles are heaped several feet high with mud, furniture, etc., that has been removed from the residences and stores. In the center of the City the water was twelve to fifteen feet deep, and the entire stock of many of our merchants was destroyed. Thousands of families have lost everything they had. This is probably the greatest calamity that has ever happened to an American City, as insurance policies do not cover damage by flood.

During the time of the highest water fires broke out in the different parts of the City and nothing whatever could be done to stop them. The large buildings immediately west of our Third Street office burned, and I went to bed the first night of the flood, thinking that my office had burned, and all of the papers and data on aeronautical matters had gone with it. A constant downpour of rain while the adjoining buildings were burning probably saved the office.

Our factory was well out of the flood district, but we have not been able to do much work as yet on account of the difficulty in getting our workmen back and forth to work. We have been without regular street car service, electric light and gas for the past four weeks.

I shall be interested in learning what the War Department has to say in reply to your letter.

Very truly yours

Orville Wright

In 1913 the British Wright Company sued the War Office through Mervyn O'Gorman (Superintendent of the Royal Aircraft Factory at Farnborough), the Government's nominee as the Defendant, for infringement of the Wrights' 1904 patent. The lawsuit concerned the Royal Aircraft Factory BE2 aircraft exhibited by the War Office (Stand No. 61) at the International Aero Exhibition at Olympia, 14–22 February 1913. This was said to have been constructed on the same principle as the Wright biplane presented by C.S. Rolls to H.M. Balloon School at Farnborough.

Clément Ader had patented in 1890 a device for warping the end of a wing, but not evidently as a means of control in roll, for which he had proposed a fore-and-aft movement of each wing.

The Wright Company
Dayton, Ohio
July 16, 1913

Dear Mr Brewer:

I am returning enclosed the signed copies of the transfer of the Belgium patents.

I have just informed M Paul Coulomb, our patent solicitor at Paris, that I do not intend to pay taxes further on any European patent. I have just received notice that the taxes on Austrian Case O are due. I do not now remember how the claim for this Austrian patent was worded, but in view of the German Supreme Court decision in writing, which by the way is very different from the oral decision, I do not think that the Austrian patent would have any value whatever. You may investigate this however, and if you think it worth while I will transfer it to The British Wright Company, if it chooses to keep up the taxes.

The oral decision of the German Court was quite brief, and was delivered by the presiding judge. It gave us the entire credit for discovering the system of control as now used. The presiding judge interrupted the counsel for the French manufacturers frequently with such remarks as, 'You know that machine could not fly'; 'That machine was never even built', etc., when the patents of Harte, Boulton, Ader, etc. were presented. The only thing in the oral decision upon which the French could base any hope were the words of the patent itself, in which the term 'coupled' was used, but the written decision evidently was prepared by one of the other judges, who was not so favourably disposed. The written decision states that the use of the vertical rudder, according to the experts called by the Court, is absolutely necessary for maintaining lateral equilibrium; more necessary, if anything, than the warping itself; and that this function of the rudder was disclosed in our original application in the patent office files; but that this function of the rudder was not properly understood by the examiner, and as a result the original specification was amended in a way to indicate that the vertical rudder serves solely for steering in a horizontal plane. The decision then gives some suggestion on how we ought to have taken out our patent! The decision holds, however, that in spite of our own disclosures and our mistakes in taking out our patent, etc. we still had the claim for the mechanical coupling of the warping and the rudder! The attempt to make the present decision appear to agree with the oral decision in the matter of warping per se is so childish that any court with any self-respect ought to be ashamed of it.

I thank you for the translation of the parts of the French decision. The French Company decided at a recent meeting to increase its stock ten per cent (80,000Fcs) to raise funds to prosecute the case before the expertise, but all of the French stockholders have refused to subscribe for any of the stock without my first subscribing 25,000Fcs. This naturally made me think that they have little confidence in the final outcome of the case, and I answered them that it would be foolish for me, who is at a distance and not informed in the matter to subscribe when those who are on the ground are afraid to do so. I asked them to have Mr Peartree give me a full statement of the case. I have received from Mr Peartree a letter giving the steps that the case must yet pass through before a final adjudication can be had, but expressing no opinion whatever upon what would be the final result. I am so far away, and it takes so long to really learn what the situation is by correspondence, that I cannot get enough information to enable me to decide whether to put any more money into the litigation or not. If you should learn anything from any of the Directors as to what is their real opinion of the prospects of success, I would be glad to have you let me know.

I have been watching the progress of your negotiations with the English Government with interest, and I am glad to have information on it as it goes along.

The Curtiss appeal from the decision of the American Circuit Court will probably come to trial some time in the coming Fall.

Very truly yours

Orville Wright

Aug. 4th 1913

Dear Mr Brewer:

Katharine and I are delighted with the prospect of a visit from you and Ogilvie this fall. I hope you will not be too disappointed if we are not able to make the 'soaring' trip south. Present prospects are that I will not be able to get away from Dayton this fall, and I will not have any time to get a machine ready. You can adjust the time of your coming to suit yourselves. The monument has had to be postponed on account of the flood. The fund with which work was to have been done, was entirely by subscription from Dayton people, most of whom were severely hit by the flood, and few of whom, could at the present time make good this subscription. We are just now having unusually hot weather but the months of September, October and the first half of November are almost certain to be pleasant.

I believe the picture you took last year of the new house showed the foundations and some piles of brick and lumber. Now, all of the brick is up and the roof on, but, at the present rate it will be the first of next year before we can move into it.

Since I last saw you I have been doing some experimenting with pontoons. We have a very good one for smooth water but it would not be suitable for rough water. With our 50–60 h.p. motor we rise from the water with four persons aboard in a distance of four or five hundred feet, about 20 seconds in time. We got off in a calm in ten to twelve seconds with two persons aboard.

We have not as yet had the chance to test the new automatic on the machine although tests of it on our training machine give us good hope of its success.

Sincerely yours
Orville Wright

9th August 1913
[To] Mr Orville Wright,
1127, West Third Street
Dayton,
Ohio,
USA

My dear Orville,

I duly received your letter of the 16th July, and have to thank you for the return of the Assignment of the Belgian Patent.

I have since also obtained a printed copy of the Austrian Patent No. 23174 and have had the claims translated, and these read as follows:

1. A flying machine with supporting surfaces arranged one above the other, characterised by the fact that on the front longitudinal side of the supporting planes, which are adjustable to the wind at opposite ends at different angles, there is mounted a horizontally-arranged

front or head rudder, which by its adjustment receives a hollow curvature turned toward the wind, and on the rear longitudinal side a vertically arranged tail rudder so connected with the adjusting mechanism for the supporting planes that it offers to the wind at any time that side which is turned toward the end of the supporting plane which is adjusted at the smaller angle.

2. A constructional form of the flying machine protected by claim 1, characterised by the fact that between the two frames which are connected by vertical supports (2) stiffened by cross bars, there are stretched two ropes in such a manner that one (5) is led from the right-hand rear top corner to the right-hand front bottom corner and thence to the left-hand bottom front corner and to the top left-hand rear corner and has between the two bottom corners a slide for the aeronaut, while the other rope (8) is led in a corresponding manner from the left-hand upper front corner to the right-hand top front corner.

3. A constructional form of the flying machine protected by claims 1 and 2, characterised by the fact that the front rudder consists of a frame with material stretched over it, and rotatably mounted rearwards below its front edge and has springs sprung in between its front edge and an abutment.

4. A constructional form of the flying machine protected by claim 1, characterised by the fact that the vertical tail rudder is connected by means of universal joints with struts which hold it, and to the rear rope (8) by a steering cord.

I should say that these Austrian claims were drawn in Austria by someone who had no understanding of the invention in any way, because it appears that not only must the adjustment of the wings be <u>connected</u> to the rudder, but the machine must have a front horizontal rudder which by its adjustment receives a hollow curvature. It would appear that the drafter of these claims either understood nothing of the subject, or considered flying was so visionary a subject that narrowness of claim could be of no importance. I think, however, the British Company would like to keep this patent in force for a year or more to see how things shape themselves, and so I will bring it before the Directors and advise them to pay the tax, and I will bring the assignment to America with me next month at the same time that I bring the Italian assignment.

I saw Dr Eberhardt at the Hague last week at the Conference of the F.A.I., and he told me that the Memorial unveiling was postponed till next year. This will not make any difference in our plans, so you can still expect to see Ogilvie and myself just after breakfast on Saturday the 20th prox.

Please give my kindest regards to Miss Catherine and Bishop Wright, and believe me,

Yours sincerely,

[Griffith Brewer]

The Wright Company
Dayton, Ohio
October 10, 1913

Dear Mr Brewer:

Your wireless, 'Must 1904 machine continue sliding during turn' received. I do not see how to answer by telegraph.

At the beginning of the season of 1904, the vertical rudder was coupled with the warping, just as shown in the original patent. Later in the season I made a flight with a mechanism that performed exactly the same functions as the mechanism of our present machine. With that arrangement we were enabled to offset the rudder with reference to the wing warping, but the wing warping still operated the rudder. Having been accustomed to the use of the warping and the rudder firmly connected, I did not handle the offsetting of the rudder properly, and as a result nearly had an accident. Wilbur would not try it at all, and as the next turn to fly was his, he put the mechanism of the patent on again.

I am not certain of the exact date on which we began using the rudder and warping disconnected. In the first flight in May of 1905, the rudder and warping were independent, and blinkers were used in front. We had trouble in handling the machine with the controls arranged in this manner, so we dropped the blinkers. All of the later flights of 1905 were made with the rudder and warping disconnected.

Sincerely yours,

Orville Wright

The Wright Company
Dayton, Ohio
November 19, 1913

Dear Mr Brewer:

Your letters of October 18th, 31st and November 7th have been received.

The machine of the patent must continue to slide towards the inside wing all of the time in making a circle. This does not mean, however, that it is actually sliding down hill inwardly. It simply means that the inside wing is brought forward in advance of the outside wing. In other words the machine is skidding towards the inside wing in making a turn. This skidding reduces the amount of the angle on the outside of the rudder, and thus permits the machine to turn. Ordinarily the rudder turns just enough to secure a pressure to balance the difference in the pressure on the two wings, so that if one wing is warped to a larger angle than the other, the rudder exactly balances the difference in resistance and the machine continues on a straight course. But it will be seen that when the machine quarters slightly the pressure is reduced on the rudder, and thus the machine is permitted to make a turn.

We are now getting up an improved incidence indicator, which we hope will indicate more closely and with less vibration of the hand the angle at which a machine is flying. I should be glad to have you make the instruments for sale in Europe. I cannot see any reason why this indicator should not be built at a cost of $10.00 or less, but all that we have built so far have cost us over $25.00 a piece. This has been on account of the experimental work connected with building the first ones.

The report on the War Office Interview is very interesting. I am very pleased with the spirit shown by your War Office in the matter.

The Curtiss trial came off at New York on the 5th and 6th of this month. We are looking for a decision some time in December.

I had a telegram a few days ago from Tharel, announcing that unless I made a subscription at once, the CGNA would have to go into the hands of a receiver. I cannot see that I am justified in investing more money in the French Company when the stock-holders, who are on the ground and better acquainted with the situation, are afraid to do so.

The new house is moving on slowly, but we hope it will be ready by the time you get over next year.

Sincerely yours,
Orville Wright

Letter from Griffith Brewer to Orville.

13th February 1914.

My dear Orville,

I received your interesting letter yesterday about the costs of your litigation in America, which appears to confirm the rough estimate we made to the War Office of your having spent over £30,000 on litigation over there.

The decision of the Court of Appeals in the Curtiss case is most satisfactory, and I am very pleased to have the copy of the Judgement which you sent.

I note from your letter that you have not applied for patents for the Stabiliser in America. What I should like to do would be to come over to you now and help to rough out two specifications, one for the longitudinal automatic balance, and the other for the lateral automatic balance, and then these could be settled by some American Patent Attorney for use in America, and we could file applications over here, either as communications from you, or in your name as inventor. Whether you file the United States applications now or not, would be optional, because we could file the British applications and prevent publication for twelve months, so as to give you time to file in the United States.

I make this suggestion because there are so many people now alive to the importance of the invention you have in your possession, and the English law would grant valid patent to anyone who could find out what you have invented, and the thief could then successfully hold his Patent against even you yourself over here.

If you approve of this suggestion and you cable me the single word 'WELCOME', I would see if I could get over to Dayton for a fortnight and would cable you what steamer I would come by.

Yours Sincerely,

[Griffith Brewer]

The Wright Company
Dayton, Ohio
March 2, 1914.

My dear Mr Brewer:

Your letters of February 16th and 18th were awaiting me on my return from New York. I have also received the proposed copy of an affidavit to be used in the English suit, but have not as yet had the time to read it.

The basic principles of the stabilizer were contained in our earlier automatic patent, that is; the lateral control is regulated with a pendulum, and the fore and aft control with a vane. The new part of the device, upon which we expect to take out patent as soon as we have it working to our satisfaction, is for preventing the machine over-controlling, so that the machine does not keep rocking over the centre. We have not been able to do any experimenting with it during the last two months on account of very bad weather, but expect to take it up again within a few days. I do not think this is of sufficient importance at the present time to justify making a special trip for it, but, of course, we are always glad to see you whenever you can get away.

In the matter of small details, I think it best to work them pretty well out before applying for a patent, as the experiments give one a better idea of the points to be claimed in the patent.

I will read over the affidavit within a day or two, as soon as I have disposed of some of the other work that has accumulated, and send it to you.

Sincerely yours,

Orville Wright

The Wright Company
Dayton, Ohio
March 20, 1914

Dear Mr Brewer:

The affidavit for the English suit had almost slipped my memory. In reading it over I find several things which are not exactly true. In the beginning of Paragraph 8, the statement is made that the aeroplane with which flights were made on the 17th December, 1903, was identical, both in construction and mode of operation, with the Aeroplanes described and illustrated in the British patent specification. The mode of operation was identical, but not the construction. The machine shown in the patent warps from end to end. The warping wire to the cradle passes along the front edge of the machine. In the power machine of 1903, only the end sections warped, and the warping wire passed along by the rear spar, exactly as it does in the Wright machines of today. This was only a slight modification made in order to get a rigidly trussed center, on which to place the motor and propellers.

At the end of Paragraph 9, appears the statement that approximately 100 successful flights were made in 1904. A total of 105 attempts were made, but quite a number of these were not successful. In some cases the machine failed to get off the rails successfully. However, I think it should be stated in this paragraph that in many of the flights made during the year 1904 with the machine of identically the same mode of operation as that described in the patent, complete circles were described, and that we were able to steer the course of the machine with as much accuracy as machines of today can be steered by pilots with the same amount of experience.

I am returning the written affidavit for these corrections. I do not understand your English law well enough to know whether I could write this on the typewriter and swear to it before a notary.

Very truly yours,
Orville Wright

Attached to the above letter is a typescript copy of the following letter from Brewer.

31st March 1914
Mr Orville Wright,
1127, West Third Street,
Dayton,
Ohio,
USA

My dear Orville,

I was very glad to get your letter of the 20th, returning the affidavit with your remarks on the two inaccurate portions. Paragraphs 8 and 9 have been redrafted to meet your criticism, and the amended affidavit has been recopied. It is now returned to you so that you may swear it before a Notary Public, and also so that the Notary may attest the exhibit which you have kept by you. If you execute these documents immediately, and return them to us by return mail, we might still be able to bring the action to trial before the long vacation, in the event of the other side deciding not to come to America to take your evidence.

It is very important that we should file the affidavit without delay, because we want to place the other side in the position of either having to accept the affidavit in time for the case to come on next term, or for them to be obliged to go to the expense of coming to America in August next to examine you on your evidence. What they would naturally like to do would be to accept your affidavit late next term, so as to make the commission in America unnecessary, so that there would not be sufficient time to hear the case before the long vacation. They could then hang the trial up until the end of the year, without being obliged to incur the expense of the commission.

If there is anything inaccurate in the affidavit as redrafted, you can either alter in writing and initial the alteration in the margin, the Notary also initialling, or if the alteration required is big, you can also recopy the whole affidavit on the typewriter and then execute before the Notary. I hope, however, it is now in such form that you can immediately swear to it as it stands.

Yours sincerely

[Griffith Brewer]

The Wright Company
Dayton, Ohio
April 13, 1914.

Dear Mr Brewer:

I signed and returned to you the affidavit and accompanying exhibit last Saturday.

The affidavit was all right, although I thought that possibly one feature should have been brought out more strongly, that was, that our patent was the first instance in the history of aeronautics in which the use of the rudder for purposes of lateral balance was disclosed. The Supreme Court of Germany said that we should have applied for a patent for the use broadly of the rudder for purposes of balancing.

I am not sure as to the point you were trying to bring out in Paragraph 3. I do not believe that it is good policy to argue that there was no one at the time of our invention that could have flown, if he had had a controllable machine, and that it was necessary to interconnect the rudder and the wings in order to acquire the necessary skill. The defence will set up the argument that machines with adequate means of control have been known for years (the Boulton for instance), but that there were no skilled pilots to fly them. They will claim that all the different elements found in our invention were old, but that no one had the skill to use them; that it was not a matter of inventing a machine that would fly, but rather a matter of training men to operate the machines already invented; that we succeeded in acquiring this skill by simplifying the method of operating the different elements of control by interconnecting them; that our invention should be restricted to the interconnection and should not cover the use of the elements themselves.

We are expecting to be in the new home in a few weeks now, and will be glad to have you and Alec come over whenever you can.

Sincerely yours

Orville Wright

Attached to the above letter is a typescript copy of the following letter from Brewer. Brewer refers to the editorial 'The Wright Patents in America' in Flight, *Vol.6 (16), 18 April 1914, which stated:*

> *...it would seem that if the Wright Co. persist in their present policy they will succeed, not in making money for themselves, but in wrecking the whole industry. Fortunately for the British industry, there is no threat of any such monopoly as that possessed in America by the Wright Co., for whatever may be the case in other directions, our own patent laws compare favourably in these matters with those of other countries.*

24th April 1914

My dear Orville,

I have already acknowledged the receipt of the affidavit, which has now been filed.

The feature of the use of a rudder for the purpose of lateral balance per se, is one of greater importance in German Patent law than in English patent law. In Germany, one patents a discovery or invention involving a new technical effect; for instance, valid patents are granted in Germany for the use of a particular known alloy for making already known objects. Such a patent really becomes a patent for the selection of a known thing for a new purpose. Mere selection in this way is not patentable in Great Britain, and the use of a known apparatus, i.e. a rudder, for another purpose, is not patentable per se, because British patents are granted only for new methods of manufacture, and not for a new use of a known object, when no invention is required to adapt the old object to the new use.

The point of paragraph 3 is to refute the objection b̲ raised by the Defendant, saying that the direction given in lines 25–30 on page 3 of the said specification is wholly inaccurate and misleading for speeds of the machine exceeding a critical speed for each type of wing section. We do not know exactly what the Defendant means by this statement, but we believe that he means that in machines of high speed flying at very small angles of incidence, the change from say 3° angle to an angle on one side 2° and on the other side of 4°, does not change the resistance in certain types of wing section on opposite sides of the machine, and therefore that the rudder is not required to be operated simultaneously with such small change in the angles of the ends of the wings for the purpose of maintaining the lateral balance.

The machine therefore which is illustrated in your patent and which is described in the specification, need not necessarily include these modern conditions, if such modern conditions are alleged to exist, because the specification related to a useful machine of slow speed, not flying at the critical speed referred to possibly in the allegation, and not possibly of the type of wing section referred to in such allegation.

It is sufficient, in order to maintain the validity of your patent against this allegation of mis-direction, that the specification and drawing should illustrate a useful machine, and not cover all machines which might be designed later. Paragraph 3 therefore explains how, in order to invent a machine which was capable of flight, you naturally described a slow machine, and the directions given in the specification are fair directions to anyone to construct and use such a slow machine.

The whole affidavit is directed against the two allegations of non-utility and mis-direction, and not against prior knowledge, which must be dealt with by witnesses in Court. Your affidavit, if accepted by the Defendant, should prove that the machine was useful, and that you did not deceive the public by misleading them in respect to machines exceeding a certain critical speed for each type of wing section, which machines, if they exist, can only have come into existence after you had made the first useful flying machine.

The British Government has not cited Bolton [sic] in the Defence, but only Harte, where independent flaps are arranged at the rear of the wings. This patent will no doubt be made a great deal of, to prove that Harte invented flaps per se, and thereafter anyone was entitled to use flaps. They will no doubt endeavour to use this specification, for the purpose of driving us to interpret your claims as meaning warping, as distinct from flaps or ailerons.

The question of breadth of the claim, as to whether they are confined to warping or to include flaps and ailerons, does not arise in the present action, because no matter which way these claims are interpreted, the construction of the B.E.2 infringes the warping method. If they can prove that the claims must include flaps and ailerons per se, and that ailerons are old by Harte, then they would succeed in defending the action owing to the invalidity of the patent because it includes flaps.

Enclosed is a printed copy of your affidavit for you to keep for reference; also a page from last Saturday's 'Flight', containing an article on the American Company and the Editor's confused views on the position in this country.

Many thanks for your kind invitation, and for my part I will say that I shall come over to Dayton at the very first opportunity I have. At present I am working at arranging the Wilbur Wright Memorial Lecture Dinner, which will be held here on the 20th and 19th May respectively. You will be receiving an official invitation to both these functions in due course.

Yours sincerely

[Griffith Brewer]

The Wright Company
Dayton, Ohio
May 9, 1914.

Dear Mr Brewer:

I am just in receipt of your letter of April 24th. I am not sure that you understand the point I was trying to make clear in my last letter. The combined use of the rudder with wing warping is extremely useful, even at those speeds at which the defendants claim the wing with the smaller angle has a greater resistance than that with the larger angle. I was afraid that if we set up the claim that the rudder was simply for the purpose of keeping the machine on a straight course, the court might then hold that it was simply a steering device, and that its function was not different from that of the rudders proposed in some of the old patents or other papers.

I believe patent law is pretty much the same in all countries. Harte has been considered by the German and the American courts, but was not held as an anticipation by either. I think that the English court will also hold that old paper patents, which were never built and never tried and from which nothing ever developed do not constitute anticipations.

A few days ago I did a little flying with an improved form of the automatic device of which you prepared some specifications a year ago. The new device is a very great improvement over the particular device we had at that time, and from the little experience we have had in using it so far, I think it is going to be a very good thing. Its simplicity is its strong point, there being no electrical or pneumatic machinery required to operate it.

Sincerely yours,

Orville Wright

34. Glenn Curtiss's reconstruction of Langley's 1903 tandem monoplane *Aerodrome* in flight over Lake Keuka, 1914. The Curtiss-built pontoons, and much else, were not part of the original.

In 1914 Glenn Curtiss at Hammondsport, western New York State, reconstructed Langley's 1903 tandem monoplane Aerodrome. *Curtiss made various alterations reflecting aeronautical advances in the subsequent decade. The reconstruction, with the addition of Curtiss-built pontoons, was flown from Lake Keuka on a number of occasions. In May 1914, whilst in America to take Orville Wright's evidence in the case of* The British Wright Company Limited v. O'Gorman, *Brewer travelled to Hammondsport to witness the flight trials of the reconstructed Langley machine.*

Katharine Wright refers to Lieutenant Kenneth Whiting, a naval aviator who learned to fly at the Wright School of Aviation at Simms Station, Huffman Prairie. The School operated from 1910–16, and a former pupil, Oscar Brindley, was the chief instructor. Alpheus Barnes was Secretary and Treasurer of the Wright Company.

Note that the Wrights have moved to their new house at Oakwood.

Hawthorn Hill
Oakwood
Dayton Ohio
Sept. 13 1914

Dear Mr Brewer

Because we have been so interested in the success of England and France against that 'crazy egotist' it has been hard to write while things were reported to be going badly with the Allies. Now that the tide has turned, we are tremendously relieved. It is amazing how 'neutral' we all are! In six weeks, I have run across just six people who are for the Kaiser. All the rest hope he will have his head thoroughly punched and we think he will, undoubtedly.

When Carrie was putting your room in order, she found two packages in your closet which looked interesting enough to investigate. So when Orv and I came in at noon on the 19th of August we found the books and the camera in the middle of the hall table. You can perhaps imagine my joy over the books. I want <u>nothing</u> so much now since the flood. The only trouble is that these four lovely little volumes may lead me into extravagance for I <u>must</u> have the rest in that very edition. I am saving these four for the long winter evenings when I can settle down and enjoy them. Thank you so much for them and for the good wishes.

I think Orv felt a little like Buster about the camera, at first sight, but when he read in your note that you had 'plenty more guns at home', he was reassured and decided to be very glad that you had! He has been experimenting but has had nothing developed so far. I think he feels a little dubious of success.

Lieut. and Mrs Whiting left just yesterday. Mrs Whiting has been ill for three weeks and is going home for a month, to recuperate, before she goes to Pensacola, where the Lieutenant has been ordered. Another Navy man has had orders to come here. Lieut. Whiting was a very satisfactory person, in every way, and Orv was glad to do all he could for him.

Mr Barnes is in California, where the army machine is going through its tests. It seems that Brindley is cross-wise and has been making no effort to get what he can out of the machine. The speed test has been passed and Mr Barnes says he expects the rest to go through without any trouble, if Brindley is not too treacherous. I am afraid he will find it unprofitable, in the long run, to be disloyal.

I have had a nice letter from Lord Northcliffe telling me to use his letter, by all means. And I shall, never fear!

Henry Woodhouse is making us another 'visitation' today. I use the term 'visitation' advisedly! He is such an unmitigated bore and has no more sense or stability than a weather cock, as you know. He has some crazy idea, I do not know what and haven't tried to understand. It isn't worth while. He says he didn't know what the original Langley machine was and therefore didn't know what Curtiss was doing!

My best to Beatrice and the children. Tell her to be thankful, as she is without being told, that Cyril isn't old enough to be sent out to be shot out. I haven't yet got over the feeling that it's all a bad dream and <u>can't</u> be true. And yet the papers say that England is settling down, for a two years war or more. The Allies are bound to win, eventually.

You haven't happened to hear anything about the de Lamberts, have you? And what are Mr Ogilvie and Mr McClean doing? We are so eager for news of all our friends and hope they are safe. Please give our affectionate regards to 'Alec' when you see him.

Tell Beatrice that you got through without being told that you weren't wanted any longer but that you did leave one great, big hole in the household, which is still felt. She had better come along next time!

Please tell our English friends that we are so neutral over here that it is immaterial to us whether the English or French administer the proper drubbing to the Kaiser. That is where our neutrality comes in strongest! We <u>can't</u> swallow the Russians but we don't have to do so. And Lorin's Katie has flopped over to the English side, after receiving a letter from home that all Ireland was united against the enemy! We have had lots of fun over that.

Buster caught another mole but now the trap has been stolen. He left it too near the road. I think Cyril might enjoy some of Buster's adventures.

Much love to all from all of us.

Katharine Wright

P.S. Orville's rheumatism is no better – worse rather, I am sorry to say. K.W

In October 1914 the claim of the British Wright Company against the War Office was settled by a lump payment of £15,000. The following extract from a typescript copy of a letter from the Treasury Solicitor, dated 1 October 1914, and held in the Royal Aeronautical Society Library records the details of the settlement:

... I am now instructed by the War Department that, whilst they do not anticipate that there will be further use of the Wright Patent No.6732 of 1904 in new Military Aeroplanes, nevertheless they will agree to pay £15,000 (Fifteen thousand pounds) in settlement of all claims in respect of past present and future use by the Military and Naval Forces of the Crown of the Invention covered by that patent, or by any corresponding foreign or colonial &c patent controlled by the Company.

The Wright Company
Dayton, Ohio
October 27, 1914.

Dear Griff:

For the past several months I have had a spell of not writing, or rather as that is my normal condition may be I should say that I am just starting a spell of writing.

I have received your letters on various matters.

I was much interested to note after your departure for Europe that the Canadian Government took up the proposition, which you suggested to it, with other parties here in America, among whom were the Connecticut Aircraft Company, Woodhouse, and Charles R. Flint. Of course, all of Mr Flint's negotiations were in the interests of our own company. We did not care to undertake the establishing of a Canadian branch without a guarantee of a considerable amount of business. I have never heard that anything finally came of the plan.

On receipt of your telegram, ordering a motor for Ogilvie, we hurried the completion of one, and shipped it off by express, as we thought it would be safer this way than by freight. We would have liked to have waited until one of the later motors was completed, on account of the finish of the cylinders. The one we sent Alec had painted cylinders. Our newest ones are plated, so that the finish is not affected by heat, as was the case with painted ones. There seems to be a very large demand for motors in Europe at the present time, but a demand which the American manufacturers will hardly be able to satisfy.

We sent to Alec a blue print of our drawings of our wheel control. The warping is done by the turning of the wheel, the elevator is controlled by the fore and aft movement of the wheel and the lever on which it is mounted, and the vertical rudder is operated through the small lever mounted on the wheel, so that when the lever and wheel are gripped together, the vertical rudder works in conjunction with the warping. Of course, it would be very easy to disconnect the rudder and operate it through a foot lever if preferred. We are now arranging to equip all of our machines with wheel controls instead of the lever, as it possesses more instinctive movements.

The dividend from the settlement with the Government was received all right by cable. The rate of exchange was unusually good, so that I received almost $5.00 per pound.

I received your letter and telegram with reference to reducing the license rate to British manufacturers to twenty pounds. I replied by cable, 'Proposed royalty not acceptable under present conditions'. These conditions are, that in America our royalty rate is just ten times this amount. If it became generally known that British manufactures were being licensed at the low rate of twenty pounds, we would have trouble here. Of course, the low rate would give the British manufacturers a big advantage over the American or other European companies in the open market. I therefore think it would be inadvisable to make such a low rate anywhere until we have our business in America satisfactorily arranged. The English output is practically already provided for in the license to the Government, so that I do not see that there is very much left to be done in England now. The recognition of our rights morally by the Government is as much as could be asked for. All that could be procured legally would hardly pay for the litigation.

I did not understand that the life of an English patent could be extended beyond its original term. A notion prevails in America that American patents can be extended, but I cannot find any foundation for it. I do not know of the life of any patent having been extended here.

We have just received your cable with reference to time of delivery of four machines if ordered by Flint. I take it you have reference to machines intended for South Africa. We will be able to complete the four, ready for shipment in about four weeks after order. We are equipping these machines with wheel control, so that it will be easier to get operators for them in Europe.

After thinking over the matter for a long time, I have decided not to be about the camera like Buster, although in this case there is good reason why I ought to be. I will later send you prints of the four negatives you exposed before you left. Out of the eight remaining, I succeeded in exposing just one. I did not understand the film packs, and found that I was pulling the sheets from the wrong side. I did not make this discovery until I got to the last one left.

With kindest regards,
Sincerely yours,
Orville Wright

In Brewer's papers the following typescript copy of a letter from him was attached to Orville Wright's reply.

Private
6th November 1914

Mr Orville Wright,
Dayton, Ohio,
USA

My dear Orville,

Several things of interest have occurred since I last wrote to you.

We have succeeded in interesting certain parties in the Wright machine, to the extent that if the machine comes up to requirements, it might be necessary to buy perhaps two dozen machines.

Our difficulty of showing what the Wright machine could do, was met unexpectedly by Hudsons' Consolidated Limited asking us if The British Wright Company would assemble and fly a new Wright machine which they had bought, through its tests down at Farnborough. We therefore quote £120., being £70 for erecting the machine, and £50 as a fee to Ogilvie, for flying it in its tests. Ogilvie intends to give his fee to a patriotic charity.

During the past fortnight therefore, Ogilvie and I have been down at Farnborough putting the machine together, and Ogilvie has made the following flights:

October 28th	1 minute ★
October 31st	8 minutes, 5 seconds
" "	15 minutes, 40 seconds
November 3rd	20 minutes
November 5th	11 minutes, 45 seconds
" "	6 minutes, 15 seconds
" "	4 minutes, 55 seconds

★ This flight terminated when the machine had reached a height of 250 feet, by the engine seizing. No.2 cylinder turned out to be badly scored, the result of the oil pump jamming owing to a bead of solder, which was afterward found between the pump teeth.

All the above flights with the exception of the flight on the 3rd November, were in windy weather, and the machine was found to be thrown off its course and sideslip badly. On the 3rd, when the weather was calm, however, Alec says that he enjoyed the flying, and found the machine responded to its controls very well.

The conclusion arrived at is, that the machine cannot safely be flown in rough boisterous weather which we get over here, and which, under War conditions, the Military Flyers have to fly in. We are therefore waiting for some fine weather, in order to put the machine through its military tests on a calm day.

The large order in view would require machines which were suitable for flying in windy weather, and so Alec and I have been discussing the problem of whether, after the machine has gone through its military tests, it would be easy to alter it so as to make it steady in the air. There are three things which are unusual in the design, all of which might contribute to the lack of control:

1. The dihedral angle of the wings;
2. The length of the fuselage and large area of its side surface;
3. The low centre of gravity of the machine.

I have suggested to Alec that we should, now that we have the machine before us, make drawings of it so as to be able to make modified drawings for your consideration, with a view to overcoming the difficulties, and with this object in view we will make drawings to a scale of 1 inch to the foot, and then if we get out any modified arrangement, I will at once send you a tracing for your consideration.

Last week I sent you a cable asking how long the four machines which were enquired for by Flint's would take to deliver. This cable was sent because the people who originated the enquiry asked me to give them further information, which I naturally wished to do as completely as possible. The question of delivery was one portion of the information they required, and they are now in cable communication with South Africa. I have not suggested any alteration in the machine to them except that as the machine they require is for landing on soft sand, larger wheels and larger tyres might be employed, and also that slightly larger wings might be used if high speed were not required, so as to make the landing safer on the undulating sand over which the flights would be made in South Africa.

With regards to the British Wright Company Licences in Great Britain, we shall probably come to a stand-still here, because it would be impossible to collect a flat rate of £60. without considerable uproar, and so for the sake of peace things will probably slide. A great deal of the objection would be met if we could charge a percentage royalty, and this would probably be better than a flat rate of £60. A 5% royalty would enable machines costing £400. to pay £20. royalty, whereas machines costing £2000., which is nearer the modern figure, would then pay £100. Would you agree to 5% substitution for the £60. flat royalty? If so, a cable saying, 'Agree five per cent' would be most welcome, as it would enable us to come to terms before the effect of the Government settlement has completely cooled off.

Yours sincerely

[Giffith Brewer]

The Wright Company
Dayton, Ohio
November 19, 1914

Dear Griff:

I have your letter of November 6th.

This is the first that we had heard of what had become of the machine which we were experimenting with when you were here. I do not altogether understand what the trouble is with the side slip to which you refer. Does this occur in straight flight in windy weather or when making turns? On account of the dihedral angle of the wings in that machine, I found it sensitive to side gusts, and until I had become quite accustomed to it, I had difficulty in making smooth turns, because when the machine slid inwards on the turn, the machine was brought out of its bank. The machine seemed to me very steady fore and aft when flown in winds. The incidence indicator showing less than a degree variation ordinarily. We have no dihedral angle in the later machines. I do not think that its sensitiveness to side gusts is due to the exposure of the side of the fuselage, because I noticed that the wing on the side from which the gust came, always tended to rise. Our experience with the older machines has been, that when we had a vane effect low on the machine, the wing that was exposed to the wind tended to sink instead of rise. I should be very glad to hear further of your experience with this machine after the dihedral angle has been removed. I myself have not been able to do much flying of late on account of a very severe attack of rheumatism.

In order to keep the motor working properly when the machine is climbing, it will be necessary to turn the carburetors [sic] around, so that the float feed tank is forward. I do not know whether this change was made in the motor sent to you. You will remember that we had trouble with this machine when making a steep climb. We have discovered that the bigger part of the trouble was due to the position of the float feed of the carburetors.

I am sorry that I cannot allow you at the present time to establish a royalty rate of five per cent on the price of machines. A royalty rate of five per cent in America would bring us in scarcely anything, and if this price were allowed abroad at the present time, it might kill some negotiations which we now have here in America. The Americans have already set up the claim that we are making the British Government a much better price than we are offering here in America. As soon as the American business has been entirely settled, I shall have no particular objection to any rate of royalty in England that may seem reasonable to you.

Sincerely yours,
Orville Wright

Copy of a letter from Brewer held in typescript. Brewer refers to discussions held with Lt-Col. William Sefton Brancker (1877–1930), Assistant Director of Aeronautics, and Brewer's plan that a Canadian air squadron be organised under the code-name of 'Brewer's Exhibition Flights'.

G.P. Wallace was one of six pilots selected to go to England for advanced training, and in May 1915 was to command the newly formed South African Aviation Corps.

Private
12th November 1914

Mr Orville Wright
Dayton, Ohio
USA

My dear Orville,

Since writing to you last Friday, your long letter of the 27th October arrived, and has been much appreciated both by Alec and myself.

I am up from Farnborough today, as a gale of wind is blowing and nothing can be done down at the flying sheds, but I am going back this evening and will take some drawing instruments with me, so that I can trace the suggested alterations in the machine in time to post this tracing to you tomorrow.

The position over here is extremely difficult with regard to the prospects of the possible sale of Wright machines, because anything sold over here direct to the British Government must be approved by the Aeronautical Inspection

Department at Farnborough. The Director of the Air Department, Colonel Brancker, has expressed fears that a 60 h.p. engine cannot bring a machine up to the standard called for under war conditions on the Continent, where it is better to let the pilot and observer risk breaking their necks in landing, rather than court being pounced upon and destroyed in the air by a hostile faster machine.

Although it is blowing 40 to 50 miles an hour, yet today and yesterday I have seen machines flying at Farnborough and at Brooklands, and a machine is to leave today to fly from Farnborough to France. You will therefore see how arduous are the conditions imposed on machines which can be made use of by the Armies in the field.

The South African enquiry has not yet matured, and the day before yesterday, Captain Wallace – who is at the Flying School here, and who would have charge of these machines if they go to South Africa – called at Farnborough and inspected the Wright machine. He talked of getting a flight of twelve machines, and said that these would first have to be tested by British Government flyers. He also said they might try to get the machines in France, so as he and his Department have such varied views, I should not expect it to come to anything.

The two dozen machines which are referred to in my last letter, are to compose the proposed Canadian Squadron, which Colonel Brancker approves subject to the machine satisfying them at Farnborough. He has mentioned the scheme to the Commander-in-chief who also approves, and if the tests come up to his requirements, the Chief would ask the Canadian Government to organise this Flying Squadron, and Alec and I having volunteered our services, would come over to America for the purpose of organising the men and machines. I did not give you these particulars last time, because I thought it best for you not to know them, but if any thing is to come of it, it will be necessary to speak more clearly.

The chief difficulty we are apparently in, is that if the machine gets through its ordinary tests on a calm day, it would be useless to go ahead with the scheme if the machine cannot be flown in gusty horrible weather, such as the other machines are flying in, and Alec says that he won't fly the machine again as it is, in a high wind, because it side-slips and won't answer its controls in the ready way in which his machine down at Eastchurch answers. We must therefore cure this lack of control, or abandon the scheme so far as a Canadian Contingent is concerned.

The questions I want answered are:

35. Wright Model H. From *Aero Digest*, Vol.67 (1), July 1953.

1. Whether, with Alec's alteration as shown in the tracing, the machine
    is likely to fly steadier in the wind.
2. If it would fly steadier, would you be willing to alter your design in
    order to attain this result?

In the event of the Canadian scheme falling through, Alex suggests that the
British Wright Company should be financed by him and should manufacture
Wright machines on this modified plan with a view to selling them to the British
Government. We will not, however, do this without we are fairly well assured
that the machines so constructed will be purchased, and that at a profitable price.

From these long letters, you will no doubt gather that Alec and I are both
extremely keen on working off superfluous energy in a direction profitable to
the British Cause, and if this can be done with your co-operation, our satisfaction will be considerably increased.

Yours sincerely

[Griffith Brewer]

The Wright Company
Dayton, Ohio
December 3, 1914.

Dear Griff:

Your letters of the 12th and 19th have arrived almost simultaneously. Most of your letters have reached me within ten days.

I should have told you in my former letter that we were getting out a faster machine than the one that was shipped to England. That machine was designed especially for slow speed, so that for purposes of training it could be flown at a speed of 35 miles or less. It was designed to make 33 miles with two men and a small supply of fuel. The faster type which we call the 'HS' is about ten miles faster than the model 'H'. The surfaces have less area and less camber. On account of the deep curvature of the surfaces on the model 'H', the drift becomes high at angles below four degrees. The uprights between the surfaces are of a streamline form, very similar to the sketch sent by Alec. The fuselage is built in two sections, the joint being about a foot back of the rear edge of the surfaces. The veneer is put on diagonally, which seems to relieve the veneer of buckling when a little damp. The gas tank has a valve operated with a lever coming up between the two seats. With regular setting of the lever, the tank cannot be drained to the bottom. By turning the valve the reserve left in the bottom, which amounts to several gallons, can be utilized. Alec's suggestion that the tank be divided into two sections so that in case one be punctured by a shot all the gasoline would not be lost is a very good one.

We are fitting all of the new machines with the wheel control similar to the print mailed to Alec some weeks ago. It is a very simple matter to change this to the regular 'Deperdussin'. A magneto short circuit button is attached to one of the wheels, so that the motor can be stopped either by holding the valves open, or by the short circuit. One of these levers and wheels is made so that it can be removed and replaced in less than a half minute.

We are using a different form of tail skid. The one on the machine which you now have tends to slue the machine around after making a landing. The landing wheels are steel rims and detachable tires. The vertical rudders are of simpler design and construction. The segments for operating the elevator are of improved construction and are quickly detached and assembled for shipment.

The wings of our present machine are wired differently from the one you have. The dihedral angle which had a disturbing effect in winds has been removed, and the angle at the tip of the wings has been increased, so that in flying at small angles of incidence no downward pressure is carried on the tips. As you already know, a one pound downward air pressure on a wing causes as much resistance as two pounds of weight carried. When flying at 60 miles an hour with the wings trussed as they are in the machine you have, about 50 feet area of the wings are exposed at a negative angle.

I think without question the trouble you are having with the power of the motor falling off when making a climb is due to the siphoning effect of the overflow pipe in the glass gauge. The vent to this tube is now located several inches below the bottom of the glass jar. It should be immediately under the jar. When the gasoline begins overflowing through this tube, the pressure in the jar is reduced in amount equal to the length of the tube. If you will remember when you were here, this little tube used to entirely draw all the gasoline out of the carburetors. An easy method of curing this trouble is to close up the top of the overflow tube and then bore one small hole in it at the top, which will maintain a small pressure in the jar when the motor is running. A one-sixteenth inch hole is ample to let the surplus gasoline escape and at the same time is small enough to prevent the siphoning of the gasoline.

I am very much interested in your account of Alec's speed and climbing tests. I am not certain from your letter what load was carried on the machine in these tests, but I take it that there was about 450 pounds altogether counting the two men and fuel. I think Alec will have no trouble making 400ft per minute climb with this load when the trouble with the motor is cured. I do not think the trouble is due to the Zenith carburetors, although it is quite possible that the Claudel may be a better one.

If your plan of organizing a Canadian flying corps goes through, we will be prepared to build machines of any type desired.

We are now planning to get out a single screw tractor machine to have a speed between 70 and 80 miles an hour using our present motor. In this machine we propose to make a small fuselage and place the men in tandem. At speeds above 70 miles an hour the gain in efficiency through the use of two propellers will not any more than compensate for the losses due to extra weight and resistance of chain guides and propeller frames. Of course, the single screw machine is simpler in construction. My most serious objection to it is the gyroscopic effect of the motor and propeller, which prevents turns to right and left being made with equal facility.

I have not had time yet to thoroughly study the sketches you sent, but many of the suggestions seem very good. I have doubts as to whether the gasoline would feed to the carburetors by gravity alone when the machine is climbing, unless the gasoline tank were placed closer to the motor.

I notice the sketch for the chassis and shock absorber. We built a chassis about a year ago, based on European designs, using rubber bands similar to those shown in your sketch, but as we were not able to get suitable bands we were finally compelled to go back to our older type. The bands we used chaffed so badly on each other, that they did not last any time at all.

We will be ready at any time to undertake the building of machines for you along any lines that may best serve your purpose.

Tell Alec I will answer his letter in a few days as soon as I have time to examine your sketches more carefully.

Sincerely yours,
Orville Wright

The Curtiss Model H America was a twin-engined flying boat built for an attempted Atlantic crossing in summer 1914. 'America' became a class name for many of its derivatives.

January 5, 1915
The Wright Company
Dayton, Ohio

Dear Mr Brewer:

We have lately entered suit for injunction against The Curtiss Aeroplane Company for infringement of our patent. The Curtiss Aeroplane Company is composed of the same stockholders and officers as the Herring-Curtiss Company, against which injunction has already been obtained.

In prospect of a suit against his present company Curtiss got out the old 'Langley' machine and attempted to fly it to try to make it appear that Langley was the real pioneer in the art. (The courts had held that our patent deserved the broadest interpretation because we were the pioneers in the art.) He also began the construction of the America, in which he operated the ailerons upward only, in this way avoiding infringement of Claim 3 of our patent, on which the court had held his former machines to be an infringement. Claim 1 of our patent covers this new operation, but Claim 1 was not involved in our former suit, and therefore, has not as yet been passed upon by any court. However, the use of one aileron at a time as in Claim 1 produces only about one-half of the controlling effect as when two are used simultaneously operating in opposite directions as in Claim 3.

I have been told (but I cannot remember who told me) that the America, while at Hammondsport, had all of the cables and pulleys necessary to operate the ailerons simultaneously and in opposite directions as they were used in the earlier Curtiss machines, but that the cables to the under-side of the flaps were disconnected, the intention being, I think, to infringe only Claim 1 while using the machine in the United States, but to connect up the extra cables and operate the ailerons in both directions when taken to Canada to make a bluff at starting across the Atlantic.

In our coming suit it will be of very great advantage to us if we can show that Curtiss actually had all of the necessary cables on the machine when it was shipped abroad, so that by simply making connection the ailerons could be operated simultaneously in opposite directions, and that the machine as now being used has these cables connected up in this manner.

I have been wondering whether it will be possible for you to see the America, if possible the original one which you saw at Hammondsport (I understand that two have been sold to the British Navy), so that you could make an affidavit accompanied by a diagrammatical sketch showing the ailerons and the cables and the manner of operating them. Also a statement as to whether these cables, guides, etc, for the cables were on the machine before it was shipped from America. Of course, you would have to base this statement upon knowledge gained from some of the Naval Officers who were acquainted with the condition of the machine when it arrived, or who would know whether any changes had been made in the method of operating the flaps since its arrival.

The points that we wish to show are:

(1) That the America as now being used has the ailerons connected up so as to operate simultaneously and in opposite directions.
(2) That all of the mechanism necessary to operate them in this manner was on the machine when it was shipped from America.

We believe that if we can show this, the court will grant us an injunction against Curtiss building machines in which the ailerons operate independently, although this Claim has not as yet been regularly operated in this manner and that the mechanism for so operating it was furnished by Curtiss.

I am enclosing three blue prints showing different types of Curtiss machines on which we are asking injunction. No.1 is the old type of machine in which the ailerons are operated simultaneously. No.2 is a newer type with ailerons or flaps at the rear edge of the upper surface which are operated simultaneously and in opposite directions, and No.3 is a type corresponding to the American as used at Hammondsport, in which the ailerons are lifted upward only and one at a time. We are not certain as to whether a shoulder brace was used for operating the ailerons in the America, or whether they were operated by means of pedals with the feet.

If you are able to furnish this affidavit for us, you should give the usual data concerning your place of residence, occupation, your connections in aeronautical societies, etc. You should also include a statement that your affidavit is made for use in a suit brought by The Wright Company of New York against the Curtiss Aeroplane Company. The affidavit should either be made before the American Consul at London, or before a Notary Public and vised by the American Consul.

Sincerely yours,
Orville Wright

The Wright Company
Dayton, Ohio
March 30, 1915.

Dear Mr Brewer:

Your letter of March 6th was received a few days ago in the same mail with your letter of March 11th enclosing patent specifications on the automatic longitudinal control and the side slip indicator. I have been so rushed lately that I have got very little of my correspondence attended to.

I fully understand the difficulty of securing information on the construction of the Curtiss machines being sold to countries now at war, and after receiving your letter I fully appreciate the impossibility of securing such information through citizens of these countries. The furnishing of this information might be held as an act of treason, in which case they would feel forever disgraced. Since writing you we have endeavored to get the information through Americans now in Europe, but so far the information has not been forthcoming. This is probably due to the fact that the flying grounds are so closely guarded that the Americans cannot get near enough to secure the information. We have the information from an employee of the Curtiss factory that the 'America' is now coupled up so that the ailerons work both upwardly and downwardly and simultaneously. But unfortunately we are not able to use the information on account of the confidential manner in which it was secured.

I hope the war is not going to continue so long that you and Alec cannot get over this year. I am planning to put up our wind tunnel within the next few months, and I think Alec would enjoy very much fooling around with it.

Sincerely yours,

Orville Wright

Orville refers to Giulio Romagnoli's patent for a aircraft-balancing device using elastically-controlled surfaces (British Patent No.20,963 of 1910).

Howard M. Rinehart was the instructor at the Wright School of Aviation when Brewer was a pupil there in 1914; Marjorie Stinson was a pupil at the same time, gaining her licence on 12 August 1914. Rinehart was later to work for The Dayton-Wright Company and Wright Aeronautical Corporation.

The Wright Company

Dayton, Ohio

July 3, 1915.

Dear Mr Brewer:

Your letters enclosing citations of the patent office are received. I have not yet been able to study them carefully, but at a glance the citations against the automatic do not amount to anything, unless it is the patent granted to Romagnoli. He seems to have had a similar idea, although I do not believe his device is a practical one. I will write again later in regard to this matter.

A short time ago when down at New York, I met Mr Danielson. He said that he had just returned from London, where he had seen you and told me of your activity in getting out instruments. We hear occasionally from the different pupils who were in the school last year when you were here. Miss Marjorie Stinson is flying in the South in exhibition work. The Whitings are stationed at Pensacola, Florida in the Navy Aeronautic Station. I see from the papers that Day is contemplating going into the exhibition business. I believe he is advertising as the 'Sixteen-year-old aviator'. And came back for a few hours more training this year, but I am afraid he will never develop into an expert. Rinehart is still doing our teaching. We now have adopted the wheel control exclusively. Rinehart found no trouble at all in changing to this system, and likes it very much better than the old lever control. He finds that he can teach pupils much more quickly. He put one pupil through the course in four days and the pupil successfully took his pilot's license on the next day. This would have been very much more difficult with the old system of levers.

I have heard nothing lately concerning the British Wright Company, or of what it is doing. As I remember it there was something like three thousand pounds left from the payment of the British Government last year in the Treasury. Should not a dividend be declared on this? The longer it stands the greater will be the taxation.

We have missed your visit this year, but we hope that affairs abroad may shape themselves so that you and Alec can come over for a month or two. I haven't got started on the laboratory yet, but I hope to do so within the next few months.

Sincerely yours,

Orville Wright

Attached to the above letter is a copy of the letter that follows from Brewer, held in type-script by the Society. It refers to the Ogilvie Air Speed Indicator, the main product of the Aeronautical Instrument Co. Ltd, which was formed in February 1915 as a development of the British Wright Company, with Brewer and G.N. Ogilvie as Directors. The Ogilvie Air Speed Indicator had been used by Alec Ogilvie and Francis McClean in their successful 1914 flight up the Nile to Khartoum in a Short Pusher S.80 seaplane. The instrument was patented in 1915 (Patent Nos 9100 and 9102 'Air-current indicators, applications of').

British Wright Company, Limited,

33 Chancery Lane

London

Orville Wright, Chairman.

27th July 1915

Mr Orville Wright,

Dayton, Ohio,

USA

Dear Orville,

Your letter of the 3rd July has escaped the German submarines and gives me welcome news of all the old pupils. I was especially glad to see that Rinehart is still doing your teaching and that he found no trouble in changing to the wheel control.

The reason you have heard nothing lately concerning the British Wright Company is because we have practically to remain inoperative during the war. At the present time we are trying to prove to the satisfaction of the Income Tax

Authorities that the payment made by the Government last year was for the purchase by the Government of the Patent rights. If it were for the purchase then no Income tax would be payable, whereas if it were a payment in the ordinary course of business of the company, then Income Tax of more than £1000 would have to be paid.

Our contention is that the Government being the sole users in Great Britain, when they acquired the free right to use, they virtually acquired all the rights conferred by the patent, and therefore that this amounts to a sale of assets and not to income on which tax should be payable.

There was as you say, something like £3000 left over after the payment by the British Government. It is the intention of the Directors to hold this sum for the future prosecution of the business of the Company under the Patent and for endeavouring to obtain an extension of time for the main patent before the expiration of the ordinary fourteen years period. The Company therefore has a sum of £2000 invested in 3½% War Loan and £1000 invested in 4½% War Loan, and if the Company is ever wound up or ceases to do business, this amount of capital would be refunded to the shareholders.

It appears however that the business of the Company in acting as Agents for the sale of Ogilvie Indicators is going to be quite a profitable concern, and when it would be possible to endeavour to collect other Royalties without disturbing the Aeronautical trade by attacking them unpatriotically during the strains of War it is quite possible that this reserve of resources may enable the Company to get its extension of life of the Patent and collect some Royalties from those firms in Great Britain manufacturing for delivery to Foreign Governments.

The Ogilvie Indicators are selling like hot cakes, and we are working all our time on orders which run into four figures. This is my first insight into manufacturing and it has proved most interesting. I am buying aluminium by the ton, copper tubing by the mile, and learning how to make things which formerly appeared to grow in some mysterious manner.

We are having enquiries from the United States for indicators but are refusing to supply so long as the Government here takes all we can make. I daresay we could spare you a couple of indicators for your own use if you would care to fit these to your machines at Dayton.

With kind regards to Bishop Wright and Katherine [sic],

Believe me,

Yours very sincerely,

[Griffith Brewer]

36. Front cover of brochure for 'The Wright Flying School' (New York: Wright Flying Field Inc., 1916). The Wright Flying School was based at the Hempstead Plains Flying Field, close to Garden City and Mineola on Long Island, New York.

In September 1916 The Wright Company, the Simplex Automobile Co. syndicate, The Glenn L. Martin Company, Wright Flying Field Inc. and the General Aeronautic Co. of America, Inc., merged to form The Wright-Martin Aircraft Corporation.

On 6 June 1916 Brewer presented the Fourth Wilbur Wright Memorial Lecture – 'The Life and Work of Wilbur Wright' – to the Aeronautical Society of Great Britain. It was subsequently published in The Aeronautical Journal, *Vol.20, July–September 1916.*

The Wright Company
Dayton, Ohio
September 18, 1916

My dear Mr Brewer:

I will have to ask you to excuse my not having answered your several letters. I have been in such poor health for the past couple of years, especially last winter, when I was confined to my bed for nearly three months. I have done almost no writing. I have just returned from a two months' vacation on the Georgian Bay, Ontario.

Your letter in regard to the prolongation of our English patent came while I was there. I had no intention to try to prolong the patent in England. If it could be done, it would not be fair, because I do not think it could be extended in other countries.

Your letter addressed to Lorin arrived a few days ago.

It may be well for you to address the company directly, but I will refer your letter to the company anyway. You should address Mr Edward M. Hagar, President, The Wright-Martin Aircraft Corporation, 60 Broadway, New York City.

We had been hoping that you would get over again this year. I was in the notion several times of cabling you from Ontario, but I was afraid that it would be too late to visit us there by the time you could get off. I am just purchasing an island in the Georgian Bay, and hope that you can come over and spend a couple of months with us there next summer. Of course, we would like very much to have Alec come along too, if he can get away; but I suspect that Alec is very busy while the war is on.

I am now putting up a small building for an aeronautical laboratory on the rear of the building on the corner of Broadway and Third Street. It will be completed some time this Fall, so that I hope to have a tunnel and instruments ready in the Winter or Spring.

I do not know whether I acknowledged receipt of the proofs of your Wilbur Wright Memorial address. It was very good, and we would like to have several copies of it when it is printed.

Hoping to hear from you often, and with best regards to Mrs Brewer and the children, as well as yourself, I am

Sincerely yours,

Orville Wright

In his autobiography Brewer recalled, 'In 1916 Orville Wright decided not to apply for an extension of the British patent. I wrote a letter to the Aeroplane giving this news to the British industry, saying that it amounted to a gift from Orville Wright to the industry. This was warmly applauded by Lord Northcliffe as another instance of the Wrights' generosity to their British friends' (Fifty Years of Flying, *London, Air League of the British Empire, 1946). An editorial entitled 'On the Wright Patents and the Aircraft Industry' was published in* The Aeroplane, *Vol.11 (14), 4 October 1916.*

A copy of the following letter from Brewer is held in typescript.

6th October 1916.
Mr Orville Wright,
Dayton, Ohio,
USA

My dear Orville,

I was very glad to get your letter of the 18th September, and if you had cabled, I should have made a special effort to come to you at Georgian Bay, Ontario. It is doubtful whether I should have succeeded, however, because while the European War is on, one is not one's own master. We all have to do our bit, if not at the Front, then at the base supplying those more ahead with the wherewithal of resistance.

You will be receiving six copies of the Aeronautical Journal containing the Wilbur Wright Memorial address, and also a copy of this week's 'Aeroplane' in which you will see that before your letter arrived, I assumed your consent to allowing the British Patent to lapse, and now have to thank you for confirming this permission.

I will write to you again very soon, telling you how things are going, but in the meantime you may rest assured that we have turned the tide, and it is only a question of how long it will be before it is made to ebb at a decent pace.

Yours sincerely,

[Signed] Griffith Brewer

On 19 September 1916 Orville Wright purchased Lambert Island – located in Lake Huron's Georgian Bay – which was to become his annual summer residence.

The following letter from Brewer is held in typescript.

9th October 1916
Mr Orville Wright
Dayton Ohio
USA

My dear Orville,

This is to be a letter with nothing in it about the war. It is doubtful therefore whether it will pass the Censor.

I am most interested in your island. It is what I have wanted ever since the age of ten, and I shall certainly not wait for a second invitation. Georgian Bay was the scene of my one back-woods experience. In 1889 I went up Georgian

Bay from Owen Sound to Spanish River, an island at the back of Manatulin Island. I got very seasick and the boat arrived very late. We found that the only boarding house in the little lumber town had a sofa in the dining room and half a bed as sleeping accommodation, so tossed up for the choice, and my friend winning, he chose the sofa. I had a look at the half bed and saw the other half occupied by a dark headed man partly dressed, so following the evident custom of the country, I only partly undressed and got in as quietly as possible. My stockinged feet struck something hard – the top boots of my bedfellow which encroached on my side, and had therefore to be gently persuaded a little to one side. This woke him and he started up with the enquiry where the —— I had come from. On explaining I had come in from the steamer which had since left, his language became more fluent, denouncing the steamer and the place and his own eyes, until when he cooled, he explained that he had been sitting up listening for the steamer whistle, and falling asleep he had missed it and there would not be another for the next three days.

I spent a week on the island wading through swamps, learning to run on the logs and drying my clothes; and when this adventure holiday was over, and I was enduring further sea-sickness in the steerage home to England, Georgian Bay stood out in my recollection as the place to return to when sufficient funds had been saved to start real life again in the wilds. You must tell me how to get to your island, and then when you cable I can come out and bring Alec with me after our work is done.

There is every prospect of my getting more leisure in the future. Cyril is growing up and will soon be able to earn his own living. Bee has abandoned her life of leisure and is now the chief bread winner, going up to London by the 8.14 a.m. train and getting back at 7 p.m. in time to serve the dinner. She recognises her responsibilities and is anxious to reform. The only bar to my permanent retirement is that Betty says she won't work to keep her Father and she has no intention of going up to London to help to earn the bread and dripping.

Your wind tunnel sounds most interesting. I am building one here 3ft diameter, circular in section, with a 5 h.p. motor driving a four-bladed propeller and giving a 54 m.p.h. wind before the honeycomb is fitted. A photo shall be taken and sent you soon.

Norman Ogilvie tells me that Alec is on crutches. In saving a machine from running into a fence, he got in front of one wing to turn it and his legs were badly bruised. No bones broken.

By same post are some cuttings from last Saturday's papers, showing the appreciation of your gift to the British Nation. The natural love of something for nothing appeals to this stout island race. Please forgive me for the liberties I have taken.

At present a lively skirmish is taking place with the Inland Revenue. The directors of an English Company are personally responsible to the Government for all taxation, so it would be no use to divide up the balance of the B.W. Co. before we are successful in testing the Revenue's demands. I am using the fact of your being an American Citizen, to resist the demand for payment of excess profits, on the ground that this was a law passed after the settlement, and if applied to you would amount to the Government striking a bargain and then bringing in a law to make you pay the money back. There is a Teutonic lack of humour in an income tax official, who can sit down and gravely say that the law as it stands makes one Department disown the obligations entered into by another Department. The situation is similar to a reward being offered, and when earned being presented with a letter of thanks. Then outside the chamber where the reward has been presented, posting other officials to take away the reward after presentation. This might be possible with a Government dealing with its own citizens, who must naturally in times of stress be made to give up all they possess, but in your case it would be equivalent to incurring debt in America and then afterwards bringing in a law to repay a less sum than that originally bargained for. For these reasons I have every hope that even the income tax officials will not prove themselves as absolutely wanting in common sense. You shall hear as things develop, whether 'the law is an ass' or whether it is only temporally blind to common sense.

Bee sends her love to Katherine, and we both hope you will take every care of your health and not overtax your strength. You will remember that Lord Northcliffe was in bad health for a long time from overwork and strain, but now he seems quite recovered and is our most vigorous indispensable over here. We therefore hope you will be quite strong and enjoying outdoor life in Georgian Bay, when we come over the other side after our homes have been made secure against the burglar who is still trying to break in.

Yours very sincerely,

[Griffith Brewer]

The Advisory Committee for Aeronautics had been formed by Lord Haldane in April 1909 with the co-operation of the distinguished physicist Lord Rayleigh, who became its President, with Dr Richard Glazebrook, Director of the National Physical Laboratory, as Chairman.

The Wright Company
Dayton, Ohio
October 24, 1916.

Dear Mr Brewer:

Your letter of the 6th and 9th of October came in together this morning.

The American papers had the report of the lapse of the British patent badly mixed up. I had been wondering what really appeared in the English papers.

Can you get for me two copies of the Technical Report of the Advisory Committee on Aeronautics for all the years excepting 1912–1913? If the others cannot be secured, I would especially like to have a copy of the 1911–12 report. These are not to be had in America any more, and I have lost my copy of the 1911–12 report. If new ones cannot be had, I would be very glad to secure second-hand ones, and I am willing to pay whatever is necessary to get them.

I am glad that we are going to have you with us at the Georgian Bay next year. We expect to go there about the first of July and stay until the middle of September. Our island has eight or nine small buildings on it, with not more than two bed rooms in any one building. We are going to have quite a job to try to beautify the buildings. While built as good as buildings generally run in that part of the country, the designer certainly had no eye to beauty. The main building is perched on a rock seventy feet above the surrounding water, and is a land mark for miles around. The houses are now all painted in white and are very conspicuous. We are going to paint them in some less showy color, probably a green or a brown. You will probably be given a paint brush when you visit us.

I am awful sorry to hear of Alec's accident, but hope that he is recovered from it now. I will write Alec in a few days. I have not heard from him for more than a year. I do not know who is owing the letter, but as I am such a poor correspondent I suspect I am the guilty one.

With kindest regards to all the family, I am
Sincerely yours,
Orville Wright

In 1917 Orville Wright established the Wright Aeronautical Laboratory.

Wright Aeronautical Laboratory
Orville Wright, Director
Dayton, Ohio
January 31, 1917.

Secretary,
The Aeronautical Society of Great Britain,
11, Adam Street,
London, England.

Dear Sir:
 I thank you very much for the copies of reports of the Advisory Committee for Aeronautics.
 Very truly yours,
 Orville Wright

Dr Albert Francis Zahm, who taught physics and experimented in aeronautics at the Catholic University of America, Washington D.C., had assisted in the flight trials of the reconstructed Langley 1903 tandem monoplane Aerodrome *at Hammondsport. Zahm subsequently published a report of these trials in the* Annual Report Smithsonian Institution, *1914, pages 217–222, 'The First Man-Carrying Aeroplane Capable of Sustained Free Flight: Langley's Success as a Pioneer in Aviation'. Dr Charles Doolittle Walcott had succeeded Langley as Secretary of the Smithsonian Institution in 1907. Charles Matthew Manly, the original pilot of the 1903* Aerodrome, *was in 1914 a consulting engineer to the Curtiss Aeroplane and Motor Corporation.*

Orville Wright
Dayton, Ohio
January 31, 1917.

Dear Mr Brewer:
 A few days ago I received a copy of the 1910–11 reports of the British Advisory Committee for Aeronautics and a number of the reports for 1911–12, but quite a number of the 1911–12 are missing. I did not realize there would be so much difficulty in getting these reports. I supposed there were a good many

second-hand ones in England that could be had easily. I thank you very much for the trouble you have taken in getting these for me.

The past ten days we have been working on the new wind tunnel. The channel itself is three feet square, connected to a distributing chamber seven feet square by twelve feet in length. The laboratory room is 60 feet by 40 feet by 16 feet. The motor is to be of ten horse power, but it is not as yet installed. If there is any difficulty in getting a uniform current – that is uniform velocity over the greater part of the channel – I think I can get it, as we did in our early experiments, by screening the parts of the channel having greater velocity. Only a part of the measuring instrument is done so far, but I expect to have it complete within the next three or four weeks.

I am enclosing an editorial from Collier's of January 6th in regard to the Zahm-Curtiss fake flights of the Langley machine. I think it was after you left America that a full account of these Langley machine experiments at Hammondsport came out in the affidavits and photographs furnished by the Curtiss side in the patent litigation. It developed that before the machine was able to make a flight – and it never succeeded in making a turn, although this was attempted many times – less than thirty per cent of the machine was either a part of the original machine or a copy of the original machine as tried out by Langley in 1903. Not only this, but they even had the nerve to use a part of our control on the machine, a system of control Langley never used or contemplated using. You will remember that Manley [sic] made some reply to your letter, published in some of the New York papers when you were over here in 1914, in regard to the Langley machine. In that letter he said that there were no changes made in the Langley machine excepting the addition of floats to enable it to be launched, and the replacing of the steering wheel by a regular Curtiss steering wheel and shoulder bracket. These affidavits show either that Manley was a terrible lier [sic] or a very incompetent observer.

Manley's own statement in the case, as well as that of Doctor Zahm and others, confirmed our opinion at the time that the machine had never flown when you had your interview with Doctor Walcott. According to their own affidavits it was not until a Curtiss motor, of nearly double the power of the original Langley motor, was put in the machine, that the machine was able to keep itself off the water.

Mr Lyman Seely, who now represents the Curtiss Company in England, was at that time connected with the Curtiss Company and was the Associated Press reporter at Hammondsport. However I understand that he has denied responsibility for those early reports of the machine having flown.

With kindest regards to Mrs Brewer, Betty and Cyril, as well as yourself, I am
Sincerely yours,
Orville Wright

*On 9 April 1917 the Dayton-Wright Airplane Company was incorporated. Edward
Andrew Deeds was Vice-President of Dayton's National Cash Register Company and
co-founder with Charles F. Kettering of the Dayton Engineering Laboratories Company,
and with the Talbotts of the Dayton Metal Products Company.*

*Orville Wright refers to George Owen Squier who was in charge of the US Army
Air Service from June 1916 to May 1918.*

Orville Wright
Dayton, Ohio
May 9, 1917.

Mr Griffith Brewer,
The British Wright Company, Ltd.,
33 Chancery Lane,
London, England.

My dear Mr Brewer:

I am this morning in receipt of your letter of April 16th enclosing check for
450 pounds, fifteen per cent dividend on my British Wright Company stock,
for which you have my thanks.

I shall be sorry and disappointed if you do not get over this year. However,
the vacation at the Georgian Bay has been given up, as I will be too busy this
summer to get away.

I am now just getting my wind tunnel in working order. I do not know what
I will have to do in the military work. I have been commissioned a Major in
the Aviation Section, Signal Officers' Reserve Corps. It is possible that I may
have to go to Washington, although General Squier told me a short time ago
that they thought they would have more need of me in the laboratory.

You may have heard of the new companies organized in Dayton. One is
called the Wright Field Company, which carry on school work, the other, The
Dayton Wright Airplane Company, which will engage in manufacturing. The
Directors of the two companies are the same. Mr Deeds is the moving spirit in
the enterprise. The Directors are, E.A. Deeds, C.F. Kettering, H.E. Talbot,
H.E. Talbot Jr and myself. I will be free of the business end.

It looks to me like we are in for a long hard fight, and I hope that we will not make so many blunders that our efforts will be of little service.

With kindest regards to Mrs Brewer, Cyril, Betty and yourself

Sincerely yours,

Orville Wright

P.S. If you know what Alec is doing, please let me know about him.

McCook Field, near Dayton, was a US Army research centre.

Orville Wright

Dayton, Ohio

July 13, 1918

Dear Mr Brewer:

Your letter enclosing check for 450 pounds dividend on my 3,000 shares in The British Wright Company has been received. Please accept my thanks.

We have been having a great deal of trouble to get good air speed indicators in America. Practically all of them have been entirely of metal construction. While this would seem to have some advantages, yet the difficulties of properly calibrating them and keeping them in adjustment seems to be greater than in the Ogilvie with its rubber diaphram.

The National Cash Register Company has made several hundred exact copies of the Ogilvie for the United States Government. I have tested a number of them and find them much more reliable than the other American indicators. The criticism made here of the Ogilvie is in regard to its rubber diaphram, which many think will deteriorate rapidly with age. I have done a little experimenting with an air proof fabric diaphram, which I think might be developed into a satisfactory instrument. My experience has been that when a metal plate is attached to the centre of the diaphragm the records are not altogether uniform; since slight tilts of this plate in different directions give slightly different readings on the indicator. For this reason I have found it advantageous to hinge the plate. I am enclosing a sketch showing roughly my idea.

I have lately put up a small tunnel in my laboratory, in which we have a wind velocity of over 160 miles an hour. McCook Field (the Government aeronautical engineers experimental station) is now making an exact copy of it with the intention of later building it on a seven foot scale.

Milton, Lorin's oldest boy, sailed last week. He is in a company, I believe, which uses one pound guns.

I am leaving Monday for some weeks in the Georgian Bay in Canada. We have a number of small buildings on our island, but we shall not attempt to furnish the buildings this year. For this reason Buster, Charlie Taylor and I are going up alone. Katharine may come up for a short time later. I wish you could be with us in camp. However, I think you would enjoy it more next year when we get the camp fixed up a little better. We will be very glad to see this war ended so that you can visit us again.

With kindest regards to Mrs Brewer, Betty, Cyril and yourself and also to Alec.

Sincerely yours,
Orville Wright

Orville Wright
Dayton, Ohio
October 29, 1918.

Dear Mr Brewer:

Upon my return from my vacation I found your letters and also one from Alec awaiting me.

I learned from the National Cash Register that they are not receiving any further orders to build Ogilvie indicators, but have been asked to quote a price on making some of the Foxboro instruments, which have been developed by some of our 'scientists' at Washington.

I hope, however, that the fact that the Ogilvie instrument is not still being manufactured will not deter you from making the trip over anyway. We certainly would be most glad to see you again. It begins to look as though the war might not last very much longer. We felt very anxious for a while that the President might be drawn into another note writing contest; but I believe this danger is now past. If you cannot get over before, we at least hope you will be able to get over next summer and go camping with us in the Georgian Bay. The simple life there is most restful.

I am enclosing a copy of a letter, which I am writing to Alec, which explains the speed indicator situation here.

With kindest regard to Mrs Brewer and the children as well as yourself.

Sincerely yours,
Orville Wright

Orville Wright refers to Herbert Wright, Reuchlin's son, and Milton Wright Jr, Lorin's son.

Orville Wright
Dayton, Ohio
December 13, 1918

Griffith Brewer, Esq.,
Park Avenue Hotel,
New York, N.Y.

Dear Mr Brewer:

Katharine has just received your letter stating that our Country has taken such a fancy to you that it won't let you depart for several days yet.

I telegraphed you this afternoon that I was sending you letters Special Delivery in care of the Park Avenue Hotel. The letters referred to are enclosed with this letter. The ones addressed to Herbert and Milton we would like to have mailed on your arrival in England, as we think this will be the quickest way of reaching the boys. I have left the letters unsealed in case there are some censors that want to look at them before you get to England. Will you please seal them before mailing?

We were very sorry that you had to be off so soon, but it is nice to think that we are going to see you again with Mrs Brewer this Summer. Bring Alec along too if you can.

Wishing you a 'Bon Voyage',
Sincerely yours,
Orville Wright

Katharine Wright refers to Karl Hotchkiss a friend of Horace 'Buster' Wright, Lorin's son.

Hawthorn Hill
Oakwood
Dayton, Ohio
December 13, 1918

Dear 'Griff',

You don't feel any worse than we do about the time you are wasting in New York. I have always understood that travelling in war times had its drawbacks.

We have admired your courage in tackling not only a trans-Atlantic voyage but a Trans-continental journey!

Next Tuesday is the fifteenth anniversary of the first flight and I am going to celebrate by having a little dinner for my 'Little Brother' with the Deeds's, Ketterings, Rikes and one or two other friends. How I do wish you (and Mr Edgerton) could be here! We have heard nothing further from Mr Edgerton and are afraid he has gone home.

Milton has been heard from. His regiment was hurried to the front, for reinforcement, but never got sight of the Germans. They were going too fast! Milton is now in a school, studying the one-pound gun. He is Corporal now and has been acting Sergeant. It seems that all the huskies in his company have been disabled in some way or other, 'flu' and such, and he, the runt of the crowd, has been flourishing.

Most astonishing of all, Karl Hotchkiss has been heard from. He was the one Orville was trying to get news of. He was <u>not allowed</u> to write – while the big drive was going on. He was in the intelligence service and when he had crawled a half mile, on hands and knees, to get a message to his machine gun platoon (from which he was temporarily detached) he found only three living. Report is general that the losses in the Argonne-Meuse drive were very heavy. Congress is demanding that the government let people use the cables to get news of the boys, some of whom have not been heard of for months, like Karl. Carrie's brother hasn't been heard from yet.

Thank'ee kindly for the pleasant little message from Woodrow. He's getting more than a 'post-card now and then' from us! Orv is writing you this afternoon, to send some letters, with money, over to our boys. Goodbye – Good luck with your passport & the US Customs!

Sincerely,

Katharine Wright

Orville Wright
Dayton, Ohio
March 3, 1919.

Dear Griff,

My argument against the very large aeroplane was from the standpoint of their present military usefulness. Of course, when the time comes that it is desirable to drop a ton or more of explosives in a single charge, the large aeroplane would be the only one with which this could be accomplished.

37. Riley E. Scott preparing two 18lb bombs to be carried by Captain Thomas Milling in a Wright B at the US Army flying school at College Park, Maryland, 11 October 1911. The aim was to demonstrate Scott's invention of the world's first practical bombsight allowing for different speeds and altitudes.

However, in the present war, where the large planes were used, the size of the bombs were not increased but only a greater number of them were carried. I believe that for a long time to come the big machines will be at the mercy of the smaller ones.

The position Alec takes in favour of the large machine for commerce is right if you accept all of his conditions.

1. I see no reason for changing pilots every four hours. In touring with an automobile we would not think of such a thing. Of course one man cannot operate a machine for twenty-four hours continuously, but I see no necessity of making a twenty-four hour flight without landing to change pilots.

2. In clear weather navigation should not be any more difficult over land than over sea; since on land you have land marks from which

to guide your course. When flying above the clouds the difficulty is greater. Yet in this case I cannot see where the two pilots are necessary. Surely the advantage is in favor of the smaller machine, which has the higher speed and therefore drifts less from its course in a given distance.

3. I cannot agree with Alec on the third point that the engines run best when watched and oiled. I believe if a record could be had it would be found that ten motors have been stopped by tinkering with them while they were running to one that was kept going through the attention of a mechanic. I would, therefore, dispense with about five of the six 'indispensable members of the crew'.

You state that Alec says that the large machines can be made as efficient per unit of surface as the smaller ones. I do not believe Alec's statement is borne out by the records. The load that can be carried on the small machines in proportion to the total load is theoretically greater than with the same factor of safety in large machines. You will find that all of the large machines use a much lower factor of safety.

We would like very much to have Alec come over if he can get away.

Sincerely yours,

Orville Wright

Orville Wright
Dayton, Ohio
March 10, 1919.

Dear Mr Brewer:

When you receive a package containing a French grammar, please remail it to Milton to the enclosed address.

Milton is teaching a class in French, but he has no grammar.

The Post Office Department here will not accept packages addressed to a private in the American Expeditionary Forces in France.

Sincerely yours,

Orville Wright

[Attached address]

Private Milton Wright,
Headquarters Company,
54th Infantry, Regulars,
American Expeditionary Forces.

Orville Wright
Dayton, Ohio
May 17, 1919.

Dear Mr Brewer:

Your letters of the 16th, 17th and 25th of April came in one mail.

The bill of lading for the grinding machine has not been endorsed by Houlder Brothers and Company. The technicalities of the Revenue Office require it to be endorsed. I am therefore returning it enclosed for their endorsement.

We have the engraving machine set up and have made a couple of our cutters on it. It does the work very well, only a little hand work is required in finishing the cutters. I believe it is going to be very useful. At the present time we are using dentist tools for the cutters. The tools that came with the machine were not quite small enough in diameter for our work. The dental tools, however, work very well.

Sincerely yours,
Orville Wright

Orville Wright
Dayton, Ohio
June 13, 1919.

Dear Mr Brewer:

I have been so rushed lately with some other work that I have not attended to any of my correspondence. (This is not uncommon, as I never do anyway.)

I am sending enclosed the signed transfer of stock. The certificates of stock were never delivered to either Wilbur or me.

We are looking forward to your visit with us in August, either here in Dayton or at the Georgian Bay. I wish Alec could come along with you and Mrs Brewer. I expect to spend July on an automobile trip through the West with Colonel Deeds and several other friends.

Sincerely yours,
Orville Wright

Orville Wright
Dayton, Ohio
August 6, 1919.

Dear Griff:

Your letter of July 11th came while I was away on our Western automobile trip. I have just got home and am now getting ready to start for the Georgian Bay. We expect to remain there until the first week in September. We probably will be back before your arrival in America. However, I believe it would be a good thing to telegraph me at Dayton immediately upon your arrival, so that we can let you know whether to come North or directly to Dayton.

We will be delighted to see you and Cyril, and are sorry that Mrs Brewer and Betty cannot come along.

Sincerely yours,

Orville Wright

3

Disputes with the Smithsonian and *Nature*: February 1920–June 1925

Katharine and Orville Wright refer to the Canadian-born Arctic explorer Dr Vilhjalmur Stefansson (1879–1962). Brewer's signed copies of Stefansson's books are held in the Royal Aeronautical Society Library. They include My Life with the Eskimo *(London, Macmillan and Co. Limited, 1913),* The Friendly Arctic: the Story of Five Years in Polar Regions *(New York, The Macmillan Company, 1921) and* The Northward Course of Empire *(New York: Harcourt, Brace and Company, 1922).*

Hawthorn Hill
Oakwood
Dayton, Ohio
February 12, 1920.

Dear Griffith,

I have just had a letter from Mr Stefansson, the Arctic explorer, who is expecting to go to England in a week or so. He wants and we want to give him an introduction to you. He came here to speak about the middle of January and was visiting us when he came down with influenza and was at our house a week and a half. We talked a good deal about you and he would like to meet you, since he knows you are a special friend of ours.

It was about a year ago that Mr Morgan – of Flood Prevention Engineering fame – asked Orv to telegraph to Mr Stefansson and see if he wouldn't stop off to spend a day in Dayton. Mr Morgan had seen that he was to be in Chicago and he thought he might come to Dayton, if Orville asked him. Well, he did come finally and we grew to be such great friends that he has been back twice since for a visit. Orv and I nearly always agree about people, you know, and we both like and admire Mr Stefansson tremendously. You will like him I know and we'll be under great obligation for anything you do for him while he is in England. Orv will write his letter of introduction but I wanted to say more than could be put in such a letter and we wanted you to know that we had more than a perfunctory interest.

38. Eugène Lefebvre adjusting his Wright A at Reims, August 1909.

Maybe you know a lot about Mr S already, but <u>we</u> didn't, so I'll tell you a little to prepare you. He has been in the Arctic three different times: 1906–1907, 1908–1912, 1913–1918. So you see he has been North for ten years. He never tried to get to the Pole. His first interest was in the Eskimo – as an ethnologist. Later he became an explorer and he evolved an entirely new system i.e. of living off the country – instead of depending on transporting supplies. He also proved that it was possible to live on the Polar ice – seals, etc. etc., for food. It is fascinating to hear him tell it and Orv sized him up right away as being absolutely truthful and therefore very interesting. He and Orv are great mutual admirers! I feel sure you will enjoy him for his own sake and I know you will receive him for ours. I'd like awfully well to have him meet some of the 'English bunch' especially Alec and Frank McLean and Maurice Egerton. We are also giving him a letter to Lord Northcliffe but I do not suppose he is in England now. We are both very well – no sciatica for Orv this winter. When are you coming again?

Sincerely,

Katharine Wright

39. A Wright A (pilot Eugène Lefebvre) at Reims, August 1909.

Orville Wright
Dayton, Ohio
February 14, 1920.

Dear Mr Brewer:

You will probably remember our talking of Mr Stefansson who is the bearer of this letter, when you were here last time.

He has spent the most of the time the past fifteen years above the arctic circle, and has developed and demonstrated an entirely new method of living in the arctic, a method which will revolutionize arctic exploration. He has demonstrated that one can live in the fartherest north off of the resources of the country, without bringing from the south anything but hunting material. He lived in this way for nearly two years, after he was given up for dead by Peary and our other explorers.

You and Mr Stefansson ought to be good friends because you can sympathize with one another, having had some of the same experiences at our house. It was Dr Spitler, however, instead of Dr Conklin, that did the business for him.

Mr Stefansson is a fine fellow, whom I know you will enjoy meeting. Anything you may do in introducing him to our friends in England will be appreciated by Katharine and me.

Sincerely,

Orville Wright

Katharine Wright refers to Paul Tissandier who had been a student pilot of Wilbur Wright at Pau. Tissandier, comte Charles de Lambert, and another Wright student pilot, Eugène Lefebvre, flew French-built Wright A biplanes at 'La Grande Semaine d'Aviation de la Champagne', an international aviation meeting held at Bétheny, five miles north of Reims, 22–29 August 1909.

Oakwood,

Dayton, Ohio

April 8, 1920.

Dear Griffith,

It's awfully nice of you to be so cordial about Mr Stefansson's coming. By this time I suppose you have seen him and I <u>hope</u> you like him. One of his striking characteristics is that he thinks it rather important to tell the truth! That's fairly rare, you know! I <u>know</u> he will like you and it will please us very much to have you two know each other.

The clock is here at last and you have no idea how much we enjoy having it. It reminds us of you every time it rings – almost literally it does that very thing – and you don't seem so far away. I <u>hope</u> Orville has written to thank you for it – but knowing his failing in that respect, I have fears that he has not. Anyway I thank you. I care a good deal for associations and you know that Orville does too. It seems to me that I couldn't have anything that I would like more than I do like to have that clock from you.

Perhaps Orville has told you that the case was cracked in the coming but we have it without the case, on our living room mantel. Orville is intending to make a little base to let it rest on and then it will be just right as it is. Now it wants to roll a little (quite in keeping with its nautical nature!) because of the circular shape.

We are beginning to think of your coming again and hope it will be before very long. Mr Deeds wants Orville to go to Europe with him & Gordon Rentschler, of Hamilton, Ohio – the man we tried to get there, coming back from Oxford, but Orville's leg is bothering him again and he is afraid to travel.

Mr Deeds is going on business. He and Mr Kettering are no longer closely associated — for which we are all sorry. Mr Deeds is evidently going in now for developing engines and 'such'. I wish Orville were not kept so close by his sciatica. It restricts him very much. I would not care at all to go to Europe now for sight-seeing but would like to get over to see some of you who are particular friends. I want very much to see the de Lamberts. A friend of Tissandier's was here not long ago and told Orv something about Tissandier and the de Lamberts.

Love to all the family from both of us.

Sincerely,

Katharine Wright

Lambert Island

Penetanguishene, Ontario

Sept. 9, 1920.

Dear Griff,

We are going to Penetang quite unexpectedly as usual and I have only a minute to write you a little note. I want to send your cable which I had the cheek to open! If it had been anything urgent I should have made an effort to reach you immediately, <u>some</u> way.

Orv has been better on the whole since you left but last Monday he was very stiff. I went to Penetang Tuesday with Mr George who just happened to come by. Wilf and the Naubic had stopped running. We are going by the Williamses this morning to see if we can get anything for them today.

I shall leave next Monday the 13th. Orv will probably come on about Wednesday. The work has stopped except when Orv stays at it. C. Taylor is a parlor boarder now! The sun isn't shinning [*sic*] so brightly just now. (Mrs McCormick would guess why.)

Stef didn't leave anything behind this time except Bartlett's book — which is a good record for him. He sent Orv a map of the Dominion which is very acceptable and I also sent another hundred pages of manuscript — which is the best of all. It is going to be a good book if this improvement keeps up!

We are wondering if you are sailing today on the Imperator. If so — I hope she doesn't topple over in the gales.

Goodbye. We both send love to you all. As always —

Katharine Wright

Hawthorn Hill
Dayton Ohio
Sept. 17, 1920

Dear Griff,

Orv found Betty's card at the post-office at Penetang just as he was leaving so he brought it on home. There are more 'cows' and 'goats'! It is certainly one of the most interesting things I know of.

The trip wasn't very hard on Orv. He seemed more free from lameness than for weeks. The 'Little One' was very dirty but otherwise all right. He ran around everywhere to visit all his old haunts.

Sorry the seeds of the 'simple life' fell on such stony ground at your cousins'! We'll resume next summer. After I came home I had four meals before there was a single bit of 'washing up' as you call it. Then Lottie did it and it only took her a few minutes. I am thoroughly converted!

We are having beautiful weather here – cool, bright and full of 'pep.' Orv seemed very lively this morning. The change has done him good, anyway – in spite of all the troubles at Lambert. He finally brought the engine back for some changes. George France took the launch and other boats – except your canoe – for the winter. Your canoe is in the house.

Of course, you know that I will gladly do <u>any</u> thing I can do to help in the book. Don't be 'backward about coming forward' to ask for anything you need or want. I am so grateful to you but it is nothing new, this devotion of yours to Will and Orv. You know that I appreciate it more than I can express.

We had a second instalment of Stef's book. It was simply <u>entrancing</u>! The story of the trip over the ice – the first trip – <u>must</u> be the best part of the whole story. If the book keeps on as it promises it will be a 'hammer'. Isn't Stef a lovely character? Full of whims and 'insistent ideas' but so gentle and considerate – and interesting and absolutely genuine and truthful.

I hope you found everything 'right side up' when you got home. I know how pleased you will be to have Cyril go to Cambridge. Love to Beatrice. I hope her arrangements are all going well. Best from both of us.

Katharine.

Katharine Wright refers to a Dr Sutton, and in later letters to a 'Dr Dick'. It is evident that this was the same person — a local doctor and friend of the Wrights.

Hawthorn Hill
Dayton,
Ohio
October 15 1920

Dear Grif,

Orv had a letter from you — perhaps two — but he has hardly been at his office since we came home from Canada. So this time he is blameless in the matter of letter writing.

After many delays and failures to get prints of all the snaps that were taken at the Bay, I think I have finally got a full collection for you and will mail the bunch tomorrow when I mail this letter. You will have evidence in the picture of the bridge that you helped build that you made yourself useful. Do tell Beatrice what Mrs McCormick said, 'your coming seemed to coincide with the coming out of the sun.' She certainly saw through that peculiar coincidence pretty keenly!

I think that Orv has finally made up his mind to go to the 'Mayo Clinic' at Rochester, Minnesota. The Mayo brothers are very celebrated surgeons and doctors who live in a little town in Minnesota. When they found themselves famous they decided to stay right at home and let people come to them. We think it is as good as any place in America for a diagnosis. They X-ray and examine in every possible way and about a dozen top-notch men will look Orv over if he goes. Of course, he could get good attention anyway but Dr Sutton has a particular friend there who will see that the very best men are on the job. I think Orv really wants to go now. He has been in bed again for a week since we came home and is barely around any of the time. But he looks <u>well</u>. It's amazing what a good color he has and his appetite is good all the time. We have a really good cook now who gives us <u>too</u> much good stuff to eat. Still we are thriving on it. The 'simple life' is all right in its time and place! I never felt better in my life. So I think we have you to thank as much as the other way — for the good vacations all around — in spite of seeming drawbacks.

Stef wrote some weeks ago that his book is about done. He has been 'remiss' as he expresses it about writing so is being punished by not getting his pictures. Yours go off first. It is amazing how we <u>can</u> look when we know we are having our pictures taken, isn't it? Orv has to laugh at our pictures in Penetang. They certainly are not flattering.

Tell Beatrice that we thank her for loaning you to us. I have told the McCormicks how to find you if they get to London. They expect to spend most of the time in Italy & southern France. O.W. joins in best remembrances.

Sincerely, etc. etc.

Katharine.

Katharine Wright refers to Otto Lilienthal (1848–96) who was famous for his gliding achievements.

Mabel Beck was Orville's long-serving secretary. Frederick P. Fish was the Wright Company's attorney in the case of the Wright Company v. Herring–Curtiss Company and Glenn H. Curtiss.

Hawthorn Hill
Dayton, Ohio
November 22, 1920

Dear Griffith –

Your letter of November 8th came today and created great interest on the 'Hill'. In the first place the picture of your mother is a <u>masterpiece</u>. Orv can't get through picking it up and looking at it. Leaving out our interest in your mother, the picture is so exquisite, your mother's beautiful face and figure, the cat and the naturalness of the whole thing. You can take good pictures. We've known that before but this is one of the very best.

I should like to see your mother. She looks so nice and interesting. Did you give her an account of the 'simple life'? Would she understand our 'wild and woolly' American ways?

Betty's letter is a <u>corker</u>! Orv says he can see how she has some uncertainty as to how she 'should continue to earn her own living'. She is her father's own daughter in her originality of tastes. She will be a joy forever.

I am sorry to have to discourage you on your idea of having a lot of contributors and having Stef act as a judge in deciding matters of dispute. In the first place, of course, Stef isn't really qualified to give any opinion on these matters, particularly, and the public wouldn't regard him as an authority, capable of passing judgment. In the next place, Orv thinks you would be in a 'mess' if you got into that sort of thing – spending most of your space in the book, trying to straighten out what the others have wrong. You would immediately be on the defensive. Orv also points out that Harry Harper hasn't any special knowledge of Lilienthal's work as far as he knows. That is only an example of what the rest would likely be. Orv suggests that if you are going to go into the work of all those men who worked on the problem, you will have to make a complete study of all the histories yourself. Nothing is known about Lilienthal's work, for example, that is not found in his book. You can tell that briefly in your own words. It will be worth more than from some one who doesn't know nearly as much as you do about it, probably. When you get over here into the bunch who are intent on giving the impression that Langley did all the important scientific work, you will have a job on your hands, <u>disproving</u> the things they say. They won't prove the things they do say, but you will have to <u>disprove</u> them or they will be given wider distribution and seem to have your approval.

Why don't you go ahead and use your main time and energy telling what Will's and Orv's work was and let your readers draw their own conclusion? When you tell how the first machine was calculated; the laboratory work that was done; the accuracy of the results, etc. etc., the reader won't get the impression that it was a matter of luck or agility of limb that made Will and Orv make the first flying machine and '<u>fly</u> it', as Lord Northcliffe said. And you won't be discrediting any one who went before either. You can tell in the words – which they themselves used at the time from letters etc. what <u>they</u> thought their indebtedness was. We have such stacks of interesting letters and telegrams and all that sort of things which is a much more convincing record of what everyone was thinking <u>at the time</u> – not now after all the controversy and when different motives enter in. For instance, Orv has letters and telegrams (or copies) from Langley in 1903 and 1902, showing that Langley thought they were ahead of him then. Let's get these published and let people see how different it all was <u>before anyone flew</u>.

We had been talking about the book the last few days anyway and were planning to get a lot of that original stuff ready for your use. There is so much French stuff too that ought to be translated. I have been wanting to take it to an interpreter but Orv thinks if you were here, you could help us select what we want, from the French, much better than an outsider could. We had thought you could tell the story of the excitement in France (Mr Lahm could give you what you want on that and there are letters and published stuff too on that). You could tell too the story of the French Commission and why their plenipotentiary powers were taken from them just as they were sailing. Then there is history of the negotiations with England and USA and Germany. The original documents in all this will be immensely interesting or I am badly mistaken. It

will show that Will and Orv didn't take up the problem after all the main difficulties were out of the way and it will show that Langley wasn't the only one
who had to have nerve to work on the flying problem.

We think you won't be doing any injustice to the other experimenters if you
don't make a feature of what some one <u>may now say</u> their work was, leaving
the burden of proof on you to begin with. You can quote Langley – not print
what Dr Walcott may say Langley thought or said or what he may twist around
or assert, <u>without proof</u>. You will have to bring proof then to dispute his con-
clusions. We think it will be confusing to everyone nearly and not convincing
to anyone.

Since we have been to Rochester (I will tell you about that later) we have
decided not to go South for the winter and I am planning to get material
picked out for you – with Orv's and Miss Beck's help. I don't know just how
I'll succeed but I <u>think</u> I can help you with your outline. I hope you'll come
over as soon as you can because the work can be done so much better here
where we can immediately check up on every thing.

I have never quite understood just how you and Stef meant to collaborate. I
understood him to say that he would plan to come here as soon as his lecture
season is over. That would be in April, I imagine. I do not know how much
time he plans to put on the book nor what his other engagements are, further
than that he intends to go North again in 1922. I do not want either of you,
out of friendship and interest, to put more time in this work than you can
afford. I want to help you all I can because I appreciate what you are undertaking and because I am so desperately interested in the undertaking. Some
thing <u>must</u> be done to get the thing straight in history. So don't hesitate to ask
me to get ready for you anything that I can get ready. What was your idea about
coming over? Are you thinking of working at the Bay or were you planning to
come earlier? The reason I am asking is that I mean now to get to work seriously to help you. We had been talking about it a good deal the last few weeks
and Orv thought I ought to be able to do something for you.

I must tell you about the expedition to Rochester. We went the day after
election (I had to stay home to cast my first vote for President. It wasn't needed however. Ohio gave Harding a majority of 401,000+!). Dr Sutton, our K.C.
friend, had written to his special friend Dr Stokes of the Mayo Clinic. While
Orv's case did not come in Dr Stokes' department (Dermatology) still it was
very nice to have Dr Stokes' interest. He took us to Dr Logan the general
examination man. A competent young doctor then took Orv in hand and in
two days he was thoroughly examined from head to foot, X-rays and all. On

the third day the young doctor got together all the reports and went over the case – then he handed all the material on to Dr Logan who went through the case carefully. There was no division of opinion nor any puzzling feature in the case. They handed the case on to Dr Henderson, the orthopedic chief and he concurred absolutely in their finding. The sacro–iliac joint was injured in the accident and mechanically irritates the sciatic nerve. The only help is to wear a tight belt to make the joint work as it should. As soon as we got back Orv got right into his automobile and drove – without any pain. He will get much better – probably never entirely free from attacks. He is working all day long now with no discomfort. We feel sure that the diagnosis was correct. That Clinic is certainly interesting. We'll tell you about it when you come. Hope Beatrice's Hotel is prosperous!

Yrs, etc.

Katharine

P.S. I don't think Orv ever need have any severe attacks again. But I mean that the cause of the trouble can't be entirely removed. The Mayo doctors were very frank about that – not promising a complete cure. He will always have to be careful I suppose. KW

I still hope that Northcliffe will write your introduction and that Mr Fish will tell of the patent situation. KW

Hawthorn Hill
Dayton, Ohio
February 13, 1921.

Dear Grif –

There is always a temptation for me to stop writing as soon as I know any-one is coming to see us soon. But it is a <u>scandal</u> that I have not written to tell you and Beatrice and Cyril how much we appreciate your being so good to the McCormicks. You gave them a wonderful Christmas and they were so grateful to all of you for it. Frank has come back but Anne staid on and is now in south-ern France or Italy – as you may know. She was hoping that her mother would join her but I think that plan has fallen through now.

Stef writes that he is very busy this Spring and won't have much time for the book – which is just what I expected. I don't blame him though the least bit. He has fifty irons in the fire all the time and is always rushed. He is as interested as can be in the book and I know will do all he can to help us. I

·

had just the vaguest idea of wanting to go to Europe this Spring. Anne wrote that Cte de Lambert wanted us to come for the dedication of their memorial to Will at Camp D'Auvours. I want to go for that if we can because, as you know, it is just Will's good friends that are interested in it. But I discovered later that no date was settled on at all. It might happen in the Fall, instead of Spring. I thought of writing you to see if you could come the latter part of the year just as well – though we had <u>no</u> definite plans for going. Stef hoped you would come later because <u>he says</u> that he will have August, September and October 'nearly free'. But I know that when Fall comes it will be the same old story. I didn't like to postpone your coming for many reasons, chief of which was your convenience, and so I didn't write you about it. Stef will do all he can. I know that. Stef only suggested your coming later when I wrote that I would like to go to Europe now that Orv is able to travel and I was very vague indeed about it.

We have never had a chance to discuss with either you or Stef what kind of a book ought to be written. Orv and I have talked about it a good deal. What needs to be told (for the 'scientists' and college profs who are continually breaking into print) is <u>what the problem of flying consisted of</u>; what others contributed; what the state of the art was when Will and Orv tackled it; what they originated; what they used that others had originated; to whom they owed most; how they came to succeed in actually flying (where the French development started, etc. etc.).

Another style of book would be more of a 'human interest' story. But the one that ought to get the people who write is the kind I indicated above, <u>we</u> think. I don't know what you and Stef have in mind. We aren't making all those copies of which you spoke in general. We can get that sort of thing done when we get right down to it and see what we need. I don't think we want much stuff actually copied but we can take extracts etc. I think the thing is for you to read the stuff and 'digest' it!

We hope you're going to go to the Bay with us. Maybe we can finish the work up there. I wish you could have heard Orv talk the other night when we were discussing the character of the book. He is so clear and so <u>convincing</u>. Of course, we'll talk all this over by the hour when you are here but I thought I never heard quite such a good presentation of what the problem of flying was, etc. etc.

Stef says you spoke of coming on the Aquitania, sailing March 12th (or some subsequent date!). He won't be in New York then I fear. He is having a vacation of two or three weeks from lecturing now but expects to be out again in

March. But he has very likely written to you. We didn't hear much from him – always busy!

You would never believe it if you could see Orv now; runs up and down stairs, weighs 163lbs, works from morning to night and isn't bothered by any pain at all. We'll have a lovely time when you come now that he is well.

This ink is old and 'splotchy' and the pen scratchy so please forgive the general sloppiness of this letter. Thank Beatrice and Cyril for me, please, for being so good to the McC's. They were <u>charmed</u> with their visit.

Sincerely,

Katharine

Don't you hope we won't get into war (US & England)? We would hate to have to sink your canoe!

On 20 October 1921 Griffith Brewer presented to the Royal Aeronautical Society a paper entitled 'The Langley Machine and the Hammondsport Trials' which was published in The Aeronautical Journal, *Vol.25, December 1921, with responses from Walcott, Zahm, Manly and Curtiss. The paper concluded that, 'It is untrue to say that Langley's machine of 1903 ever has flown or ever could fly...'*

Arthur W. Page was the editor of World's Work. *He had known the Wrights for some years. Frederick Handley Page was an early pioneer of British aviation who formed his own company in 1909. Katharine Wright refers to Dr Raymond Pearl (1879–1940) of Johns Hopkins University.*

Hawthorn Hill
Dayton, Ohio
June 18. 1921.

Dear Beatrice,

It is characteristic of me to loaf around when the weather is fine but when it gets so hot – as it is now – that there is no rest, I get very industrious! So you know to what you owe this letter!!

I am glad Griffith is not here in this frightful heat. Yesterday was the hottest June 17th since 1880 – except one. So we are thinking longingly of the Georgian Bay 'where cool breezes blow and black bass bite' sometimes, though the advertising folders give you to understand that the 'blowing' and 'biting' are about continuous. Scipio will be as glad as anyone to escape from this heat. He is lying at my side now in the breeze of an electric fan.

Mrs McCormick is still in Europe and as her mother has <u>said</u> she would go over soon; she will probably stay until Fall as Frank wants her to do. He is so lovely and unselfish about her. I know of no one who is more lonely without his wife and still he insists on her having all the advantage and pleasure that her stay in Europe – Italy particularly – can give her. We are all made after a different pattern. I can't think of anything I'd like less than just what she likes best in the matter of traveling. I like to travel <u>some</u> but home is my preference for most of the time, unless I have very good company when I am away.

Mrs McCormick has been busy a good deal of the time. She has been serious in her study of people and conditions but it all seems so hopeless to me. It takes a life-time to get a real history of the people and a life-long living among them to get anything more than a superficial view.

Tell Griffith that I have heard from Stef about the paper. The most serious question that he brings up is whether it is good policy to 'fire the opening gun abroad'. But we have settled that definitely. He suggested that Arthur Page's opinion on that would be valuable. But, of course, Page already knows about it but Stef doesn't seem to realize that. Stef also asks whether he may consult his friend Dr Pearl of Johns Hopkins as to his opinion of the effect of the paper, as it is, on the scientific world. With Orv's approval, I have told him he may, but suggested that it would not want to be talked about too much, except where we were sure of our people. Dr Pearl was Stef's neighbour last summer in Vermont. They went where they did to be together. Stef has already told him about the Langley business and he is the one who said that Walcott was a 'crook' and that his power was declining. Dr Pearl is one of the directors of the American Academy of Sciences and is a very influential man. Stef thinks he is about the best of the whole 'scientific' bunch. You know how much he always admires his friends. They have no faults. I shall send a copy of Stef's letter for Griffith. There is not much in it, however. Stef is lecturing every day but Sunday. He started in Louisiana in April, has gone across Texas into California, up through California, across Nevada into Utah and is now in Idaho. He is coming East to Ann Arbor Michigan on June 30th to have the degree of Doctor of Laws conferred on him by the University of Michigan. It is a great honor and distinction to get an <u>LLD</u> from Michigan. But alas: he has to go right back <u>toute de suite</u> and can't spend a minute with us at the Bay. It is awfully hot and wearing for him. Griff will explain to you who 'Doctor Dick' is. In his last letter he says 'Poor old Stef! Chautauqua work in the good old summer time is the zero of joy.' That just about expresses it.

I had a nice letter from Arthur Page about seeing Griffith in N.Y. He said,

'Before leaving your house I asked Mr Brewer to let me see him on his way through N.Y. but from my observations of his aggressive, pushing nature I feared he wouldn't do it. It was as I suspected. Nevertheless he did not escape me. I found him in the tobacco shop on Pennsylvania station, where common evil habits took us and invited myself to his room and read his paper from beginning to end', etc. etc. I'll send a copy of the whole letter with Stef's next week when Miss Beck gets them copied for me.

Mr and Mrs Deeds are just home yesterday. We haven't seen them yet. It was tough luck for Griff to have so much discomfort on his voyage home. Every boat is jammed, they say.

Do let us hear from you and about Cyril and Betty, too. I suppose the latter has returned from her school in Switzerland. Cyril certainly made a hit with the McCormicks. Frank was speaking of him again the last time he was here.

Oh. I nearly forgot. Did Orv (I suppose <u>not</u>) tell Griff that Handley-Page came back to Dayton and staid with us over Sunday and Monday, May 29th and 30th? Mme Curie did <u>not</u> come finally. Praise be!! The daughters grew to be 'impossible' – aged 15 and 20!

Affectionately
Katharine.

In the following letter Mabel Beck, Orville Wright's secretary, refers to R. Luther Reed. He was Superintendent of the Smithsonian Institution's carpentry shops, and had assisted Langley in the development of the Aerodrome.

Wright Aeronautical Laboratory
Orville Wright, Director
Dayton, Ohio
June 30, 1921
My dear Mr Brewer:

At Mr Wright's direction I am enclosing herewith copy of Mr Reed's affidavit.

I am also sending you under separate cover three half-tones and one zinc etching as follows; one showing the machine on track ready for launching; one showing the machine diving after leaving the launching car; one showing reinstatement at Hammondsport in June, 1915, and one zinc etching showing front view diagrams of the Langley and Hammondsport machines (Figs 3 & 4).

As per your suggestion we have today sent to Messrs Serrell & Son the assignment and agreement and a copy of Mr Wilbur Wright's will for legalization by the Italian Consul. We have asked them to forward these papers direct to you after they have had them legalized.

Very truly yours,

Mabel Beck

Secretary.

Wright Aeronautical Laboratory

Orville Wright, Director

Dayton, Ohio

July 11, 1921.

My dear Mr Brewer:

Under date of July 9th we sent you by Parcels Post 16 slides of the Langley machine. This included slides of 14 plates and 2 diagrams. Altogether there should be 18 illustrations, but as we did not have the original photographs of two of the plates – one as it now stands in the Smithsonian and one Hammondsport photograph, we could not have slides made of them.

Very truly yours

Mabel Beck

Secretary.

Lambert Island

July 15, 1921.

Dear Griff:

Before leaving Dayton I had the papers for the Italian business executed and sent on to your New York correspondent. I hesitated some about executing them, for fear they would lead to a law suit in Italy, and I don't propose to take part in any more suits. In fact I think it would be foolish to risk an adverse decision now after winning all our cases.

I have your letters announcing the date of your lecture on the Langley Machine. I see no objection to sending advance copies to the parties concerned. However, before it is printed, I will write making some suggestions. We have just sent the copies to Page and Haskell. I will also send you any suggestions they may make.

The plates were sent before we left Dayton two weeks ago, and Miss Beck tells me the slides have been made and are also on the way to you. After you are through with the slides and plates I would like to have them for use over here.

We have been having roasting weather since our arrival here, the thermometer running up to 90 to 94 almost every day until today, when the highest was 78.

Sincerely

Orv.

The following two letters are typescript copies taken from Brewer's papers. They are headed 'The British Wright Company Limited, 33 Chancery Lane, London W.C.2'.

Lt-Col. W. Lockwood Marsh was Secretary of the Royal Aeronautical Society from 1920–25.

Mr Orville Wright,

Lambert Island,

Penetang,

Near Toronto,

Ontario, Canada.

28th July 1921.

My dear Orv,

Your letter of the 15th gave me much welcome information. I was able on this to write to Lieut.-Col. W. Lockwood Marsh, telling him your approval of the paper being circulated to the parties concerned in America, and therefore of my acceptance of the Council's condition. I also wrote to Mr Zanardo, suggesting that if success could not be obtained without a law suit, it would be best to take no further action. Copies of both of these letters are enclosed.

All the plates are here now, and the slides have arrived in perfect condition. After the lecture, all the plates and slides shall be returned to you.

Our heat wave over here has broken at last, but we are still without rain and a partial famine is beginning to set in. No grass has grown during the past two months, and the cattle are eating up the little hay which has been gathered and which should be preserved for the coming winter. Our thermometer went to 92.

Alec has just got his new boat the 'Kittihawk', which runs 10½ knots, is 60ft long and has a tonnage of over 30. It is propelled by two Coatalen-Sunbeam engines, and ran from the Thames round to Lymington behind the Isle of Wight, a distance of 200 miles, non-stop, in just over twenty hours. In spite of the enormous expense of this new plaything, he seems somewhat worried over it, owing to the instructions in building and fitting not having been carried out satisfactorily. A fast motor yacht does not satisfy my imagination. There is no skill required, and to have the monotonous throb of the engine going all the time, together with the smell of the oil, is anything but pleasant. I hope some day, however, to go up behind Vancouver Island in amongst the thousand forest islands between Vancouver Island and the mainland, and this shall be in a sailing vessel fitted with an auxiliary engine taking up very little room. The charm of sailing can then be enjoyed, and when the wind fails, then the motor will save us from being absolutely stationary. Would such a cruise attract Katharine and yourself next summer or the summer after next, if the boat showed her seaworthiness in coming out via the Panama Canal?

Yours sincerely

[Griffith Brewer]

Comm. G.B. Zanardo,
Messrs Barzano & Zanardo,
Palazzo del Popole Romane,
9, Via due Macelli,
Rome, Italy.
28th July 1921.

Dear Commander Zanardo,

I have just received a letter from Mr Orville Wright, in which he says – 'Before leaving Dayton I had the papers for the Italian business executed and sent on to your New York correspondent. I hesitated some about executing them, for fear they would lead to a law suit in Italy, and I don't propose to take part in any more suits. In fact I think it would be foolish to risk an adverse decision now after winning all our cases.'

The papers referred to, which Mr Wright executed subsequently were received by our New York correspondent, who returned them to Dayton because the Notary's signature had to be verified by the County Clerk in order to enable it to be legalised by the Italian Consul. Ultimately, however, I should expect to receive the Assignment and Will duly executed and legalised.

The paragraph quoted above from Mr Wright's letter, will show you the attitude which he adopts, and I should like you to give this your consideration before we decide to proceed any further. No doubt Mr Orville Wright, whose health has been so shaken by the worries entailed through long litigation, does not want to be dragged into litigation again, but would rather sacrifice what he is entitled to in Foreign countries than take part in any more legal battles.

If, therefore, when I am able to send you the documents, you will be able to make use of them without litigation, I think it would be well for you to see what you can do, but if litigation is the necessary corollary, then I think for Mr Orville Wright's sake we must sacrifice the royalties to which no doubt he is entitled.

Yours faithfully,

[Griffith Brewer]

We have noted that Griffith Brewer was to give a lecture to the Aeronautical Society of Great Britain on the subject of the tests made in 1914 of Langley's flying machine. The original had crashed on take-off in 1903; but in 1914, Glenn Curtiss, with the connivance of the Smithsonian, had rebuilt and modified the machine with the aim of demonstrating that Langley's design was capable of fight. It was thought that this would undermine the Wrights' position as the first to develop a successful flying machine.

Wright Aeronautical Laboratory
Orville Wright, Director
Dayton, Ohio
August 6, 1921

My dear Mr Brewer:

On July 9th we sent you a box containing 16 slides of the Langley machine. Will you not kindly inform us whether or not you have received same?

Very truly yours,

M. Beck.

Secretary.

Henry J. Haskell was Associate Editor of the Kansas City Star *and had been a class-mate of Katharine Wright's at Oberlin College (near Cleveland) in the 1890s.*

Lambert Island
Penetang, Ont.
Aug 15, 1921.

Dear Griff:

After receiving the letters from Dr Pearl and Harry Haskell, suggesting that the authorities for the different statements in your paper should be given, I sent for the papers at Dayton (thinking you may not have all of them) and have inserted the sources of information for the statements.

Dr Pearl wanted to know the authority for the statement that the Smithsonian had not paid for anything except the transportation of the machine to and from Hammondsport. Dr Walcott told me that Zahm had been paid nothing by the Institution, and that the only expenses the Institution had had in regard to the 'tests' was the cost of transportation. I believe you have a letter from Lamb in regard to the matter. Will you send me a copy of it? However nothing needs to be put into the paper in respect of this matter.

The paper as it went to Dr Pearl, Haskell and Page, had nothing to connect it with the plates, so that it was not strange that they did not get the authority for your statements. I have written a paragraph (Insert 'a') which covers this matter, giving the source of the different plates and figures.

Dr Pearl is expecting the paper to start a fight. He thinks several sentences should be modified, as they might be hard to prove. He also suggested several changes to make the statements more positive. All three of them (Pearl, Haskell and Steff), did not like the sentences in regard to Reed shedding tears, so I have scratched the sentences out which they in any wise have criticized.

I have also made some suggestion for changes which may obviate an argument. I think we had better not give them a chance to get off onto quibbling.

Both Haskell and Pearl think the reference to the machine making short hops (top of page 15) not convincing. I have written in a suggestion which I think will clear up this matter. It is apparent from their letters that they do not understand some of the points made in your paper. Where this occurs, Katharine and I have suggested the addition of a sentence or two which ought to bring out the point. Such a case is that in regard to the lack of propeller thrust (page 15).

I am sending a set of plates showing the numbers referred to in the paper. These are not at all in the order in which they should appear. You can change the numbers to correspond with the plates as you use them.

It is very clear from the letters of Haskell and Pearl that it is important to give in the printed paper the reference to authorities. We have looked this up and inserted them in the copy I am sending.

On page 17, I have suggested slicing out several sentences. Dr Pearl suggested leaving out the sentence beginning 'I must leave Dr Zahm to explain it.' I think we are all agreed that it will be best to leave the personal references out. I would strongly recommend leaving off the last sentence of this paragraph. It is the only statement in the paper on which Zahm could base an action, and it would be rather embarrassing to defend the sentence, because Zahm does not say the Hammondsport machine had the Langley trussing. It is true that he was 'deliberately attempting to deceive'. The sentences above this statement clearly make him out a liar without calling him one.

We have been trying for a long time to get from the Associated Press a letter giving Lyman J. Seeley's connection with us in 1914, but so far have not been able to get it. We will cable if we get it. I am sending inclosed a copy of a clipping which you saw when you were at Dayton in regard to Seeley, which may be of use to you.

Katharine has had a copy of Steff's letter made and asks me to inclose it. We have incorporated in the proposed changes in the paper all of his suggestions which we thought good.

We think the paper now covers the criticisms that have been made. Dr Pearl didn't have the diagrams and only one or two plates, so that it is not strange he thought it lacking in proof, on which he insists strongly for the scientific world. I think the paper a very good one, and that it will be convincing to everyone who understands anything in aeronautics.

Please send us a half dozen or more advance proofs. I may have use for them.

Also send me an account of <u>all</u> of your expenses in connection with this matter. I want to pay them.

Sincerely yours,

Orv.

Lambert Island
Penetang Ontario
Sept. 13, 1921

Dear Griff –

Orv and I are leaving the 'Blessed Isles' day after tomorrow. We have been alone for a week, Buster and Miss O'Hare having left a week ago today. The latter is Mrs McCormick's sister. Buster is in school today, I suppose.

The only reason I haven't written you long ago was that there was so much to say that I couldn't get started! and it is very hard to write a letter requiring any thought when you have no place but the general living room for writing. We must arrange for some kind of a writing and reading room.

First, about the copy you sent over, with your own alterations, and Alec's suggestions. We think every change you have made is an improvement. We haven't heard from you since you received our suggested changes. Dr Pearl has taken the greatest interest in the whole affair. He will undertake – at his own suggestion – to get a lot of publicity in scientific journals. He has shown a fine spirit. Stef says he is very influential. He is evidently very fond of Stef and has been well 'fed up' on the subject. You remember that Stef spent last summer in Vermont in a colony of college professors. Dr Pearl was the one who got him to go there and they had houses side by side, Dr Pearl's sister-in-law chaperon-ing Stef's house.

Harry Haskell is on the job every minute. He saw Wickham Steed of the Times, who came into the Star office several weeks ago. Harry talked to him about your paper and said that Steed seemed very much interested. Harry is also busy writing to Mr Grasty in London whom he thinks is still the head of the European Bureau for the N.Y. Times. He has also written to Richard Oulahan of the Times and to Mr Van Anda the managing editor. We can use all the advance copies you can let us have. Harry wants you to let Mr Grasty have an advance copy – if he finds out for sure that he is still a chief N.Y. Times man in England. Be sure to let him know about your having the letter in Times in 1914. No paper can be so good for us as the Times as it is read by just the class of people we want most to reach. I think we can get extra attention and interest there. We have always noticed that the person who writes the editorials on aeronautical subjects is always very friendly to us. We do not know who it is, however. I'll write again when we find out about Mr Grasty, unless Harry writes to you directly.

Now about Northcliffe. We <u>must</u> have his special support and we must let him know about this thing before hand? If you will not be where you can reach him i.e. England or the continent – please let us have a cable address for him, if you can get it through the Times. We will cable him ourselves. I think he will like it and I know he will give orders to send the stuff everywhere. We want it in France, especially.

I think the paper is all right. We needn't worry any more over that. Now the problem is to get every one we can to know about it and read it. That reminds me about the lists. We will get to work on that <u>immediately</u> when we get home. I shall ask Dr Pearl to help on the lists of 'scientists'. Stef can help us on that, too I shall get lists of important librarians, writers of history for schools, etc. etc. I'll make myself busy on that job when I get home. All this reminds me to tell you that Carrie is coming back, <u>is</u> back now, in fact, and will have everything ship shape for us when we get back. So now this year, I can get my mind off of that house – not that it ever was so much on it but I felt that it should be!!

I had a letter from Mr Page not long ago saying that he was going to the Oregon mountains for a month but would be back in plenty of time to take care of the editorial for the World's Work, which will not appear however until the December number. The November number goes to print before October 20th and he wants to be sure it has been read before his comment appears. He is so friendly and interested and so <u>sensible</u>. He is one fine friend for whom we have Stef to thank.

Stef is back in N.Y. since August 24th. He lectured all spring and summer <u>seven nights a week</u>. We hope to see him in Dayton before he commences lecturing for the winter. His book is coming out now. I won't forget your two. I had a nice letter from Beatrice and will answer her when I get home. We are very busy packing up. We have missed you.

Sincerely
Katharine

P.S. Please thank Alec for me for the great interest he has taken. His suggestions were <u>good</u> but I like especially to have <u>him</u> so interested. KW

In January 1920 President Woodrow Wilson appointed Orville Wright to serve on the National Advisory Committee for Aeronautics.

Orville Wright
Dayton, Ohio
October 3, 1921.

Dear Griff:

I am in receipt of the advance printed proof of your paper.

In one of my letters from Lambert Island I gave the sources from which the different plates had been taken. I gave Plate 9 as being from the Secretary's Report. I later discovered that it was printed in Zahm's official report. Although it also appeared in the Secretary's Report. But being from Zahm's report gives it more force.

On the third sheet of the proof in the first quotation, 'Manly' should be in brackets instead of in parentheses; and in the second quotation beginning, Mr Reed the foreman 'according to Manly' should be in brackets also instead of parentheses, since these words are not a part of the quotations.

On page 4 near the bottom of the page there is a paragraph beginning, 'Several so-called flights have been made with this Hammondsport machine, etc.' I consider the point we are attempting to prove by Zahm's quotation in this paragraph the most important in the whole paper, but I find that not one person out of about eight or ten who have read this paragraph has grasped the idea. Of course, these were not aeronautical experts, although they were practically all of them more or less technical people. They have all failed on first reading to see the admission that is made, and to comprehend that if the machine was really flying more thrust would not be necessary. I think something should be added to this paragraph which will bring out the idea more clearly. Of course any aeronautical engineer ought to see at once that the machine did not really fly but the non-technical man does not get the idea from reading the paragraph until his attention is called to it.

On receipt of your telegram I telegraphed to Lord Northcliffe and received a reply that he was cabling London.

The National Advisory Committee meets on the 6th. I am wondering how Dr Walcott is going to greet me and whether he will be a cordial as he was the last time I was at Washington.

We have been trying now for three months to find out from the Associated Press as to whether Seeley was their representative in 1914. As we can get no answer at all it is evident that Seeley was, and that they do not want it to be known. I am now trying to get some evidence from other sources. Katharine has written to Haskell to see whether the Kansas City Star can get the information for us. I have also written to one of the newspaper men that was present at the trials, who I think was one of the reporters that told me that Seeley was the Associated Press representative at that time. I have not been able to learn the address of Stiles, the Tribune reporter, who also gave me this information in 1914. Can you get any information on Seeley's standing in England at the present time? Is he still under indictment, and on what charges was he indicted? I think it probable that we can use some of this matter later.

We will send you in a few days a list of several hundred to whom we would like to have marked copies of the Journal sent. I think the 20 advance proofs, which you are sending, will be sufficient.

Sincerely yours,

Orville Wright

A discussion followed the presentation of Brewer's paper 'The Langley Machine and the Hammondsport Trials' to the Royal Aeronautical Society on 20 October 1921. Frederick Handley Page, who earlier had stated that '...he felt in a little quandary in discussing this paper, as he happened to know the parties on both sides', referred to the Curtiss 1914 Hammondsport trials of the reconstructed Langley's 1903 tandem monoplane Aerodrome as '...an extraordinary procedure to have adopted. He thought everyone, from a historical point of view, owed a great debt of gratitude to Mr Brewer for going so patiently and persistently through the details of all the experiments that were made.'

Katharine Wright refers to Mr Wm. Ers. Lamb, an attorney and counsellor of law based in Washington D.C. The Royal Aeronautical Society's Library has a letter to Lamb from Walcott, dated 11 April 1921. In this Walcott says that, 'In reply to your letter of April 6, I beg leave to say that the payment made to Mr Glenn H. Curtiss for carrying on tests of the Langley aeroplane in 1914–15, was merely to cover the expenses of these tests, and was made from private funds of the Smithsonian Institution, and not from any Governmental appropriation.'

Hawthorn Hill
Dayton Ohio
October 27, 1921

Dear Griff,

There is always so much to tell you that I don't know where to begin and so don't begin at all!

First about your household affairs. What a lot of bad luck you have all been having. I do hope that Beatrice has come home quite well. Mr McCormick had a letter from Mrs McCormick (who is home now but we haven't seen her yet) saying that she had Beatrice's letter weeks and <u>weeks</u> after it was written. She and her mother spent a month I think on the coast of Brittany.

We did reach Lord Northcliffe at Sydney and had an immediate reply 'Affectionate greetings. Cabling London'. I hope you will send the London Times and the Daily Mail. We were sorry the Associated Press did not carry the story but of course you couldn't expect that on a 'scientific (!)' paper. 'Scientific' has become a term of derision with me.

Did Orv ever tell you that he never did receive any letter at all from the Secretary of the Aeronautical Society? So I had 'one on him' when I got the card of invitation from you.

Didn't I tell you that Harry Haskell saw Wickham Steed in the Star Office and told him what was coming off? I suppose that Harry didn't write to Mr Grasty. He told me that he had been unable to get any word about him – that was some time ago.

The reasons your replies from Walcott, Zahm, Curtiss, etc., were late was that Walcott was in the West and got home the 13th. See if the replies were not mailed after that. We were sorry that Orv did not have a chance to see Walcott at the Advisory Committee meeting. He might have been able to drop some suggestions about what kind of stuff he has on Zahm and Curtiss. Then, unless he is tied up with Curtiss and Zahm and is more guilty than we know, he might have hesitated to be associated with them. But now he has chosen his course, it will be a long tiresome fight but he will be sorry, <u>in the end</u>.

Of course we haven't seen the replies which you cabled you had sent, but the N.Y. Times gave a report of them. I <u>hope</u> they are as weak as the report makes them out to be. Orville is anxious to see Mr Lamb's letter and he thinks he asked you for a copy of it some time ago. Of course, he remembers that Walcott told him that it did not cost the Smithsonian a cent for the Langley tests except for transportation <u>to</u> Hammondsport. He says Walcott did not even say 'and return' but he supposed he meant that. If that is the only fact they deny it will be fun to publish that letter of Lamb's, if it is what we remember it to be.

Yesterday we received the editorial Mr Page is getting ready for the December World's Work. It is a <u>corker</u>. Certainly Mr Page is no coward. He wants to see that there are no errors, because as he says since he is coming out in such a flat-footed way, he wouldn't want to put his 'flat-foot in the sands of error'! He is trump – that man. There are a few things to be corrected in the editorial but it is a good one I can tell you.

Harry Haskell worked like a horse doing all he could to 'spread the gospel' abroad. He and Stef and Mr Page certainly did all they could. Stef got a fine story in the N.Y. Times. I haven't heard of anyone Stef has seen in the last six months that he hasn't talked to about your paper. It was a very good thing that he and Harry both knew you personally. That made it natural for them to be receiving your advanced copies. We have been very careful to keep out of sight in the preliminaries. Orv hasn't written a word to anyone, I think, and I only to Harry, Stef, Mr Page and Dr Pearl. The latter is doing what he can with advance copies and personal letters to editors of 'Science', etc. etc. He will be a valuable ally and is thoroughly stirred up.

When Orv saw the reply in the Times of the 22nd he said 'The conflict deepens. On ye braves' and looked as if he enjoyed the prospect of a good scrap. Of course, no one of us really wants to get into another fight but if we <u>have</u> to do it we will and as Dr Pearl expressed it, we'll 'make them everlastingly sorry they started it.'

I don't see how we're going to 'collaborate' on this job with the Atlantic between us. But one good thing we don't have to get together to see that we don't contradict each other in 'facts' There is always a considerable advantage in that respect when you are on the right side and can tell the truth! We'll be crazy to hear how the meeting went and everything. Handley-Page [*sic*] was 'true to form'. <u>Bah</u>!! What a moral hero he is. No opinion on this thing because he knows all parties concerned. Really I should have thought he would have kept still instead of saying an imbecile thing like that. You'll have to come over soon just to <u>talk</u>. We'll have a lot of fun before we get through with it.

Carrie is here and I have a good cook. All serene.

Katharine

P.S. I suppose Betty is home this year. How I wish we could come see you all. KW

Orville Wright
Dayton, Ohio
November 9, 1921.

Dear Mr Brewer:

The proofs of the replies of Walcott, Zahm, Manly and Curtiss were duly received. Your reply also came several days later.

The sentence which you have added on the fourth page of the proof is very good, and it seems to me that it makes the meaning entirely clear. On the top of the page in paragraph 5 I have inserted the word 'front'. We think it probable that the rear wings did not have these additional spars in the early tests. They did have them in the later flights. That is the only correction I think needed in the paper.

I started to read to Miss Beck from your reply, leaving out some of your paragraphs and inserting others containing suggestions for covering the points involved, but I had to quit when I got as far as Manly in order to try to get the paper off on the first mail. That is the reason no letter accompanied the paper. As it was I am afraid it did not reach the boat in time.

I am now returning the copy of your reply which you sent me with a few suggestions of little importance in the parts relating to Manly and Curtiss.

Your second paragraph I struck out entirely because I believe that the fact is exactly as you stated in your paper, that only the transportation was paid by the Smithsonian. Walcott stated to me on the 21st of April that the Smithsonian had no expense in connection with the trials excepting the transportation to Hammondsport. I noticed at the time that he stated 'to Hammondsport', but supposed that he probably meant transportation both ways. As Mr Lamb had it the same way, I suspect that he really only meant to Hammondsport.

I telegraphed you a few days ago as follows:

> Walcott does not say paid two thousand nor specifically deny your state-
> ment. Note Zahmesque language. Walcott told me also exactly your
> statement. Make no concessions. Your quotations proper. Hold if possi-
> ble for important suggestions.

Since Walcott does not specifically deny the statement that only the transportation to Hammondsport was paid by the Institution, I do not think it is
necessary to make any correction until further proof has been produced. If the
Institution did pay $2,000 then Walcott was lying when he told me that only
the transportation was paid.

As the replies of Walcott, et al. are so lengthy, I believe that your reply will
be more forcible if the paragraphs which are not in answer to their main arguments are left out.

No apologies are necessary for the brevity of the quotations in your paper.
The quotations are not garbled and are not misleading. All that I can see that
you have left out is that 'the workmen set to work straightening out and arranging the various parts, fittings and accessories and cleaning up the engine, which
fortunately had sustained no injury whatever, etc'. and the fact that Mr Langley
considered business engagements of more importance then seeing the test of his
machine. All the other facts in the long quotation are stated in your paper.

Your 'ostrich reply' to Zahm is a corking good one. It is exactly to the point
as well as humorous. We have read it over and over and enjoyed it exceedingly.

The changes which I have recommended are merely suggestions to be used
or not as you see fit. But I would strongly advise that no apologies or corrections be made until they produce evidence to show that you were wrong. So
far they have not done this.

We will send you in a few days clippings from some of the American papers
which noticed your address, and also copies of such editorials as come out from
time to time in the American weeklies and magazines. Mr Page will have a
good editorial in the November World's Work. The New Republic of
November 9th has a strong editorial.

Sincerely yours,

Orv

P.S. In the suggestions which I offered I mentioned that changing the camber
of a wing from 1 in 12 to 1 in 18 produces a gain in efficiency of about thirty
per cent. In some surfaces the gain is even more than this. I have now made
measurements of a thin surface of the Langley type and having the same aspect

ratio, and I find that the gain in efficiency when the camber was a little over 1 in 17 was 27 per cent more than the 1 in 12. If you use this I would merely state that the gain is over 25 per cent. You are then well on the safe side.

Orville Wright
Dayton, Ohio
November 12, 1921.

Dear Griff:

My suspicion of Walcott's statement in regard to the payment to Curtiss was well founded. The Smithsonian Report of 1914, page 120 gives the expenditures of the Langley Aerodynamical Laboratory for the year ending June 30, 1914, as $723.73; The Smithsonian Report for 1915, page 113, expenditures for the year ending June 30, 1915, $418.58; The Smithsonian Report for 1916, page 121, expenditures for the year ending June 30, 1916, $70.95.

I am considering a trip down to Washington to see the receipt held by Walcott from Curtiss 'for the payment made me in accordance with the above proposal'.

Miss Beck tells me that I have never sent you a copy of the letter I received through Mr Haskell from the Associated Press regarding Seeley. I now enclose it.

Sincerely,

Orv.

Brewer's paper was also published in US Air Service, *Vol.6 (3), October 1921 – the official publication of the Army and Navy Air Service Association of Washington D.C. – edited by Earl N. Findley, formerly a news reporter for the* New York Tribune. *He had known the Wrights for some years.*

Under the heading 'A New Langley Controversy', a short summary of Brewer's paper together with the responses from Manly and Walcott in full, was published in Aviation and Aircraft Journal, *Vol.11 (19), 7 November 1921. This magazine was published and edited by Lester Durand Gardner.*

Katharine Wright refers to Professor Raymond Herbert Stetson (1872–1950) of Oberlin College.

Hawthorn Hill
Dayton, Ohio
November 17, 1921

Dear Griff,

It is really dreadful trying to write to you! I want to tell you everything at once – with the result that I don't get much anything told.

Of course it's about the scrap. In the first place, though, I am enclosing you some clippings about Stef and his book – as well as some editorial comment from the New Republic, which is a regular 'high-brow' publication. As Harry Haskell says it is just the <u>very best</u> publicity we could get. I have heard nothing from Stef for ages. He is very busy getting ready for his expedition north next year. But he was in Kansas City a week or two ago and spent the evening with Harry Haskell. Harry wrote me telling me that Stef had furnished the material to the New Republic. I suspected it for he admires that bunch more than we do and knows many of them personally.

Arthur Page's editorial is the best thing of all. As soon as the World's Work is out we will send you some copies. Undoubtedly Mr Page will send you a copy too.

Mr Findley, our great friend you may remember, is now editor of Air Service, the paper published by the Army and Navy Air Service Club. He reprinted your paper in full, with Walcott's and Zahm's replies and will publish Manly's and Curtiss'. But <u>Aviation</u>, whose editor is L.D. Gardner, who has always been a friend of Orv's, printed your bare summary, without any evidence to back it up, and gave Walcott, Zahm and Curtiss <u>in full</u>, with Langley's picture mixed in with their defence. We can't imagine how Gardner fell for such stuff. Curtiss is of course an important advertiser, but Orv had a letter from Gardner on this very subject expressing the fear that Air Service was going to take the other side. Orv wrote him that while he had heard nothing at all from Earl Findley, he was not afraid that he would not get fair treatment in any paper that Findley edited. Findley also has editorial and a quotation from you on the outside page. We are sending you copies of Air Service and Aviation and I will send also the November World's Work because it has an article by Stef, one about him and an excellent full-page picture of him.

A friend of Harry Haskell's, also our friend, a professor at Oberlin, wrote to Harry that he thought that to clinch our point about Langley's not being the inventor of the aeroplane, an article should be written showing what Langley's scientific work actually was and then what Will's and Orv's work actually was.

He thinks that 'if you put the Wrights' case before scientific men in that way there will be no question about the acceptance of the right priority, and with proofs as to the "tests" of the Langley machine, the thing will be nailed.'

Of course, that is Arthur Page's idea also only he thought of a book by Orv as the way to get that information out. Mr Stetson's idea is to get out an article right away to be published soon under some else's name. That looks like an awfully big job to me.

Orv and I thought your turning Zahm's illustration against him by substituting the ostrich for the eagle was one of the <u>richest</u> things we every saw. I hope we can show Walcott's deception up – about what he paid Curtiss. What a liar he is! He probably remembers what he told Orv and what he told whoever answered Mr Lamb to say. His answer was 'slick'. If Zahm just talks a little more we'll get the whole story – not that he means to tell the truth about a single thing but he keeps letting things out. Isn't it 'rich' how innocent Walcott and Zahm were of any idea that this Langley business might have something to do with the patent fight. The N.Y. Tribune's correspondent says that 'for some reason or other the populace of Hammondsport feel that a successful flight of the Langley machine will give Curtiss an advantage over the Wrights' and the London Times correspondent said what you found. Everyone else knew what the object was except the Smithsonian!

Then what is the use of Walcott's pretending that the Smithsonian suggested the thing? We have the dispatch telling of Beechey's proposal and Zahm says 'When in March 1914 Mr Curtiss was invited to send, etc. etc.', he replied, 'I would like to put the Langley, etc. etc.' Learning this, Secretary Walcott soon authorized Mr Curtiss, etc. etc.' I <u>can't</u> see how they hope to get away with all these conflicting stories. But we'll have a long hard fight before we compel the Smithsonian to make the thing right. But you have done <u>one good job</u> on that paper. Every one thinks it is good. I hope it won't make you too much trouble. We didn't say much about it but we do feel under great obligation. You are such a <u>good</u> friend!

Stef's book is held up again, I hear. It was to have been out November 3rd. You shall have two copies – one as soon as it is out; the other when Stef autographs it. That will be your Christmas present! We are both very well. Don't be surprised to get letters from me type-written soon. I am getting to be such a miserable writer. Love to all the family.

Sincerely
Katharine

Orville Wright,
Dayton, Ohio
November 23, 1921.

Dear Griff:

On the 21st I sent you a list of 150 addresses to which I would like to have copies of the Journal sent. If this is more than you have printed you can cut out whatever number is necessary. I am not certain of the correctness of a number of the French addresses, as these were taken from publications prior to the war. Most of the German addresses are of a later date.

I find I was a little mixed about dates in my cable to you, but as the papers in question were received by you before the telegram it did not make much difference. As soon as you can I would like to have you send me a copy of your reply as it will appear in the Journal. As it is, the other people have had the final say.

A few days ago I sent you a bunch of clippings, and will send others from time to time. I think your paper shows very clearly the changes that were made in the Langley machine at Hammondsport, so any one who has any technical knowledge can easily understand it.

I wanted the papers sent out as coming from you and not from me. It is my understanding that you intended to send them that way unless you received advice from me to do otherwise.

Sincerely,
Orv.

Katharine Wright refers to an editorial in Nature *(Vol.108, 3 November 1921) entitled 'The Langley Flying Machine'. In referring to Brewer's paper to the Royal Aeronautical Society, the editorial said that its theme was '...the attempt to rob the Wright brothers of the credit for inventing the aeroplane'. The writer claimed that the issue of the Hammondsport trials was unimportant, stating that the 'transaction appears to have been rather sordid and reflect on the commercial system of the world which exalts "profitability" at the expense of solid service'. Extolling Langley while belittling the Wrights, the editorial concluded that the key objection to Brewer's paper was that it tended to give the erroneous impression of the importance of the part played by the Wright Brothers.*

40. Samuel Pierpont Langley (1834–1906).

Hawthorn Hill
Dayton, Ohio.
December 14, 1921

Dear Griff:

Here goes for a letter on the typewriter, I am practicing on an old Underwood but Santa Claus is going to surprise me with a new machine for Christmas! The new one will be a Hammond, I think. I am trying to go in for 'looks'. It would be sad if that doesn't pan out and I find that I have only suc-ceeded in getting a fancy machine which is not any too convenient.

Stef forwarded to us a letter from Dr Pearl enclosing a copy of an editorial in 'Nature' which Dr Pearl seems to think will have a good deal of weight with the scientists. You probably know what the standing of 'Nature' is, since it is a British publication. Dr Pearl is discouraged because in trying to get suitable people to write answers to these unfavourable comments he meets with the reluctance of all associated with aeronautics in any way to mix up, as they say, 'with patent litigation'. In fact Dr Pearl says he has been told by the 'aeronautic sharks' that the US Navy has stopped paying royalties and the whole legal fight is about to be reopened. It is possible but certainly not probable that Zahm has tried to start some such move. But Dr Pearl thinks that some one whose word would carry some weight in aeronautical matters should write to 'Nature', calling its attention to the fact that the editorial missed the point entirely. I am enclosing in this letter a copy of my reply to Stef which with the copy of the editorial will give you the story.

Stef asked for fifty copies of your paper and we felt sure he would make good use of them. That was what brought us to the point of cabling for the hundred copies. As near as I can make out Stef discusses this matter with every man, woman and child that he sees! Orv had a short letter from Arthur Page, enclosing a letter from Dr Vernon Kellogg of Washington. Dr Kellogg says that Dr Walcott is much worried about an editorial in the World's Work, which he says is based on a misunderstanding of the facts. Dr Kellogg wants to know if the World's Work will publish the letter in explanation by Dr Walcott. Mr Page replies that certainly he will publish a letter from Dr Walcott but that he will reserve the priviledge of commenting upon it or <u>the whole situation</u>. He adds that he feels very strongly on this posthumous attempt to prove Langley was the inventor of the flying machine, especially with a machine that was tinkered with. Of course they will never be able to touch Page. It will just give added publicity.

We hear from Dr Pearl that Walcott is good and worried. Dr Pearl is very active in this matter and is very outspoken about it but he thinks that the fact that he does not have a good opinion of Walcott had better not be talked about.

We are undoubtedly in for a hard, long fight which is not to be wondered at. Mr Page keeps urging Orv to get to work on the book which he thinks is the effective way to win. He says that this skirmish is a 'good fight' and necessary but that it will never settle the question finally. Dr Pearl's advice is to 'let Dr Walcott do all the talking for the next few months.' He thinks that the cause will be 'helped the most and done the least harm' that way. I wish Alec would feel like writing to 'Nature'. His standing would command respect but of course I do not want to drag him into anything he doesn't care to mix up with. You know how Orv feels about that too.

Stef's book is not here yet though I think there are some copies out. I have finally written him asking him to send you two copies from New York but they will be too late for Christmas. However they are a gift from Santa Claus. Stef was here about two weeks ago for a few hours. We drove him up to Piqua for his lecture and then brought him back to Dayton for his train. We sat in the automobile in the Station at midnight and ate sandwiches and drank hot cocoa, which I had taken with us.

I think that on the whole I have not made any improvement by using the typewriter but I can learn. I haven't put my paper in right, Orv says. That accounts for this atrocious spacing.

Merry Christmas to all and a Happy New Year.

Sincerely,

Katharine.

In Nature *of 26 January 1922, an editorial entitled 'The Langley Aeroplane and the Hammondsport Trials' observed that the Americans most associated with Langley had written to the Royal Aeronautical Society and to* Nature *complaining about Brewer's paper. The editorial, which again gave most credit to Langley for having demonstrated the feasibility of flight, noted that there was an issue of practical men not recognising Science — which, it said, really leads the way forward.*

The reference to Lilienthal is to Gustav, the brother of Otto Lilienthal.

Hawthorn Hill

Dayton, Ohio.

January 7, 1922.

Dear Griff:

I don't know just where I left off in my tale the last time I wrote. I think I told you of Dr Pearl's concern about the editorial in <u>Nature</u>. Dr Pearl says that the Lockyer family controls that magazine. I have been wondering if it is the family of astronomers. If it is, Mr McClean, if he is interested, could point out to them the error of their ways.

The <u>Literary Digest</u> took advantage of their opportunity to re-publish that editorial, omitting any adequate extract from your paper, but using Langley's picture to give the desired impression. The editorials in the <u>World's Work</u> and <u>New Republic</u> were not noticed at all. It was pretty bad, altogether. But Stef telegraphed a day or two ago that the <u>Digest</u> had agreed to re-open the discussion and asked us to send on all editorial comment that we had. We found the following editorials from the London <u>Times</u>, <u>Daily Mail</u>, New York <u>Times</u>, <u>Kansas City Star</u>, <u>New Republic</u>, <u>World's Work</u> and <u>Winning Post</u>. We have since an editorial from the New York <u>Evening Post</u>. I will enclose a typewritten copy for you. It is the best we can do. I copied it myself! Please praise my industry.

Of course we are having some ups and downs in the course of the fight. Harry and Dr Pearl get awfully discouraged. I don't see what they expected. We are establishing some important points. The public now knows for the first time that there <u>were changes made</u>. We haven't convinced some of them that the changes were important but we will, in time. People are now realizing that the two machines were contemporaneous. There has always been an impression that the Langley machine ante-dated the Wright by many years – no one knew just how many years, but 'years'. In time we'll get all the facts established, thanks to you!

Stef is a zealous missionary, sure enough. He never loses interest or quits. He is a good friend but I'd hate to have him for an enemy! His admiration for Orv is touching. He told me one day that he admires Orv more than any living man he knew. Then in his careful way he stopped to think, just to make sure that he meant just what he said. 'Yes, I mean just that.' Do you know, Griff, he reminds me of Will and Orv, in some ways. Any way he is an everlasting friend.

We read Lilienthal's letter with greatest interest. Orv says to tell you that he (Lilienthal) is mistaken, however, in thinking that Will and Orv ever had one of his brother's gliders. Orv doesn't remember that Chanute had one. Dr Pearl was delighted with that letter. He said it went to the root of the 'essential viciousness' of the Smithsonian's methods.

That was a nice letter from Mr Lahm. Wouldn't it be nice if you and we could go to the dedication of the 'stone' at Avours? Mr Lahm always sees through the neat little schemes of designing politicians – like our friend D'Estournelles. He is very agreeable without being one bit compromising.

We are to have some more poets, I hope, next Thursday. Robert Frost has been invited to read his poems before the same 'Ladies' that heard our poets last year when you were here. Percy MacKaye says that he will come over at the same time, for a visit. He and Frost are friends. I do not think I shall have to cook the dinner this time but any thing can happen. However Carrie does not allow much to happen that is not pleasant for me. I am in clover, again. Better come over quick while the pastures are fair.

I hope you all had a nice holiday in Switzerland. We had a nice Christmas, the chief joy being Leontine's arrival home that very morning. She had been away for more than six months. Mrs McCormick said she was writing a Christmas letter to Beatrice. They certainly did appreciate your kindness to them at Christmas time last year. They are well and flourishing.

This typewriter tempts me into awfully long letters, I think Orv really feels that he ought to protect my friends from these long effusions! But he can't. I am fairly contrary, as you know! Many good wishes

Sincerely, etc.

Katharine

I did not send the <u>World's Work</u> because Orv said you could get it.

Katharine Wright refers to Dr Vilhjalmur Stefansson's book My Life with the Eskimo *(London, Macmillan and Co. Limited, 1913).*
   'Scipio' was the name of Orville Wright's St Bernard dog.

Hawthorn Hill
Dayton Ohio
February 1, 1922

Dear Griff,

Your letters of January 17 to Orv and of January to me came today. As Dr Pearl would say, we were 'vastly amused' at the attempt of 'the Editor' of *Nature* to give you a few lessons on how to address such august persons as himself and on manners in general. I hope that hereafter you will observe the amenities of polite correspondence with the proper forms.

We think that his letter indicated that the first article come from the Smithsonian. Orv thought that when he saw that quotation from him and Will. I think we have told you that it came from Mr Chanute's address when the Langley tablet was dedicated. Mr Chanute, in his address, says that this is from a private letter to him from Will. It is so well buried that we knew someone like Walcott would have been the person to unearth it.

Harry Haskell has been insisting on someone writing an article dealing with Langley's work, as I told you. Orv and I have been thinking today that perhaps this would be a good chance to get in a few strokes on that. We will get to work on some suggestions tomorrow.

You certainly had rather tough luck on your 'Winter Sports'. I don't blame Betty a bit for looking about to see if there is not something available, to reach which no Channel passage is necessary. And then it was disappointing to have so little snow. We have had a very mild winter here. But we have just had a cold spell of ten days with a good fall of snow. You could have used your skis on our hills, as the neighbour's children did. We miss having Buster home. He was always out whenever there was a bit of snow.

Stef was here for a day about ten days ago. He was on his way South from Michigan on a lecture tour. He had another talk before that Cleveland 'Ad Club', where you heard him last year. Evidently they enjoyed him too. His new book is selling splendidly, the third edition being just off the press. That means that 4,500 have already been sold. His publishers as you will remember he told us, are too big a concern to deal with profitably. The 'World's Work' articles are to be published in book form, and the manuscript is ready, I think Stef said. But he has not given this book either to his old publishers McMillan's, nor to Doubleday, Page & Company. There is a comparatively new firm, Harcourt, Brace & Company which has made some of the big successes of the year. Mr Harcourt has been fairly following Stef around to get him to let him do his publishing. He told Stef that his 'Life with the Eskimo' was a regular Robinson Crusoe story and that if he had it he could make it 'a best seller'. However McMillan's would not give it up, though as Stef says, not a person around the place had ever even read it until Mr Harcourt tried to buy it. I think Stef is getting very uncertain about starting out for another trip to the North. He thinks now of devoting himself to writing. Orv advises him not to go for another expedition, on the ground that anything he does now will be an anti-climax. I think Stef sees it about the same way and I do not believe he will go. His lectures are very successful. Isn't the new book good? I suppose you have seen that Dr Anderson has begun an open fight now. He has been talking incessantly, ever since the return from the last expedition, against Stef. Mr Akeley said that Stef just let him talk himself out in New York, leaving all the sympathy with Stef! He certainly cuts a poor figure in Stef's story. What a charming person Stef is! It comes out in his book as strongly as in his conversation. You got three copies finally, didn't you? I ordered two for you and Stef sent you one, so we called it all a partnership affair.

We'll be writing again in a few days. Best remembrances to you all.

Sincerely

Katharine

Scipio's rheumatism got so bad it affected his heart & we took him away yesterday. 'Master' is broken-hearted.

Katharine Wright refers to Sir Richard Arman Gregory, author of the book Discovery, or, the spirit and service of science *(Macmillan, 1916).*

Hawthorn Hill
Dayton, Ohio.
February 9, 1922.

Dear Griff:

We expected to get off a letter to you by the Aquitania last Tuesday. But Orv has been so knocked out about Scipio that I couldn't push it through.

This last article in NATURE is much worse than the first, in our opinion. It is very shrewd and very snippy both toward you and Will and Orv. We can't see how you think it is any better in tone than the first.

About the reply. They are now off the subject entirely but they have shifted the ground so shrewdly that most people won't see the evasion. We think now that the only kind of an answer that is worth while at all is one that will go into their arguments and insinuations about Langley's scientific work. Don't you think it will pay to wait until we have a real answer to their stuff on Langley? It is awfully unfortunate that Orv is feeling so badly just now. He is some better already and will be able to send you some suggestions soon. However of course you should use your own judgement since it is your reply, not ours.

It certainly would be convenient to be closer together when these questions are coming up all the time. We have never underestimated Walcott's shrewdness nor lack of scruples about the Truth. But he will have a fall some of these days, maybe not right now but it will come. I do think it is pretty bad to have a paper in which Mr McClean has interest and certainly some influence playing the game for Walcott as it is. I marvel at Orv's attitude. He merely remarks that he observes that human nature is just about the same in all times and all places. Not one word of discouragement or disappointment. That NATURE business is a serious matter and there isn't a particle of use dealing with it in any except an adequate way. I think Dr Pearl has kept SCIENCE from doing any damage, at least, over here.

DISCOVERY is a <u>scream</u>! I wish you could see Orv go through it. Our learned Doctor, Sir Richard, still believes the Langley Law is correct and his remarks about the whole business of the sacred class known as 'scientists' run true to form. I hope we can make him eat some of his silly words before we get through with it. But I don't know. The 'scientists' have built up such an impervious wall against all but the 'elect' that they may succeed in maintaining it. Griff, I actually believe your English Bunch is even more opinionated than ours and that's saying a good deal. That snippy air toward you and your kind and us and our kind would be hard to beat. I am not particularly discouraged but certainly am DISGUSTED.

Now I have to laugh when I look back over what I have just written. It isn't anything to have such a fit about!! I am just a little more impatient than usual because Orv isn't in any condition just now to help and I realize how it would be if he does not get what he knows about this whole business on paper.

Thank you for 'General John Regan'. It came yesterday; also the copy of NATURE. I have to go down town for luncheon and I want to post this so it will get off on a Saturday boat. As soon as Orv is able to do it we will send you some material on the subject of Langley's scientific work. I wish Orv felt that he could give the lecture but I doubt a little the wisdom of giving it this year, anyway. He wouldn't want to be under any suspicion of 'using' the Aeronautical Society in any way. The book is the important thing now. That MUST be done.

Best remembrance to you all.

Sincerely,

Katharine

Orville Wright refers to S.P. Langley's Experiments in Aerodynamics *(City of Washington, Smithsonian Institution, 1891).*

J.P. Seawright was a director of the British Wright Company. Robert G. Ingersoll (1833–99) was an American agnostic.

Orville Wright
Dayton, Ohio
February 14, 1922

Dear Griff:

The copies of the second editorial in NATURE and the copy of your reply were received by Katherine some days ago. Last Thursday I sent a cable suggesting that you hold the reply until you heard from us. The editor of NATURE has never made any reply to your paper. He has kept almost entirely off the subject and has attempted to befog the issue by bringing in an entirely new matter. The matter he has introduced, however, is the very one that Stef, Haskell and Professor Stetson of Oberlin, have all suggested ought to be brought out; that is, some sort of a comparison of the work done by Langley and the Wrights. Heretofore we have been at a disadvantage from the fact that the Smithsonian for years has been quietly spreading its propaganda, and we have been in the position where an answer to it would have been an appearance of an unprovoked attack on Langley. However, the editor of NATURE has now, through the urgent appeals of the Smithsonian people, deliberately brought this point into the issue. They assert that Langley did the scientific work and that the Wrights only contributed the mechanical device which brought this scientific knowledge into practical use. This now gives you an excellent opportunity to go into this matter.

Not wishing this chance to answer this propaganda to escape, I have written the enclosed paper in reply to the editor of NATURE, after talking the matter over with Katharine. We offer this as a suggestion, to be used or not as you see fit. The matter pertaining to Langley is correct as you probably remember from your reading of Langley's AERODYNAMICS when you were here last spring. I think you already have the copies of the Langley correspondence, but to make sure of it I will have Miss Beck send you another set.

None of us here can find anything in the editorials in NATURE that makes any reflection upon your honor. There is a suggestion at the end of the first article that the squabbling of the Wrights and Curtiss over what really belonged to Langley was not very creditable to them. However, I do not think it is good policy to recognize this and we, therefore, make no reference to it.

It has been so long since I have written any letters that I cannot remember 'where we were at'. I had resolved to begin the New Year by doing a lot of writing but my resolutions went for nothing. I have done less writing the past several months than at any time for a long while.

I got your letter in regard to Seawright's and McClean's proposal that the British Wright Company bear the expense that you have been at in this controversy. It was awful nice of them to think of this and to want to do it, but, of course, I would not want it to be done that way. I want to bear all of this expense. If there are any dividends from the British Wright Company it can be taken out of my share of them, and if not, I want to send you a draft from here.

I had a letter a week ago from Colonel Lockwood Marsh inviting me to give the Wilbur Wright Lecture this year. I have withheld answer to it with the thought that I might possibly be able to accept the invitation, but I telegraphed him today that I could not give the lecture this year.

For some time we have been collecting and arranging our papers with the history of the invention in view, but I have done no writing as yet.

I am sending you under separate cover a copy of the December number of the US AIR SERVICE, containing a reprint of your reply. I have just received a letter from Findley from which I quote the following:

This is intended to beg your forgiveness for delay in thanking you for kind letter of December 13th.

We were delighted to receive from you the copy of the AERONAU-TICAL JOURNAL containing Mr Brewer's comeback. I should say that he came back with éclat. Just between ourselves and not in the capacity of Charles Evans Hughes, the editor, advertising solicitor, but as one so called human being approaching a 100% American, it seems to me that running the article by Mr Brewer in the same issue with the statement by one Curtiss was more than the Curtiss crowd could be expected to enjoy. It is a long story which I will tell you about sometime about the Curtiss company and me, but anyway you know now and so does Curtiss company that this magazine has printed in full both sides of the controversy which never should have been a controversy, any more than that Ingersoll should have raised doubts as to the integrity of Moses. Mark Twain said he wouldn't give ten cents to hear Ingersoll on Moses but would pay $100 to hear Moses on Ingersoll.

I am enclosing a clipping from the New York Post which you have probably have not seen.

Sincerely,

Orv

Wright Aeronautical Laboratory
Orville Wright, Director
Dayton, Ohio
February 15, 1922

My dear Mr Brewer,

Mr Wright has instructed me to send you the enclosed copies of the Langley correspondence. Also copy of letter from Dr Walcott of December 17 1910, and Mr Wilbur Wright's reply of December 23 1910.

I am also enclosing herewith one copy of the US AIR SERVICE for December 1921.

Very truly yours,

Mabel Beck

Secretary

Hawthorn Hill
Dayton, Ohio.
March 11, 1922.

Dear Griff:

You get the very first sample of my 'swell' paper! When I get my letterheads the result ought to be overwhelming.

Your letter of February 24, to me came yesterday and today Orv received the one of the 28. You certainly did get that reply to NATURE in good shape. This collaboration business is working to perfection. The '3-in-1' combination of the NATURE outfit has nothing on us! The more we see and understand about it the less we think that Walcott was wholly responsible for it. Sir Richard being a 'pure' scientist knew that the scientific work had to be done by another 'pure' scientist and the Lockyers being astronomers were doubtless friends of Langley. But Walcott must have supplied that quotation which was used so handily. I mean he used it more skilfully that the author of Discovery did.

However, I have some patience with Langley's friends who undoubtedly think that the chief part of the work was done by him.

The snow-house letter to Stef is good enough to print and I hope it will be printed. It would especially interest boys. You are a charming writer, Griff, and you ought to do more writing. I suppose you have written up your early balloon experiences, probably for the Aeronautical Journal, but I was wondering if you couldn't get that all together, as well as your experience in being the first Englishman to fly and so on. I believe you could make a good book of it.

Stef has deserted us entirely. We haven't heard from him for weeks but I saw an editorial in the Kansas City Star about the prize his book got from the National Geographical Society as the best contribution of the year to knowledge of Geography. Percy MacKaye was here two weeks ago and he told of seeing Stef in Washington and New York and about how pleased he was over the award by the National Geographical Society. I think Stef has made up his mind not to go North this year at least. Percy MacKaye wanted to be remembered to you very warmly. He is getting out a new volume of poems and among other features he has a series of ten on 'Great Americans'. The book is intended for a school text-book and he thinks he can do something to help in our campaign. He was very much interested in your paper and evidently took it in all right. He has the loveliest young daughter whom he brought with him. She does good work in sculpture and had some poems in HARPER'S when she was NINE YEARS old!! On the strength of them Roosevelt asked her to come to see him and she spent a wonderful day at Oyster Bay with 'Teddy' and a house full of interesting guests, Amundsen among them. But she is absolutely unspoiled and is as lovely as a young girl could be. We like the MacKayes very much. We haven't seen nor heard of the other poet who was here last year when you were here.

We sent you two copies of CURRENT OPINION, which has some comment on your paper. Stef is responsible for it as usual. The only fault I could find with it is that it is almost too violent.

Isn't it about time for another visit? This is an awfully big house for two people and we really need an occupant for your room. Besides, I can drive the automobile now so I can 'chauff' you down town. You had better have a good insurance policy before you entrust yourself with me, however.

Mrs McCormick is home and doing a good deal of writing. She will have a poem in the NEW REPUBLIC soon. Most of her stuff is political in praise of Wilson so we can't appreciate it as much as we might otherwise! She would want to be remembered to you all if she knew I were writing; Frank likewise. We send love to all.

Sincerely,

Katharine

Nature *of 9 March 1922 published a letter to the Editor from Brewer which referred to the editorials published in the 3 November 1921 and 26 January 1922 editions. Brewer emphasised that the Wrights first established the science of a practical aeroplane, and then invented the means of putting that science to practical use. The 'Editor' then commented on Brewer's letter, making the point that the scientific work of the Wrights had not been published, whereas 'men of science' always published their work – as had Langley.*

Isaac K. Russell was a newspaper reporter assigned to aviation by the New York Evening Sun *in 1909, who then worked for the* New York Times *1910–15 and the* New York Evening Mail *1915–21. He had followed the Wrights' story ever since Wilbur Wright's 1909 flights at the Hudson-Fulton Celebration, which was held in the area of New York Harbor. At the time of this letter he was Editor of* Baking Technology, *published by The American Institute of Baking.*

Hawthorn Hill
Dayton, Ohio.
March 21, 1922

Dear Griff:

I have the disadvantage of trying to answer your letter without having it to read over again. I let Orv take all your letters out to his office for filing – not because I don't keep my letters but he seemed to want yours so I let him have them.

Your correspondence with the Editor of NATURE is the funniest thing! I should think he would be almost tired of 'presenting his compliments' to you but I guess you can stand it if he can. It will be interesting to see how the 'distinguished authority on aviation' will come back on this third round.

The magazine with your Snow-house Story came today. It is as interesting as can be. Orv and I had to smile at least a little over the picture of you reposing? on the platform à la Stef's description. You may remember that you told Stef in the letter of which you sent us a copy that about once in so often you turned over and <u>tried</u> to sleep, being cold from not having proper insulation from the cold. Well, we roared as we pictured the actual situation – you heroically spending the night in the snow-house to show how comfortable it was and is and can be!! We suspect that many of Stef's theories would turn out about the same way in actual practice but Stef would never admit he was not perfectly comfortable if his theory called for comfort. You are such a splendid disciple because you really try to give a thing a fair test. It must have been lots of fun for you. I was just thinking what an ideal party for exploration you and Stef and Orv would make. What one couldn't think of and do another could and would do. I am sending you a clipping from the TIMES which came today. It explains itself as far as I could explain it. Also I am sending some clippings about Mr Akeley and his African party. They may interest you too. You will notice Stef says in his interview, which sounds like the real thing, that he is planning to go to England this Spring. We don't seem to be on speaking terms – at least we haven't heard from him in months, literally – but he will doubtless let you know if he does go.

Orv suggests that I tell you a little about Isaac Russell. I think I have but I am not sure. He is a very decent sort of chap but he is so violent in his expression that his stuff would never be of any value. While there is always some foundation for his stories, he does not remember things just as they were. For instance you could see that what he quotes Will as saying about Chanute could not possibly be correct. Still he got the right idea about Chanute never really getting the wing-warping. At least if he did he forgot it again. But we all know Will never said Chanute 'snooped'. He gets the general idea pretty well but is incorrect when he tries to give details. I suppose you already have him sized up even if we have said nothing about it before. He means to tell the truth – which is more than can be said of some!! Orv has sized up your Mr Lamb as a sensible, level-headed man. Orv says 'he always shows good sense'.

Ask Betty how she would like to shoot lions, elephants and gorilla with Mr Akeley. Wasn't that an adventure to go into the jungles of the Congo with a party consisting of two men, three women and a child of six? I had a letter from Mr Akeley as he was on his way home and he said that all had been in perfect health all the time, maybe not quite that but at least all were returning in perfect health.

Have you engaged your passage over yet? I would like to come over and descend upon you and Beatrice but I think Orv doesn't look on any travelling with favor. I may get up and come on my own account some day if he doesn't experience a change of heart on that subject. Some special friends of mine are going over this Summer and want me to join them but I am not considering it seriously.

Please give my love to the family, all of them. Best remembrances from us both.

Sincerely, etc.

Katharine Wright

On 5 October 1922 Professor Leonard Bairstow, Professor of Aerodynamics at Imperial College of Science and Technology in London, presented a paper to the Royal Aeronautical Society on 'The Work of S.P. Langley'. It was subsequently published in The Aeronautical Journal *(Vol.26, November 1922). During the discussion following his lecture, and in response to questions from Brewer, Bairstow admitted that he was the author of the editorials in* Nature *to which Brewer had responded. It is relevant that some years earlier Bairstow had given the 1919 Wilbur Wright Memorial Lecture to the Royal Aeronautical Society. His paper was entitled 'Progress of Aviation in the War Period: Some Items of Scientific and Technical Interest' (*The Aeronautical Journal, *Vol.23, June 1919). In this paper Bairstow had referred to Curtiss's flight trials in 1914 of the reconstructed Langley 1903 Aerodrome, and said, 'That Langley was correct in his estimates of weight and horse-power has been shown during the war period by the flight of the man-carrying aeroplane which he designed and made'.*

Katharine Wright refers to Chief Justice William Howard Taft, former President of the United States, who was at the time Chancellor of the Smithsonian Institution. Frank

Jefferson Patterson and his brother John H. Patterson had founded The National Cash Register Company in Dayton, which had been formative in the incorporation of the Dayton-Wright Airplane Company in April 1917.

Hawthorn Hill
Dayton Ohio
May 18, 1922.

Dear Griff:

I don't know where I am in my letters to you. I am still so shiftless that I don't make copies of my letters. Anyway I know I owe you one but, as Doctor Dick says, 'What's the Constitution between friends?' I suppose the reference is to the differences of opinion as to the Constitution, during the Civil War.

That reminds me to tell you about Harry Haskell's wife, first of all. A week or so ago she had a very bad turn and they thought she couldn't live but a week or so at most. There was a severe pressure on her heart and lungs. But that has been relieved temporarily and she writes me a cheerful letter which came today. She is really remarkable – the way she keeps up her spirits. It is almost too much for Harry sometimes. He has had to keep up an elaborate system of deception and nothing could be further from his nature or practice, generally. Their son is at Harvard, as you know, and they are both looking eagerly for his coming home for the summer. Isabel may live until he gets home. I hope so for the sake of all of them. It has been so hard for Isabel to have him away but she has been so plucky.

Doctor Dick has been gathering in a degree at the University of Missouri, an L.L.D. Stef writes that he is to be in Iowa City on June 6th so I suppose he is getting a degree at the University of Iowa. That's the place he went through in a year, starting in, classed as a Freshman and graduating at the end of the year. Don't you remember the tales he told us of his escapades at college – that night at the Island? I can imagine that he was a fairly trying specimen as a student!

I spent last week promoting a girls' camp for a friend of Stef's. He is always sending his friends to us for all sorts of reasons. This time it was frankly to help a young woman friend of his to get her camp to the attention of people who can afford to send their daughters to a summer camp. You can imagine how much I enjoyed the business of 'promoting'! But I like to do things for Stef and there are few things I can do.

We looked on the Taft reply to your letter as just what should be expected. Of course, he wasn't going to say anything to you in criticism of their Secretary.

We thought it was making it pretty embarrassing for Walcott to have Taft ask him to reply to you. It seems important to us not to get Taft edgewise in advance. He will be inclined to be at least not unfriendly to our side. Of course, though, backbone is not his strong point – but a good understanding is. I am sorry Bairstow is about to break forth with some more of their glittering generalities but it can't be helped. We'll have to exercise our patience and wait for our innings later!! Orv must write to you about that. I am not in a very brilliant frame of mind tonight (not that I am ever that but tonight I am just recovering from a very bad cold and am a little denser that usual!). Mrs McCormick is giving a talk at the Literary Club but I wasn't well enough to go.

I sent you, several weeks ago, two magazines – one with Stef's article on Conan Doyle, and the other the NEW REPUBLIC, with Anne's poem. I thought Beatrice would be especially interested in that. Stef wrote me that he was terribly behind on his correspondence and had not answered your letters. He didn't write to me for weeks and weeks but was unable to understand why I did not write to him. I gave him a little time to think and he finally guessed the riddle! Isn't he a nice person – so boyish and so grown-up all in one! He says he is to lecture for forty days this summer. His territory is Indiana, Ohio and western Pennsylvania. I suppose he won't be able to visit us at the Island. He expects to stop here in June for a day or so.

I hope you won't think we are too unsympathetic if I tell you that Orv smiles a good deal over your tilts with your various Boards of Awards. Of course you mustn't expect much in the way of gratitude, for a contribution to 'pure' Science (unless you are one of the pure scientists); and you mustn't expect much in the way of cash when you are trying to have a really scientific contribution appraised in terms of dollar and cents, or rather in terms of pounds and shillings. The best way is not to expect much, I guess. It would seem that experience would teach us that but it doesn't does it?

I was interested in your plans for building but if it as hard to get anything done in England as it is here, and as expensive, I don't envy you your job of getting it done. I actually spent $450 in getting the house cleaned this spring. That included new paper in my room and one of the maids' rooms. Otherwise it merely paid for cleaning walls and freshening ceilings downstairs and a few other items such as dry cleaning portieres and such. I was charged a dollar and a quarter an hour and at the rate of eight hours a day for some loafers who sauntered in about half-past nine in the morning, gave me the pleasure of their company until eleven-thirty, when they departed for two hours and a half, at lunch. They returned a little after two, as a rule and favored me with an upheaval and commotion till four when they had to leave to get a good start for the next day!! Honestly, it was almost that, day after day, and I was paying ten dollars a day for it! I heard Orv telling someone that we were kept in a constant uproar by these people coming and going but I corrected him by pointing out that it was only a few hours in the day that we were so annoyed! Meanwhile, Carrie and her aunt (WOMEN, you observe) were working eight good hours a day and more for three dollars per. I am getting more rabid on the WOMAN question every day. Better come over and help me get it out of my system. Orv is a great comfort; he goes me one better on all my ideas of that sort.

I suppose that you know of Mr Patterson's death. He died on the train, with no one but his valet with him. I can not say I was much surprized. You remember how feeble he was when you came over with him last year. It is a great loss to Dayton. Few of us realize how great the loss is. Every day I think of some new way in which he will be missed. The funeral was a week ago yesterday.

I hope circumstance will bring you over but certainly for more than two or three days!! I don't want you to have such a chore as that on your hands. How are Betty's 'sweet' cows and horses? I would like to see that child. How she would hoot at being called a 'child'! I hope Cyril's year at Cambridge has been satisfactory. Love to Beatrice, As ever –

Katharine

In the summer of 1922 Brewer accompanied Oswald Short on a visit to aircraft firms in the United States to seek support for Short's concept of stressed-skin metal aircraft construction. During this trip Short visited the Wrights in Dayton.

Hawthorn Hill
Oakwood
Dayton Ohio
June 29, 1922.

Dear Griff:

Behold the new letter-heads! You are getting the first letter written on them. As you probably can imagine (your imagination being fairly good!) I can't find a minute to write a real letter but we have talked a good deal about you and thought still more. Tomorrow Katharine and her mother are departing and I shall then have much more time on my hands than I want! Katharine has been an ideal visitor, being all over the idea that her mother can do nothing without her.

No wonder you couldn't find Earl Findley. Orv had a card from him yesterday from some place in Maryland where he has gone for convalescence after a bad case of flu. The curious part about him is the worse things go with him, the funnier he is. His letters are always good.

Glad to hear from Mr Short as well as from you that prospects are rosy at Washington! Please tell Mr Short that I had his nice letter and appreciated it. I know the possibilities at Atlantic City so I understand that it was no great feat to accomplish your fell purpose there!

I hate to have you wasting your days in America – not with us. I'll send the snap-shots to England for I haven't much hope of your getting anything at hotels in Washington or New York.

We shall probably go to the Bay in about a week. The weather is still very cool and pleasant here and we had a fine rain last evening. I hope you are not melted in Washington. It is ALWAYS hot there. Our best regards to Mr Short, whom we enjoyed very much, and something more to you!

'Yrs' (as Dr Dick says),
Katharine.

Lord Northcliffe died at the age of fifty-seven on 14 August 1922.

Lambert Island
Penetang, Ontario
August 8, 1922.

Dear Griff,

Your 'log' of the boat has been duly received and Orv has had your letter to him, both forwarded from Dayton. I can't answer your letter exactly because I haven't it here now to read over. I sent it on to Stef. I knew he would enjoy it. I don't usually do that with letters but I did this time.

I am glad you found such pleasant companions on the boat. Your ex-Governor from Missouri must have been a Democrat. Missouri is usually Democratic but the present Governor is a Republican who went in on the Republican landslide two years ago – or was it last year? Anyway, I don't care whether he is a Democrat or Republican any more than you do! The only thing that concerns me is that they made you have a nice time on the boat. Missouri is having – or has had but we haven't heard the result yet in this 'neck o'woods' – a hot primary fight for Senators. The Star is Republican of course but everyone has been interested in the Democratic contest because it

41. Lord Northcliffe (in the fur coat) helping to haul the Wright A at Pau, 1909. The former Conservative Prime Minister Arthur Balfour is standing to the left of Lord Northcliffe.

is really a Wilson and anti-Wilson fight with other factors mixed in, of course.

I had a letter from Mr Short just the day we left home, saying that he had not sailed with you and that he would probably be in Dayton again for a short stay. I wrote him immediately that we were leaving but that the McCormicks would like it if he would call them up. They asked me to tell him that. I have no idea that he ever got the letter though. Sending letters to transients in New York Hotels – or any other hotels over here – has now become merely a ceremony. You don't expect anyone to get them. The McCormicks say nothing of having seen Mr Short so I suppose he either did not go to Dayton or did not get my letter.

Orv came home on Saturday morning, as you know, and we left for Canada the next Wednesday. Lorin came with us and staid two weeks. Miss Ryder has been here for a ten-day visit but she too is gone now. So Orv and I are alone and have been since a week ago yesterday. We are having a nice time but we would like it better if you and Stef were here, as you were two years ago. It was about this time that you came. Your canoe reposes on the boat-house platform – such as there is. We certainly do need a new boat-house. But you know how it will be. Orv will plan and plan and then one day he will suddenly begin to move and in less time than it takes to tell it – almost – the thing will be done. We both worked on the hill in front of the house, making the path down to the new boat-house site more passable. We cleared out underbrush and Orv rolled stones in place so that the footing is fair now.

The launch is in fine order now. The starting is very easy – one improvement after another has been made until 'she' starts on the first or second pull every time. Orv has just finished a fancy spray-shield – one that can be folded up and put out of the way when not needed. All I am concerned about is that it shall not fold up when we do need it! It is really very nice and a very neat job.

The fishing has been unusually good this year, everyone says. Lorin got some nice ones when he was here. Orv hasn't had very good luck landing his. Either his hooks are not right or something else is wrong in his fishing gear for he never had such trouble before. Of course, black bass are very game.

We see very alarming news of Lord Northcliffe. Harry Haskell writes that the news at Washington is that it is some peculiar nervous disease; that Lord Northcliffe started talking to Lady Northcliffe, talked all day and all night and then talked to Steed, who relieved Lady Northcliffe, until he had to have help. I saw a dispatch in the last Star we have that his condition was very serious. Makes me feel awfully sad. I can't imagine the world without him. He was so full of life and interest and such a loyal friend of ours. Mrs Haskell is better again – goes out riding and so on. Hers is a remarkable case, Doctor Dick says. The latter is off in Minnesota, with his whole family, fishing and rusticating.

Stef is nearly through with his lectures for the summer. He had two weeks of independent Chautauquas after the schedule I gave you but I have not had his addresses. I am sending you a page from the N.Y. Times, which explains itself. Isn't Stef dear about Orv? I told him he had made himself 'solid' with me now – no matter what he did!

I hope you found Beatrice and the children (!) well when you got home. Please give her my love. We both send love to all – as a matter of fact.

Sincerely

Katharine

Griffith Brewer was the sole British entry in the eleventh James Gordon Bennett Balloon Cup contest which started in Zurich on 6 August 1922. His balloon Bee *landed near Zurich, forced down by heavy rain. After some deliberation, the adjudicating committee declared M. Demuyter, pilot of the balloon* Belgica, *the winner, with Captain H.E. Honeywell, pilot of the American balloon* Uncle Sam, *placed second.*

Katharine Wright refers to the third Rhon international gliding competition held in Germany from 9–24 August 1922.

During the summer of 1922 Stefansson organised an expedition to take possession in the name of King George V of the uninhabited Wrangel Island, 100 miles off the north-east coast of Siberia in the Arctic Ocean. He believed that this island had potential as a stepping-stone for flights between England and the Far East.

Frederick Brant Rentschler was President of the Wright Aeronautical Corporation from 1920 to 1924. The Corporation had been formed in 1919 and had taken over certain assets and liabilities of the then dissolved Wright-Martin Aircraft Corporation, including the Wright patents and the Hispano-Suiza engine licence for the United States. Rentschler was to later form the Pratt & Whitney Aircraft Company which was incorporated on 23 July 1925 with Rentschler as President.

Lambert Island
Penetang, Ontario
August 31, 1922.

Dear Griff,

Whether you intended it or not, your card and the enlargements of the photographs of 'The Tour' arrived for our birthday – which you know we celebrate together. Many thanks for both. We had seen in the paper that you landed near Zurich at one in the morning. I am glad to hear that it was a lovely trip over the mountains. I hope the thunderstorm didn't spoil it altogether. I am enclosing the N.Y. Times which shows the 'Bee' in a prominent place. Who did win that race, anyway? First it was reported that the Belgian did; then that Westover did; then that Honeywell did. Then I saw there was a dispute about it and that's all we know about it.

We get papers so late that it doesn't seem much worth while to read the old news. You know things are sure to be some other way while you are reading the old stuff. We got the first news of Northcliffe's death on the Thursday after it occurred, from Stef's letter! We opened it at Penetang and we didn't open the papers. We sent Lady Northcliffe a cable and had a wireless (I suppose) in reply. 'My love to both. Grateful thanks kind message.' I knew it was coming – the news seemed hopeless for a couple of weeks but still it was a blow. He was a powerful friend but – much better – he was such an affectionate and loyal one. The last time we saw him was in Dayton. He was so lovely that day to us both. I shall never forget it.

It is sad about 'Pat'. Our surmises as to his entire accountability seem to have been about right. 'Mum's the word'! But we do both feel awfully sorry that he is in such a plight. He is too old to adjust himself to different ways of living and so on. I don't see what he will do. Give him our kindest remembrances if you think of it, when you see him, please.

Hasn't there been a great 'hullabaloo' over the gliding? The German gliders have done well. Such nonsense, though, as comes out of it. One reporter was describing the propellers! Another tells that experts are now planning a trip across the Atlantic, in the wake of a steamer – à la the gulls.

Stef writes to ask how long we will be up here, thinking that maybe he can come. He is getting his 'Hunters of the Great North' through the press and, of course, it will be delayed. He is the most exasperating and still the most 'friendly' friend! He has been worried about his Wrangel Island men but finally has a boat sent to see how they are and so forth. The Canadian Government is acting as governments generally do act. They never have any money for sensible things. We see in the papers – and do not know that it is not true! – that our government has bought three Fokker planes and some future plans, I believe. I'd like to see Mr Short get something out of them while the 'getting' is good.

We suppose you will be getting the copy of the Bairstow paper before long. We are interested to hear about it, of course.

I am going to New York for the christening of a new Loening flying-boat which the Wright Aeronautical Corporation has bought for its own use to try out Wright engines on. The President of the W.A.C. is Fred Rentschler, a brother of Gordon Rentschler of Hamilton, Ohio (we stopped at their home with Mrs Deeds you may remember, when Orv's Franklin was cranky, at Oxford). They are naming the boat 'Wilbur Wright'. I suppose, of course, that Orv will go with me.

I had a little note from Arthur Page enclosing a clipping, giving the parrot story as Orv's! Mr Page remarks, 'If your brother's comments are all like this it is more that ever a shame he does not take pen in hand.' I set him straight on whose story it was but agreed about it being a 'shame' etc. Orv seems so well – and I haven't felt so well for years – there will be no excuse for not getting to work this Fall.

42. Loening Air Yacht *Wilbur Wright*, owned by the Wright Aeronautical Corporation. From C.G. Grey (ed.) *All the World's Aircraft* (London, Sampson Low, Marston & Company Ltd, 1923).

We have had a splendid summer. If you had been here to paddle around, quiet mornings in your little green canoe, it would have been about perfect. The weather had been fine – no hot days at all and not much rain or wind. Today was like our best October weather at home and that's our limit of perfection. We are all alone, Orv and I, and have been for nearly five weeks. I don't know where the time goes, but it never hangs on our hands. We expect to stay two weeks yet, anyway until the 15th. Orv is busy laying out his docks etc. He has been driving down inch and half pipe, to rest his dock on; but he has trouble finding the bottom. I don't know just how he will come out. But next year we shall have to have a new boat-house and dock.

Please give my best to 'Bee'. Tell her I'd like awfully well to see her. I'd enclose another of Anne's poems but fear the consequences! Mrs Haskell is much better. Dr Dick says it's her courage. But it can't be real – the improvement – only apparent. Our love to all of you.

Sincerely

Katharine

I miss the typewriter and I'm getting awfully short on paper. K.

On 26 September 1922 Katharine Wright christened a Loening Air Yacht Wilbur Wright. *It was owned by the Wright Aeronautical Corporation.*

Katharine refers to Dr Joseph Sweetman Ames, Professor of Physics and Director of the Physical Laboratory at Johns Hopkins University, who had been a member of the National Advisory Committee for Aeronautics since its formation in 1915.

Hawthorn Hill
Oakwood
Dayton, Ohio
October 16, 1922.

Dear Griff:

Since I wrote last I have seen the whole gang – Stef, Mr Akeley, Mr Page, Harry Haskell, Doctor Dick, etc. etc. I was asked to christen a flying-boat for the Wright Aeronautical Corporation so that took us to New York later in September. I smashed the bottle of champagne without any fluke and afterwards Orv, Bus and I had a dandy flight over the Hudson. It was a great view of the city and the rivers and the Bay.

While we were in New York, Stef and Mr Akeley had a 'studio tea' for us, which was very interesting, You know how much Orv enjoys 'teas' and such!! But I do not think he was bored by this one. The people were interesting. You remember Mr Akeley's studio perhaps – where the pickled gorillas were!!

We heard this summer that a niece in Kansas City was not well. So I decided to go out after we got back from New York. We got another doctor on the case and have done about all we can. I am afraid it will be a serious case, perhaps pernicious anemia.

Mrs Haskell is still living and is actually better than she was last Spring but it is hopeless, of course, and the whole thing is about as sad as anything could well be. They are both as plucky as can be but Isabel is very weak and Harry is worn out with worry and suspense. However he doesn't show it at all – except in talking to me alone when he could be himself. He asked about you and wants to see you again.

Doctor Dick is certainly one big bunch of energy and enthusiasm. I went to his house for dinner one night. They have one of the loveliest houses I have seen. I think you didn't see Mrs Sutton. She is one of these beautiful women who knows just how to dress and just how to run her house well. She is friendly and I like her but I do not think I would find her companionable but for Doctor Dick. The children are lovely – so interesting and nice in every way that I noticed.

I liked Doctor Dick better than I expected. I don't mind the breeziness in him that I would object to in other people. It is a part of him and goes with his other qualities. I saw him in action in his office!! You have some idea of that. What interested me was to see how everyone in the entire place brightened up when he stepped in. I told Orv I felt better myself when he told me I 'looked like a million dollars – and thirty cents'!! He is so warm and full of life and interest. I believe he is an able man of high principal. Certainly he is interesting. You know how open-hearted he is. He poured books and magazines and candy and flowers on me, just as he does on anyone he likes. There is just one Doctor Dick!!

Bairstow's paper came Friday. It certainly is a lame effort for a man of his standing. But it is a fine thing for us. Won't Walcott be furious at what he says of the 'Hammondsport trials'? Orv says that it is the best possible proof of the effect of your paper for he was a partisan who had believed that the Langley machine had flown and was on record as saying it HAD FLOWN. Orv thinks this will pretty much settle that particular thing in England.

He is very vague in describing Langley's scientific contributions. If we can just get a few more people to at least glance over Langley's book it will be all to the good for us. Orv doubts whether Bairstow has read it all now!! In any event this paper will do us no harm and some good for he makes no claim for Langley that has not been made and he does make some valuable admissions – on the Langley Law, for instance, and on the Hammondsport machine. I suppose Orv will write to you more fully on this.

We were much interested in your two papers, the one on Soaring Flight and the one on your balloon trip. What a furor that German gliding did cause!!

It interests me to see Dr Ames of the Advisory Committee calling attention to Orv's 1911 feat. Orv has thought that Dr Ames was pretty friendly with him; he thought he detected a not great enthusiasm toward Walcott. I think the stage is getting set for 'grief' for our friend Walcott. Now certainly is the time to come in with the real story and settle a lot of the irresponsible talk for good.

We had a delightful time at the Pages in spite of the fact that Mr Page was suffering intensely from asthma. He tried so hard to conceal how badly he felt so as not to spoil our visit. Mrs Page is lovely. We staid over night but left as early as we could in the morning so they could get away to the mountains to get relief for him. I am delighted with the impression that his father's letters are making. Burton Hendrick did a fine piece of work on that. No doubt Arthur Page's good judgment came in too.

Ridgley Torrance was here to dinner Friday night. I asked Frank and Anne to meet him. He is the one who accepted two of Anne's poems for the NEW REPUBLIC. He asked about you and so did Percy Mackaye in New York. Better come again to see us all!

Sincerely etc.

Katharine

This is your friend Gardner referred to in the clipping. K.

Orville Wright refers to S.P. Langley's The Greatest Flying Creature: Introducing a Paper on the Pterodactyl Ornithostoma. *The paper was by F.A. Lucas, published by the Washington Government Printing Office in 1902. It had earlier been published in the Smithsonian Report for 1901. In his introduction Langley described his tandem-wing model aeroplane* Aerodrome No.5, *which made a successful flight of 3,300 feet on 6 May 1896 over the Potomac by Chopawamsic Island.*

An early enthusiast of aeronautics, Patrick Young Alexander (1867–1943) had visited the Wrights in Dayton in December 1902 following an introduction by Octave Chanute. Convinced that he would not live beyond the age of fifty, Alexander donated large sums of money to charitable causes and became financially destitute. Brewer, learning of his circumstances, sought donations to a fund for Alexander's welfare that was subsequently administered by the Royal Aeronautical Society. In former years Brewer and Alexander had compiled Aeronautics: an Abridgement of Aeronautical Specifications Filed at the Patent Office from AD 1815 to AD 1891 *(London: Taylor & Francis. 1893).*

Orville Wright
Dayton. Ohio
March 15, 1923.

Dear Griff:

When I got your letter about the Patrick Alexander fund I intended to write you immediately sending a subscription of fifty pounds, but like so many of my other intentions it did not get any further. However I would want all of my subscription to go to Alexander himself, and not merely the income from it. I do not think it is good policy to establish endowment funds except where the purpose is definite and permanent. In a few years there will be no need of help to the injured of the last year. The income off two thousand pounds would not be sufficient to help Alexander very much. I am sending you a draft for the fifty pounds.

I suppose Katharine has been keeping you pretty well informed on what has been going on over here. Bairstow's paper as published certainly will do no harm and, on the other hand, I think, will do a great deal of good in showing non-technical people the conviction which your paper carried to technical people. Of course, a great many who read your paper and the replies from Walcott, Zahm, Curtiss, et al. were not able to judge the merits of the arguments presented by the different ones. Considering Bairstow's bias when he first entered into this discussion I think his paper is remarkably fair.

I have not seen any mention in American papers of Bairstow's paper since its delivery excepting an editorial in the Kansas City Star, a copy of which I am sending you. Haskell was mixed a little in several particulars. The Smithsonian evidently has taken no pains to circulate this address as they did Bairstow's former papers in 'Nature' replying to your address. I did see one notice in an American paper (I think 'Science') that Bairstow would deliver a paper on the 'Life and Work of Langley'. I thought at the time this notice was prompted by the Smithsonian; but I suspect since they have read the address their interest in it has died.

I have been under the impression that I read a statement from Bairstow (but not in his address) that Langley found, as we find today, that the angle of maximum lift/drift ratio is in the neighbourhood of three or four degrees angle of attack. I was surprised at the time that he could make such a statement. Langley's actual measurements did show this but Langley did not find it. On the other hand he did profess to find and published that the higher the speed (therefore the smaller the angle of incidence) the greater the lift/drift ratio. I wonder whether I really did see this statement from Bairstow some place? I can not find it now. I thought I had read it in the 'Nature' article which you sent us, but I do not find it there nor in the account of his address in the London Times.

On page 427 of Bairstow's printed address I notice the statement that to Langley 'there was no noteworthy distinction between demonstrations on a model and on a man-carrying aeroplane'. Langley did know the difference, as is shown in his 'The Greatest Flying Creature' published by the Smithsonian in 1902, in which the following statement appeared:

> 'From the obvious mathematical law that the area in bodies in general increases as the square of their dimensions, while their weight increases as the cube, it is an apparently plain inference that the larger the creature or machine the less the relative area of support may be... so that we soon reach a condition where we can not imagine flight possible... The difficulty grows greater as we increase the size... This is a consequence of a mathematical law, from which it would appear to follow that we can not have a flying creature much greater than a limit of area like the condor, unless endued with extraordinary strength of wing.'

This is not of much importance. I only mention it because the people who write about Langley's work seem always to give him credit for some of the things he did not know and do not give him credit for some of the things he did know. It is quite possible that he did not realize at the time he was making his model experiments in 1896 that such experiments did not demonstrate the possibility of man-flight, but he did know it thoroughly six years later before he had his full sized machine completed, as is proven by his statements quoted above.

Katharine has just returned from a trip to a number of cities including Boston and Kansas City in the interest of Oberlin College. While in New York she saw both Stef and Akeley. You may have heard that Stef has definitely announced his retirement from Arctic exploration, and that in the future he will devote his time to popularising knowledge of these Northern regions. I hate to see Stef become a professional lecturer. It will gradually lead him into the use of the professional tricks for creating 'interest'. While in Kansas City she saw the Haskells and the Suttons. 'Dr Dick' is planning an African wild game hunt for next year and is stocking up with all sorts of hunting paraphernalia.

I have been spending a good deal of time the last five or six weeks in going over Father's letters and papers. I have found hundreds and hundreds of letters written by Reuchlin and Katharine, probably two hundred or more written by Wilbur and a much lesser number written by myself. These range in date from 1881 to 1912 or 1913. Quite a number of the letters are of the years from 1899 up to 1905 and give some record of what our thoughts on the flying problem were at that time. These letters will be of some use to me when I begin writing of our work, but I have not as yet made a start in actual writing.

We are looking forward with pleasure to your visit with us this year. Katharine has just received a letter from Mrs Brewer stating that you have been suffering from sciatica. You know my six years' sciatica made me an expert on sciatica. If doctors there do not cure you promptly come and see the 'expert'.

With kindest regards,

Sincerely yours

Orv

Orville Wright
Dayton, Ohio
November 13, 1923.

Dear Griff:

Your suggestions with regard to the disposition of the 1903 machine have been thought over a good deal since you left. If you are right in thinking that the officers of the Museum would be keenly interested in securing this machine for exhibition in the Kensington Museum, I should be inclined to let them have it. The fire risks are too great where it is now stored and I have no better place for it.

Of course the machine ought to be in the National Museum at Washington. But when one considers the way the officials of that Institution allowed the original Langley machine to be taken out of the Museum and the original materials of its structure to be destroyed for the purpose of private parties to a patent litigation, so that the machine now hanging in the Museum is not the original but is mostly a new machine with many of the restored parts of different construction from the original; and when one further considers that they have hung upon this new machine a misleading label true neither of the new nor of the original machine, one can have little faith that our machine would be any safer from mutilation or that it would receive a label from the present officers of the Institution any more truthful than that on the Langley machine.

If I were to receive a proposition from the officers of the Kensington Museum offering to provide our 1903 machine a permanent home in the Museum, I would accept the offer, with the understanding, however, that I would have the right to withdraw it at any time after five years, if some suitable place for its exhibition in America presented itself.

Sincerely,

Orville Wright

In the summer of 1923 Brewer initiated a 'Wrangel Island Relief Fund' to finance a relief ship Donaldson *for Stefansson's Arctic explorers trapped on the island by surrounding ice. In his book* The Adventure of Wrangel Island *(London: Jonathan Cape Ltd, 1926) Stefansson revealed that the largest single contribution to the Fund was from the British Wright Company, of which Brewer was the major donor, and that Orville Wright had loaned Stefansson money to send the relief ship* Teddy Bear *in an earlier attempt to reach the island the previous summer.*

Orville Wright
Dayton, Ohio
November 13, 1923.

Dear Griff:

I have just written you a letter in regard to the disposal of the 1903 machine. The letter states the conditions under which I would be willing to let the machine go to the Kensington Museum. I do not feel at all easy about the machine where it is. It is not likely to have to go through another flood, but it is liable to fire. I would suggest that you sound the management of the Museum on the matter before letting them know that I have written you anything concerning it.

Katharine has just had a letter from Harry Haskell telling of his visit at Burvale. He was very much pleased. In his letter he sizes up Stef in just about the same way I have come to think of him.

A letter from Taylor arrived the next day after you left. As your letter to him had not yet been mailed when his letter was received I did not suppose that it had anything in further explanation of the expenditures in connection with the 'Relief Expedition'. I have not received any carbon copy of a letter from Taylor, and so assume that he has not as yet made any reply to your letter.

I have only been in the office a few days since you left. While bending over the washbowl in my bath room the Monday morning you were arriving in Washington something seemed to give way in my back. I had not yet put on my belt. I managed to get to the office that day and the next but was at home all of the time following up to last Friday. I will hereafter be cautious about washing my face without my belt on.

Sincerely

Orv.

On 30 April 1925 Orville Wright announced that he was presenting the original 1903 Wright Flyer to the Science Museum in London. Orville refers to Colonel Sir Henry Lyons, Director of the Science Museum.

Orville Wright
Dayton, Ohio
May 6, 1925.

Dear Griff:

I am sending you enclosed a few of the many publications of my statement of my reasons for sending our 1903 machine to the Science Museum, and the replies of Dr Walcott in defense of the Smithsonian Institution. I am sending you mostly clippings from the Dayton papers because I have extra copies of these.

I will write you in a few days when I have more time and will also send you more additional clippings if there be any of interest. Has anything appeared in the British press, and do you happen to have any clippings of the London papers of December 17th last? The American papers stated at the time that the Daily Mail and other London papers carried my statement on the twenty-first anniversary of our first flight. But I have not seen any of the London papers.

Sincerely yours,

Orville Wright

Orville Wright refers to the 1925 Pulitzer Trophy contest organised by the National Aeronautic Association which was for the highest speed achieved by an aircraft in competition. Established by the four Pulitzer brothers, American newspaper owners, the contests were held annually from 1920 to 1925 after which the contest was discontinued.

Orville Wright
Dayton, Ohio
June 4, 1925.

Dear Griff:

I have been sending you some of the clippings from the American press on the Smithsonian controversy. You will see from these that not many really understand the matter, but that a big row is being made over the machine going out of the country. One congressman has threatened to introduce a bill in Congress to prevent the exportation of such historic relics.

This newspaper controversy has so interferred with my work that I can not tell just when the machine will be ready for shipment. But I now think it will not be before October or November. I had hoped to get it out of the country before news of its going got out. But there was a leak at New York. I suspect Haskell told confidentially some one out there, and like most confidences, it didn't keep.

You will find in the clippings a good deal of talk about keeping the machine here. Tell Mr Lyons to not let this talk disturb him. I have no intention of asking to be relieved of my obligation to the Science Museum. In fact I have no intention of ever having the machine come back here unless all of the sinister machinations of the Smithsonian are fully rebuked, and a sincere attempt is made to make matters right. If requests should come from others to Mr Lyons, he may be able to save himself embarrassment answering that he leaves that matter entirely for my decision.

We were pleased with your change of mind about coming to America this year. If it is the excitement of the 'scrap' with the Smithsonian that you are 'hankering after', may be you had better postpone the time of your visit to the end of September and the first of October. The NAA officials have asked me to hold the machine here till that time for exhibition at the time of the Pulitzer races at New York. I have not decided as to this, but I doubt whether it will be ready before that time anyway for shipment. You could attend the races with me. I think matters will become warmest about the time the machine actually leaves. But, anyway we are glad that we are going to see you, either at the bay or at Dayton.

Sincerely yours,
Orville Wright

4

EXILE AND RETURN
OF THE WRIGHT FLYER:
FEBRUARY 1928–DECEMBER 1943

On 31 January 1928 Orville Wright shipped the original 1903 Wright Flyer to the Science Museum in London, his intention being to lend the aircraft for a period of five years. Brewer's copy of Orville's instructions for assembling the Wright Flyer is given in Appendix IV.

Orville Wright
Dayton, Ohio
February 18, 1928.

Dear Griff:

I have been delayed in getting off the instructions for assembling the machine at the Science Museum. I am sending enclosed a copy of the instructions sent Sir Henry Lyons. I also have sent him several photographs, which I am not sending to you because I have no more copies.

If the parts having the same numbers are carefully kept together there will be very little difficulty in assembling the machine, and the written instructions will hardly be necessary. There were quite a number of holes in the old parts of the machine, due to changes made at different times. These may cause confusion if the tags are taken off before the machine is completely assembled.

When you were here the old parts of the machine had been cleaned only to the extent of having the flood mud brushed off. The new parts were bright in contrast. After cleaning up, the old and the new are not so easily distinguished. However, we have kept a record of the parts which are old and which are new, which I shall send on at a later date.

I have several of the original parts here which could not be used again, such as the cloth and the propellers. The propellers on the machine now are not the originals, and I neglected to examine them to see whether they exactly corresponded with the originals in details in angle, width, etc. They have the general appearance of the originals.

I am intending to make up a set exactly like the originals and have them tested on a manometer to ascertain the amount of power actually developed by the motor at Kitty Hawk.

I was interested a few days ago in looking over our 1903 Kitty Hawk notebook to find that before having any test of our screws our calculations predicted a standing thrust of 100 pounds at 305 revolutions per minute. By actual measurement we got 132 to 136 pounds of thrust at a speed of 350 revolutions. As the thrust should vary as the square of the speeds, this would indicate 100 to 103 pounds at 305 revolutions. The Smithsonian would say this was a pretty good 'guess'.

There has been but little in the papers about the machine going off. I will send you, later, notices that may be of interest. Findley writes that he has an attack of the 'rams', which he says are ten times worse than the 'heebe-jeebies', if you know what they are. This attack has been brought on by reading an editorial in the Washington Star. He is going to have something on this subject in his magazine this month.

Miss Beck thinks that I ought to tell you that the incidence indicator arrived. (I am <u>not</u> very prompt.) Many thanks. Also she wants me to tell you that this letter is being written on the portable Royal typewriter which was delivered at Dayton by being dropped from an aeroplane on a parachute. It was delivered to me in the original package undamaged.

Sincerely

Orv.

Following the death of Walcott, Charles Greeley Abbot was elected as Secretary of the Smithsonian Institution in January 1928. The Journal of the Royal Aeronautical Society, *Vol.32, April 1928, published a letter from Abbot to Orville Wright which defended the Smithsonian Institution's labelling of Langley's 1903 Aerodrome. The label stated that, 'In the Opinion of Many Competent to Judge, this was the First Heavier-than-Air Craft in the History of the World Capable of Sustained Free Flight under its own Power'. Brewer responded to Abbot's request that Orville acknowledge the Smithsonian Institution's statement, saying that, 'It amounts to an invitation to Mr Orville Wright to make an insincere statement, in return for which Dr Abbot would withdraw the incorrect description on the Langley machine'.*

In the Journal of the Royal Aeronautical Society, *Vol.32, June 1928, Abbot began his response to the Society's Secretary with the words, 'The spectacle of my statement sandwiched between your salutatory and Mr Griffith Brewer's valedictory has a Daniel-in-the-lion's-den aspect that amuses one, while arousing other impressions. It has been sufficiently obvious for several years that nothing the Smithsonian could do or leave undone would meet with Mr Griffith Brewer's approbation'.*

Captain J. Laurence Pritchard was Secretary (1926–51) of the Royal Aeronautical Society. At the time of this correspondence he also edited the Society's Journal.

9th May, 1928
The Secretary,
The Royal Aeronautical Society
7, Albemarle Street, W.1

Dear Pritchard,

I am returning the letter addressed to you by Dr Abbot dated April 27th, of which I have had copies taken.

It is a beautiful piece of composition, and a most welcome one, because it is the first in which the Head of the Smithsonian Institution voluntarily states that the Wright Brothers 'mastered the problem independently by their own experiments'. Once having recognised this fact, the Head of that great Institution has made a big step towards righting the wrong which has been done by earlier Smithsonian publications.

I will read Dr Abbot's letter again, with a view to letting you have a comment for consideration and possible publication in the Journal simultaneously with the publication of Dr Abbot's letter.

Yours sincerely
Griffith Brewer

Formerly the Society's Chairman for the years 1926–27, Colonel the Master of Sempill had been elected President of the Royal Aeronautical Society on 8 May 1928.

On 8 June 1928 a banquet at the Savoy Hotel was organised by the Royal Aeronautical Society, the Royal Aero Club, the Air League of the British Empire and the Society of British Aircraft Constructors in honour of Alliott Verdon Roe. It was in 'recognition of his pioneer work on machines of his own design and construction, and of the great debt which British aviation owes him' (Journal of the Royal Aeronautical Society, Vol.32, July 1928). Pritchard had originally suggested that the banquet be held in honour of the twentieth anniversary of the first flight in England, but Roe's flight in his Roe I pusher biplane of June 8 1908 was much disputed, and consequently the terms of the banquet were amended. The controversy led the Royal Aero Club to form a committee under the chairmanship of Lord Gorell to investigate early British flight claims. The Gorell Committee's conclusion was that J. T.C. Moore-Brabazon's flight of 2 May 1909 in a Voisin biplane at Shellbeach was the first flight by a British subject in the British Isles.

Orville Wright
Dayton, Ohio
June 12, 1928.

My dear Colonel Sempill:

At the time I received your telegram I may have been under the misapprehension as to the nature of the dinner that was being given to Mr A. V. Roe. I had read in the Aeronautical Journal that a testimonial was to be given to Mr Roe in June in recognition of the twentieth anniversary of his first flight, and knowing that Mr Roe had not made a free flight, as early as June, 1908, I hesitated to send a congratulatory telegram, as it might appear to be a recognition of that date.

I have a letter written August 14, 1908, by Mr Roe, and addressed to Wilbur, at Le Mans. In the letter he states: 'In all I managed to get six trials since receiving the 18–24 h.p. Antoinette engine last May. I managed to make several flights towed by a motorcar, the power being very slight. At the present time the machine is detached and stored away'. The rest of the letter mostly is a recital of his many difficulties with the Brooklands track people and his plans for the organization of a company to finance a flying field where 'would-be aviators' could keep their machines and experiment. This letter makes it clear that no free flight was made before the 14th of August, 1908.

Although I have failed to follow closely Mr Roe's later work, which has given him the high standing as an aeroplane constructor in England, yet his name will always be familiar to me because he was among the early ones in England with whom we had correspondence.

With pleasant remembrance of your visit to Dayton in 1918, and with kindest regards.

Sincerely yours,
Orville Wright

Typescript copy held in the Royal Aeronautical Society Library

4th July, 1928.

Dear Mr Orville Wright

I was delighted to receive your very kind letter of June 12th, and quite understand your views with regard to the banquet recently given to Mr A. V. Roe. I think it is highly probable that Mr Roe may have mentioned nothing about his early flights when he wrote to your brother at Le Mans as he was not then aware that they had been seen by three witnesses, and he possibly thought that it was better to say nothing.

No doubt you will by now have received my other letter, together with the vellum, which I hope was in no way damaged in transit through the post.

With very kind regards and pleasant recollections of your kindness to me in Dayton some ten years ago.

Yours sincerely,

President

Walcott had been not only Secretary of the Smithsonian but also Chairman (1919–27) of the National Advisory Committee for Aeronautics. At his request, two members of that Committee, Joseph S. Ames and David Wilson Taylor, compiled 'A Report on the Langley Machine' in June 1925. Ames succeeded Walcott as Chairman of NACA, and served until 1939; for some years Taylor was his vice-chairman.

Orville Wright refers to a meeting held with Abbot at the Carlton Hotel in Washington D.C. In his book The Wright Brothers *(New York, Harcourt, Brace and Company, 1943), F.C. Kelly says that,*

> *In the course of their talk Dr Abbot expressed the wish that they might come to an agreement by which the Kitty Hawk plane could be returned to America and placed under the care of Smithsonian in the National Museum.*

Abbot's response to Orville's concerns, which are reiterated in the following letter, was published as 'The Relations between the Smithsonian Institution and the Wright Brothers', Smithsonian Miscellaneous Collections, *Vol.81 (5) (Washington D.C., Smithsonian Institution) on 29 September 1928.*

Orville refers to the Congressional investigation concerning the 'First Heavier-than-Air Flying Machine: Hearing before Subcommittee No.8 Committee on Military Affairs, House of Representatives, Seventieth Congress – First Session April 27 1928'. This took place as a result of the introduction of a resolution on 29 February 1928 by Congressman John J. McSwain of South Carolina to ascertain which was the first heavier-than-air flying machine. Orville Wright's statement to the Hearing is given in Appendix III.

A typescript copy of the following letter is held in the Royal Aeronautical Society Library.

Dayton, Ohio,
September 28, 1928.

My dear Dr Abbot:

I have just returned to Dayton after several months in Canada. When I left Dayton I was compelled to leave several hundred letters unanswered. As your letter of May 31st required a long answer it had to be one of them. I am sorry for this, but I am taking up your letter the first since my return.

In our friendly conversation at the Carlton Hotel last April you expressed a desire to settle the controversy between the Smithsonian Institution and myself without the intervention of outside parties, and stated that you would be willing to correct the matter to which I objected, if it could be done without vilifying either your predecessor or the Smithsonian Institution. I stated that all I required was a correction of the erroneous impressions created by earlier Smithsonian publications. I have hoped that you might see your way clear to make a frank and full statement of the changes made in the Langley machine in the tests at Hammondsport. With that matter cleared up most of the others would dispose of themselves, for then any competent aeronautical engineer would know that the original Langley machine was not capable of flight, and that the scientific data from which it was designed could not have 'formed the foundation of modern aviation', as the Smithsonian Institution has claimed. I regret that the statement enclosed with your letter of May 31st is not the frank and full statement which I had hoped for, and that it will not correct the false impression already created.

I have been under the impression that you had no part in these earlier acts of the Institution to which I have taken exception, and I have had no inclination to make you personally suffer for the acts of your predecessor. However, I feel that you now, as Secretary of the Institution, can not escape the responsibility of correcting errors committed at any time by its officials.

First let me suggest that the term 'Langley-Wright Controversy' used in the statement is a misnomer. There was never any controversy between Dr Langley and ourselves, and Dr Langley was not responsible of any of the conduct of the Smithsonian Institution to which I have taken exception. This has been a 'Walcott-Wright' or a 'Smithsonian-Wright', but not a 'Langley-Wright', controversy.

If this thirty-six-page statement entitled 'Aeroplane Pioneers', is intended as a 'correction of history', as it suggests, it falls far short of its purpose. The few corrections contained in it are presented in such a way as to leave unaffected the false impression created by the earlier statements. The present paper appears to be a defence of the past conduct of the Smithsonian Institution rather than a correction of history which it has perverted.

I will take the points treated in your statement in the order you have given them.

Point No.1 pertains to the prominent mention of the achievements of Langley in the addresses at the time of the first presentation of the Langley medal. This brings up a new matter not raised by me; so that any discussion of that point by me is uncalled for.

Point No.2 pertains to the misleading account of the exercises of February 10, 1910, printed in the Smithsonian Report for 1910. On page 4, you 'acknowledge with regret that the summary of the proceedings given at an earlier page of the Smithsonian Report for 1910 (pp.22–23) is misleading.' This misleading summary created an impression, wherever it was read, that our early machines were based upon Langley's scientific data. This was not true, but your statement will not correct this impression.

Point No.3 pertains to the matter of a Wright exhibit for the National Museum. On page 8, after quoting the letters between Dr Walcott and ourselves, you say: 'I can not but feel that Mr Wright has erred in ascribing to Dr Walcott any but a sincere invitation to the Wrights to make their own selection of whatever they thought best suited and most available to deposit in the National Museum for the purpose of illustrating their achievements.' Dr Walcott's letter plainly shows that it was the 1908 machine both in full size and in model form that was desired. It states that a model of the 1903 machine would be appropriate 'if there were any radical differences' between that machine and the 1908 machine. There were no radical differences, and therefore the condition here imposed eliminated a model of the 1903 machine. It also is stated that the Fort Meyer machine of 1908 would be 'most suitable', but that if the Wright Brothers thought the Kitty Hawk machine would answer the purpose better, their judgement 'might decide the question'. (It did not say 'would decide'.) I will here call your attention to the fact that this statement in Dr Walcott's letter is not properly represented in the 'chronology' presented by you to the Subcommittee No.8 of the Committee on Military Affairs of the House of Representatives. The word 'to' is there substituted for the word 'might', giving a different meaning. It is apparent that the 1903 machine was not appreciated nor particularly wanted, and we did not wish to have it exhibited by any institution that did not properly appreciate its importance in the art. It is a significant fact that if the preferences of the officials of the Smithsonian

Institution, as expressed in that letter, had been complied with, the aeronautical exhibit in the National Museum would have contained an 1896 Langley flying model, a 1903 Langley full-size aeroplane, a 1908 Wright full-size aeroplane, and a quarter-size model of the Wright 1908 machine.

Point No.4 pertains to the employment in 1914 of Mr Glenn Curtiss, a defendant at that time in a patent suit brought by the Wright brothers, to make tests of the Langley machine. I agree with you when you say that you 'concede to Mr Wright that it smacked of unfriendliness to put the tests of the Langley plane into the hands of his opponent, Mr Curtiss'. Heretofore I have called attention to this fact more to show that fair tests could not be expected when made by one who might be financially benefited by the outcome of the tests.

Point No.5 pertains to the tests of the Langley machine at Hammondsport in 1914; to Smithsonian reports of these tests; and to claims of priority in capacity to fly for the Langley machine.

On page 10 you quote a statement from the Annual Report of the US National Museum for 1914, p.47, as follows: 'Owing to a defect in the launching apparatus, the two attempts to fly the large machine during Dr Langley's life proved futile, but in June last, without modification, successful flights were made at Hammondsport, N.Y.' You then state that this 'certainly was not literally true'. And further on in the same page you say there were 'many differences'. Among these changes you mention only a new carburetor, and addition of pontoons and their supports, and the strengthening of the wings and the modification of their supports. You give no exact information as to the nature of these changes so as to enable one versed in the art to form an opinion for himself as to their importance. The attitude of the Smithsonian Institution in this regard has been unique in scientific procedure. A test was being made to determine whether the original Langley machine was capable of flight, but the test was not made with the machine as designed and built by Langley, nor with an exact copy of it, and yet no list of changes was furnished.

In giving an account of the result of these tests, the following statement, remarkable in coming from a scientific institution, appears on page 11 of your statement:

> Of the resistance in the air, there was a considerable increase in 1914 over 1903, owing to the pontoons and their supports.
>
> On the other hand, there were other differences which favoured success by increasing the strength of the wings and modifying their supports.

Just what effects, favourable or unfavourable, the sum total of these changes produced, can never be precisely known. In the opinion of some experts, the tests demonstrated that Langley's machine of 1903 could have flown, and in the opinion of others these tests did not demonstrate it. It must ever be a matter of opinion.

If the information concerning the changes which I enumerate below had been furnished by the Smithsonian Institution to competent aeronautical engineers it could no more have been a 'matter of opinion' as to whether or not the Langley machine could or could not have flown in 1903, than it could be a 'matter of opinion' as to which direction a man would fall, up or down, if he were to tumble out of a balloon.

I here name a number of changes made in the Langley machine at Hammondsport which were not reported. Some were of fundamental importance and without which there could have been no possibility of a flight of the machine in 1903.

1. The wing trussing posts were moved thirty inches rearward. This brought the centre of pressure of the wings in front of the posts and eliminated the backward pull which instead of the launching device, had bent this post backward and wrecked the machine in the tests of 1903. This was a fundamental change in design, without which the machine never could have carried its weight. No mention of this change ever was made in any report of the tests put out by the Smithsonian Institution.

2. Three fundamental changes were made in the design of the wings: (a) the camber was changed from 1 in 12 to 1 in 18; (b) the shape of the leading edge was entirely different; (c) the aspect ratio was slightly increased. These three features are the most important characteristics in determining the efficiency of a wing. No mention of these changes ever was made in any report of the tests put out by the Smithsonian.

3. The rear spars of the wings, which collapsed in the tests of 1903, were reinforced by two additional members. No mention of this change ever was made previously in any report of the tests put out by the Smithsonian. On the contrary the official report of the tests, page 220, Smithsonian Report, 1914, states that 'notwithstanding these surplus additions of 40 per cent and 85 per cent above the

original weight of the craft, the delicate wing spars and ribs were not broken, nor was any part of the machine excessively over-strained'. This statement would seem to be intended to give the false impression that the wing spars, without change, had carried the original weight of the craft and 40 and 85 per cent additional load.

4. The wing trussing used by Langley was changed to a different type at Hammondsport. Also the angles and the places of attachment of the wires were changed, giving the wings greater strength. Yet not one of these changes ever was mentioned in any report of the tests put out by the Smithsonian. On the contrary the official report of the tests, page 221, Smithsonian Report, 1914, stated that 'apparently the machine could have flown much higher', but that 'higher flying did not seem advisable with the frail trussing of wings designed to carry 830 pounds instead of the 1520 pounds actual weight.' This statement evidently was intended to give the false impression that the wing trussing used at Hammondsport in 1914 was the same as the original wing trussing designed and used by Langley in 1903.

5. The large fixed vertical keel surface, situated below the main frame in 1903, was entirely omitted in 1914. This omission improved the inherent stability of the machine, yet it was not mentioned in the Smithsonian reports of the tests.

6. The small split vane rudder of the Langley machine was omitted at Hammondsport and was replaced by a larger and more effective single surface rudder having less resistance. This improved the control of the machine, but was never mentioned in the official report.

7. The position of the Penaud tail was raised about twenty inches in 1914. This change increase the inherent stability of the machine, and no mention of it was made by the Smithsonian Institution.

8. The forward corners of the original Langley propellers were cut off after the fashion of the early Wright propellers to increase their efficiency. The official report made no mention of it.

9. The Penaud tail was connected to a regular Curtiss steering post, instead of to a self-locking wheel as provided by Langley in 1903. This increased the controllability of the machine. No mention of this change ever was made in any report of the tests put out in a Smithsonian publication.

10. The cloth was varnished in 1914, increasing the efficiency of the wings. This cloth was not varnished in 1903. No mention of this change ever was made in any report of these tests.

11. The original Langley engine was changed in several respects; A modern type carburetor, a new intake manifold, a magneto ignition, and a modern radiator replaced those provided by Langley. These changes were not reported in the report of the tests.

In addition to the above mentioned changes there were many others of more or less importance, only a few of which received even casual mention in the official report of the Smithsonian. My most strenuous protest has been against the Smithsonian putting out the opinion that the tests at Hammondsport in 1914 had demonstrated that the Langley machine was capable of flight, and then suppressing the above mentioned important changes made at Hammondsport, from which any competent engineer would have come to exactly the opposite conclusion.

The Ames and Taylor report is so long that I shall not attempt to correct it here. It is mostly a repetition of matters already put out by the Smithsonian, to the misleading nature of which I have already called attention. If the Institution continues to broadcast these, while you are secretary, you can not avoid becoming responsible for them. As an example I cite the statement at the bottom of page 31, paragraph number 23: 'A complete wing, one-quarter of the sustaining area, showed by sand load test, ability to carry a total weight of 260 pounds without damage, while one-quarter of the weight of the original machine and pilot was 207½ pounds, only.' In the first place the one-quarter weight of the original machine is erroneously stated. The total weight of the machine in 1903 was 850 pounds, one-quarter of which would be 212½ pounds, instead of 207½ pounds. This error in itself is not a serious matter, though it is strange that all of the misstatements coming from the Smithsonian should tend to favor its side in this controversy. The error in the general purpose of the statement however, is a serious matter. The statement would give the impression that one wing of the Langley machine had been sand load tested and had shown an ability to carry 52½ pounds more than would be its load in flight. On the contrary, this load imposed in the sand tests actually was less than the load either of the forward wings would have to carry in flight. One competent to give an opinion of the Langley machine should have known that the forward wings, in a tandem system such as Langley's, would have carry from 62 to 65 per cent of the total load instead of their proportionate share, as was figured by Dr Ames and Admiral Taylor.

The label proposed in the Ames and Taylor report is misleading, it states: 'In the opinion of many competent to judge, this machine was the first heavier-than-air craft in the history of the world capable of sustained free flight under its own power carrying a man'. This is not true. No machine is capable of sustained free flight which has not adequate means of being launched. It can not fly unless it has some way of getting started. The Smithsonian Institution has always maintained that the device provided in 1903 was defective in both trials. That device was not changed in 1903 to remove the defects. Therefore, it can not truthfully be said that the machine was capable of flight that year.

If one wishes to continue to believe that the Langley machine was capable of flight in 1903 in spite of all evidence to the contrary he has the privilege of doing so. But no one has a right to lead others to this belief through false and misleading statements and through the suppression of the important evidence I have mentioned before.

Point No.6 pertains to the failure of the Smithsonian Institution to recognize the Wrights as research men. This is another point which has not been raised by me. My complaint has been against the Smithsonian's giving credit to Langley which belonged to other pioneers in aviation, such as Lilienthal, Penaud, Mouillard, etc., as well as ourselves.

I must again express my regret that you did not see fit to make a full and unbiased statement of the controversy, and I regret that the only apparent way of settling it will be through a congressional or some other impartial investigation.

Sincerely yours,

Orville Wright

Following the 16th Wilbur Wright Memorial Lecture, delivered to the Royal Aeronautical Society by Frederick Handley Page on 30 May 1928, the Society sent Orville Wright an illuminated address signed by members of the Society's Council and selected others. It said,

We are grateful to you for having so carefully restored the original Wright machine, evolved through the mechanical genius of your Brother and yourself, in which, on December 17th, 1903, you separately made the first flights ever achieved by man in a power-driven aeroplane. Further, we greatly appreciate the renewed evidence of your goodwill in sending this historic machine to England and not less the distinction you have thereby conferred on our renowned Science Museum where it is now exhibited for all the world to see.

Orville Wright
Dayton, Ohio
November 17, 1928.

My dear Colonel Sempill:

The beautiful memorial, signed by the Council of the Royal Aeronautical Society and its distinguished guests on the occasion of the sixteenth Wilbur Wright Lecture, was gratefully received by me just before I was leaving for a two months vacation in Canada.

The sending of our first plane to the South Kensington Museum, and the resulting public interest, so greatly increased my mail, that I was compelled to leave for my vacation with hundreds of letters unanswered.

Please accept this apology for my tardy acknowledgment of the receipt of the memorial and express to the members of the Council my most sincere appreciation of its testimonial.

Sincerely yours,
Orville Wright

At the suggestion of Colonel the Master of Sempill, on 17 December 1928 — the twenty-fifth anniversary of the Wrights' first flight — the Royal Aeronautical Society held a dinner at the Science Museum under the original 1903 Flyer. At the dinner Brewer gave an address summarising the Wrights' early flight experiments (subsequently published in the Journal of the Royal Aeronautical Society, *Vol.33, January 1929).*

The Air Minister Lord Thomson was amongst those killed in the R.101 airship crash near Beauvais on 5 October 1930.

Orville Wright
Dayton, Ohio
December 29, 1928.

Dear Colonel Sempill:

Please accept my thanks for your letter, handed to me by Lord Thomson, expressing the congratulations of the Council of the Royal Aeronautical Society on the twenty-fifth anniversary of our first flight.

Sincerely yours,
Orville Wright

43. The Royal Aeronautical Society's dinner at the Science Museum under the original 1903 Flyer on 17 December 1928 – the twenty-fifth anniversary of the Wrights' first flight.

On 3 March 1929 Katharine Wright died in Kansas City of pneumonia. Her engagement, and marriage on 20 November 1926, to Henry (Harry) J. Haskell had caused a major rift with Orville Wright.

Brewer's obituary of Katharine Wright is given below; it was published in the Journal of the Royal Aeronautical Society, *Vol.33, December 1929.*

'WRIGHT HASKELL. On Sunday March 3, 1929, from pneumonia, at Kansas City, Katharine Wright Haskell, wife of Harry Haskell, only daughter of the late Bishop Milton Wright and sister of Wilbur and Orville Wright. Funeral at Dayton, Ohio, to-day (Wednesday).'

The above notice appeared in the Times *on the 6th March and it seems to have passed unnoticed. It is sad to think that human memory is so short that twenty years can obliterate the memory of some of our best friends. Yet twenty years ago, Katharine Wright accompanied her brothers, Wilbur and Orville*

Wright, through France, Italy, Germany and England, in the first demonstration in Europe of actual flying. During that time she met King Edward, King Alphonso, and the leading Presidents and people on this side of the Atlantic, and her charm made her fast friends with many people in this country. She did not forget her friendship for England; for, on the 6th June 1916, Lord Northcliffe, in speaking before the Royal Aeronautical Society before America had come to our assistance in the Great War, quoted a letter he had received from Katharine Wright, in which she said: 'We here make no pretence at being neutral – we are heart and soul for England and her Allies in this great struggle.' Members of the Society will remember that it was after this that Lord Northcliffe went to America, and by his eloquence and earnestness played such a valuable part in securing the wholehearted co-operation of America in the European struggle for freedom.

We have therefore, not merely to remember Katharine Wright for the encouragement and help which she gave to her brothers at a time when sympathy and comfort were most required in the attainment of flight; but we, as nation, have to remember her with grateful feeling for the part which she contributed in securing the co-operation of an ally of overwhelming power, at the time when our very existence was in peril.

G.B.

On 8 April 1930, during a fiftieth anniversary celebration held in Washington D.C. of the founding of the American Society of Mechanical Engineers, Orville Wright was presented with the first Daniel Guggenheim Medal for Aeronautics, '…for design and construction with his brother now deceased, of the first successful engine-propelled airplane'. The Daniel Guggenheim Fund for the promotion of aeronautics had been founded in 1926, and Brewer was the Royal Aeronautical Society's representative on the Daniel Guggenheim Medal Board of Award.

Letter to Mr J. Laurence Pritchard, Secretary, The Royal Aeronautical Society.

Dayton, Ohio
April 16, 1930.

Dear Mr Pritchard:

Please extend to the President and Council of the Royal Aeronautical Society my sincere thanks for the congratulatory resolution on the Daniel Guggenheim Medal Award.

Sincerely yours
Orville Wright

44. Captain Kenneth Whiting, Colonel E.A. Deeds, Orville Wright and Major-General Henry H. ('Hap') Arnold at the Wright Memorial, Kill Devil Hill, which was dedicated on 19 November 1932.

The Journal of the Royal Aeronautical Society, *Vol.33, March 1929, incorporated the Sixty-Fourth Annual Report of the Society's Council which included a brief report of the Society's dinner at the Science Museum under the original 1903 Flyer on 17 December 1928.*

Dayton, Ohio
July 9, 1930.

Dear Sirs:

I beg to acknowledge with thanks the receipt of the copy of the Journal for March, 1929, which you so kindly sent to Mr Wright.

Very truly yours,
Mabel Beck.
Secretary.

On 17 December 1933 – the thirtieth anniversary of the Wrights' first flight – Abbot suggested that a committee, headed by the famous transatlantic aviator Charles Lindbergh, should be formed to settle the differences between Orville Wright and the Smithsonian Institution.

Orville Wright
Dayton, Ohio
January 11, 1934.

Dear Mr Brewer:

To keep you posted in regard to the recent gesture on the part of the Smithsonian Institution, which has started all this 'hubbub', I will go back to the 17th of December. On that day the Women's Aeronautical Association arranged for Dr Abbot to place a laurel wreath on the Wright case in the Smithsonian Institution. In his speech that day (a copy of which I enclose) he suggested that Colonel Lindbergh be asked to act as an arbitrator in trying to secure the plane for the Smithsonian Institution.

Several week ago I sent copies of Dayton newspapers, giving Dr Abbot's speech in part, and Mr Wright's reply through the press. I am herewith enclosing copies of the correspondence, which has passed back and forth to date:

> Dr Abbot's letter to Mr Wright of Dec. 17, 1933.
> Mr Wright's reply of December 23rd.
> Dr Abbot's letter of January 3, 1934.
> Colonel Lindbergh's letter of January 4th, and Mr Wright's reply of
>   January 11th.

Of course, you know the copies of these letters are to be kept confidential.

I am also enclosing an editorial from one of our local papers, which is very good.

I do not know whether you are on Mr Findley's mailing list or not. In case you do not get US Air Services I am sending a copy for January 1934, under separate cover.

Mr Wright thinks the last move is only another gesture on the part of the Smithsonian, but he is going to try to use it to force an investigation.

Sincerely yours,
Mabel Beck
Secretary.

P.S. Mr Wright had been intending to write to you but has not got it done. He says that it will be all right to allow the motion pictures to be taken of the plane in the Museum. M.B.

Typescript copy of a letter held in the Royal Aeronautical Society Library, addressed to Dr Charles G. Abbot, Secretary, Smithsonian Institution, Washington D.C.

Orville Wright
Dayton, Ohio
December 23, 1933.

Dear Dr Abbot:

I am in receipt of your letter of December 17th inclosing a copy of your remarks made on that day in accepting a laurel wreath for the Wright case in the National Museum. In your letter you ask me to give consideration to the suggestion contained in your remarks that a committee of three be appointed to act as an intermediary in removing the obstacles which stand in the way of bringing the Kitty Hawk plane of 1903 back to America.

No one in the world deplores so much as I the necessity of sending the Kitty Hawk plane out of our country; it was sent abroad for but one purpose and that purpose was to bring about eventually a correction in the history of flight.

The points involved in the straightening of the record are not on matters of mere opinion. They are on matters of fact, which at this time can easily and definitely be established. All that I have demanded in the past has been that there be an impartial investigation of the matters in controversy and that the record then be made to agree with the facts.

The suggestion made by me in 1925, three years before the plane left this country, that a committee be appointed to make an impartial investigation and settle the controversy, received from the Smithsonian no response. Nevertheless, I shall be most happy now to join with you in the selection of such a committee, with the understanding that the committee will fully investigate the matter in controversy and will make a full report of its findings.

If the committee finds that the charges which I have made against the Smithsonian Institution are unjust and untrue, I shall make every effort to free the Institution of the obloquy which these charges may have brought upon it, and to give equal or greater publicity to the corrections than were given to the charges. On the other hand, if the committee finds that the charges are justified and true, then the Smithsonian Institution, on its part, shall make every effort to rectify the offences committed by it in the past in its own publications by printing full corrections in these same publications. These corrections shall be unequivocal, and shall be given a prominence and circulation equal to that given to the former statements of which they are a correction, so that in the future the matter involved can not be misunderstood.

I heartily approve of your suggestion that Colonel Lindbergh be asked to serve as one of the members of the committee. There being full agreement as to his suitability, the invitation should be extended to him on behalf of both parties. If the committee is to consist of three members then the other two may be chosen between us – one by the Smithsonian Institution and one by myself.

If this plan for arbitration is carried out and the plane is returned to America, your invitation to place the Kitty Hawk plane in the National Museum will be given consideration.

Sincerely yours,

[Signed] Orville Wright

A copy of the following letter from Charles A. Lindbergh is held in the Royal Aeronautical Society Library.

Jan. 4, 1934

Dear Dr Wright:

Dr Abbot has suggested that I might be helpful in arranging to bring the original Kitty Hawk plane back to the United States to be placed permanently in the National Museum in Washington. You and your brother have brought honor to this country by many accomplishments and by being the first to achieve sustained flight with a power-driven airplane. Consequently it seems fitting that your original machine should be preserved for future generations in the National Museum. Naturally I would be very glad if I could be of assistance in bringing this about.

Sincerely

[Signed] Charles A. Lindbergh

January 11, 1934.

Dear Colonel Lindbergh:

I am in receipt of your gracious letter of January 4th and am greatly pleased that you seem inclined to accept the invitation to act as an arbitrator in settling the differences between the Smithsonian Institution and myself.

From your letter I infer that Dr Abbot did not make it clear to you that the invitation was extended in behalf of myself as well as the Smithsonian Institution. I enclose a copy of a letter I wrote to Dr Abbot on December 23rd in which I ask him to extend the invitation to you on behalf of both of us.

The letter also states the reasons for which the Kitty Hawk plane was sent to a foreign museum and the conditions which would have to be fulfilled before it could, in justice to the memory of my lamented brother, be brought back.

I would suggest that you, Dr Abbot and I have a conference at Washington to arrange details on the afternoon of Tuesday, January 23rd. I suggest this day because the three of us have other duties calling us to Washington on that day. Will you let me know if this is agreeable to you?

Sincerely yours,

[Signed] Orville Wright

On 14 December 1933 at a meeting of the Royal Aeronautical Society under the chairmanship of C.R. Fairey (the Society's President, 1930–34), the recommendations of the Society's Council that Griffith Brewer and Orville Wright be elected Honorary Fellows of the Society were unanimously carried. Previously, Wilbur and Orville Wright had been elected Honorary Members of the Aeronautical Society of Great Britain in November 1908.

Orville Wright
Dayton, Ohio
January 12, 1934.

Dear Mr Fairey:

I was much pleased to receive your telegram bearing the congratulations of the Council and Members of the Royal Aeronautical Society on the occasion of the thirtieth anniversary of our first flight. Wilbur and I had always believed that the aeroplane would be an instrument tending to bring about peace rather than war. Your opinion that it is accomplishing this end is gratifying to me.

Sincerely yours,

Orville Wright

Letter to Mr J. Laurence Pritchard, Secretary, The Royal Aeronautical Society,

January 12, 1934.

Dear Mr Pritchard:

Please accept my thanks for your cable informing me of my election to honorary fellowship in the Royal Aeronautical Society. This is an honor which I appreciate greatly. Please extend to all the members of the Council an expression of my appreciation.

Sincerely yours,
Orville Wright

In the British weekly journal Flight, *Vol.26, 30 August 1934, an editorial notice commenting on the recent hundredth anniversary on 22 August 1934 of the birth of S.P. Langley included the following observation:*

'His work in developing practical aeronautics was of the greatest value, and yet it is hard to find a special niche for him in aeronautical history as being certainly the first in either design or in practical flight...'

In a letter published in Flight, *Vol.26, 11 October 1934, A.F. Zahm responded to this editorial stating,*

'From the flight of the monoplane model, Dr Langley and other competent judges, including Chanute, Manly and Wilbur Wright, concluded that the quite similar full-scale machine was competent to make a successful pioneer flight, if suitably launched. All of them have recorded this opinion which has been endorsed by many subsequent engineers...'

Brewer responded in a letter published in Flight, *Vol.26, 25 October 1934, questioning Zahm's sources; he wrote, 'Wilbur Wright made so few prophecies that it would be interesting to know where the record may be found of his having shared this mistaken belief with Dr Langley. Will Dr Zahm very kindly mention his authority?'*

In the following letter Orville Wright refers to a group photograph taken at Sheppey. This is reproduced here as Illustration 17.

Orville also refers to the Langley 'Memoir on Mechanical Flight' edited by Charles M. Manly (Smithsonian Contributions to Knowledge, *Vol.27 (3), Washington D.C., Smithsonian Institution, 1911) and to S.P. Langley's* The Greatest Flying Creature: Introducing a Paper on the Pterodactyl Ornithostoma *by F.A. Lucas (Washington: Government Printing Office, 1902).*

M.J.B. Davy's Henson and Stringfellow: their Work in Aeronautics: The History of a Stage in the Development of Mechanical Flight *(London: His Majesty's Stationery Office, 1931) described the early aeronautical designs of William*

Samuel Henson (1812–88) and John Stringfellow (1799–1883). They developed various models based on Henson's advanced fixed-wing monoplane configuration known as the 'Aerial Steam Carriage', first published in 1843.

In 1934 Colonel E.B. Macintosh was Director of the Science Museum.

Orville Wright
Dayton, Ohio
November 20, 1934.

Dear Griff:

Your several letters, received since you left us at camp in the Bay, have been read with much interest. From the photograph sent I can readily understand the meaning of your expression 'top-sawyer'. A short time ago I ran across an illustration in a magazine showing the top sawyer on the surface of the ground and the other down in a pit. When one considers the position of the under man the superiority of the top one is quickly appreciated.

Your photos of the upper sides of the clouds were beautiful. In my flying I never but once had the experience of flying with nothing in sight below but clouds. That was at low altitude. The day was calm, and the upper surface of the clouds was a series of undulations, beautiful in the sunlight, but lacking the majesty of the storm clouds shown in your pictures.

I was very glad to get the photograph of the group at Sheppy [*sic*] Island. I had forgotten that Lockyer was there. He and McClean visited us at 7 Hawthorn a year or two later, with the weather at 100 degrees in the shade!

I have not written as yet to Colonel Mackintosh, but I will get to that before long. Since my return I have read Davy's book on Henson and Stringfellow. I saw at once, in glancing through his manuscript on the 'Wright Aeroplane', that Davy's lack of knowledge of the history of the Wright aeroplane and the work of the Wright brothers rendered him incompetent to write such a book. I also observed that he made too much ado over matters of little importance and then almost entirely omitted matters of great importance. I thought this probably was due to a lack of knowledge rather than to a lack of understanding. Reading his book on Henson, however, convinces me that it is in the latter respect that he is most lacking. The next to last paragraph in his Preface can bring only a laugh from anyone who has the least comprehension of the problem in Henson's time. There could have been a thousand Hensons and still no flying today. What I have said here refers to Henson and not to Stringfellow. Stringfellow made a valuable contribution.

Dr Zahm has been quite busy of late. He heard in October several compli-
mentary references to Wilbur at the F.A.I. convention in Washington. This
was too much for him. So the interview in the enclosed clipping took place.
This interview was the target of Findley's editorial in the November issue of
'US Air Services'. I do not take 'Flight' any more, but when I got your letter I had a photostat copy made of the page containing Zahm's letter to the
editor.

I do not know when Wilbur 'recorded' the opinion mentioned in the letter.
Zahm as librarian of the Aeronautic Section of the Library of Congress has
access to Wilbur's letters to Chanute, and it may be that he is basing his statement on something in one of these letters. But knowing Zahm as I do, and
knowing that he has no apparent scruples about lying, I place no credence in
his assertion that Wilbur ever made such a statement as he attributes to him.
Wilbur may have expressed the opinion that the 1903 Langley machine had
enough power to fly. Langley was only attempting to carry 16⅓ pounds per
horse power, while we in our 1903 machine actually carried 60–65 pounds per
horse power.

I feel sure Wilbur never expressed the opinion that Langley's machine was
strong enough to fly, for we both thought the primary cause of its failure in
1903 was its structural weakness. Wilbur never saw the 'Langley Memoir of
Mechanical Flight' from which the exact details of construction of the 1903
machine have been obtained. If he had been acquainted with the arrangement
and location of the original wing trussing, which collapsed in 1903, he never
could have thought the machine capable of flight.

It seems that Zahm never can be truthful in matters, where a misstatement is
more advantageous to him. In the second paragraph he says, 'His quarter-scale
model of the one-man monoplane on August 8, 1903, flew publicly with good
inherent equilibrium and landed upright on the water according to schedule.
Previously in private it had flown successfully many times, both with monoplane and with biplane wings.' This quarter-size model was launched just three
times altogether. On June 18, 1901, fitted with monoplane wings, it made its
first flight in which it remained in the air 'between four and five seconds'. In
its second flight on the same day it remained in the air 'about ten seconds'.
(Langley Memoir, p.232). In both trials the launchings were successful but the
flights ended quickly on account of lack of power. Manly said the flights were
'very disappointing', and that, 'the Aerodrome was accordingly returned to
Washington for the purpose of making new cylinders for the engine' (Langley
Memoir, p.232). After increasing the engine power, which in the first two

flights had been only 1.5 to 2 h.p. (Langley Memoir, pp.230 and 233) to 3.2 h.p., this quarter-size model with monoplane wings was again tested on the 8th of August, 1903. In this third trial it remained in the air only 27 seconds (according to schedule?) and again landed on account of the motor failing to furnish enough power.

Without further trials the small launching device was dismantled to prepare for launching the full-size machine (Langley Memoir, pp.258 and 261). The quarter-size model was never flown with superposed wings although superposed wings had been built for it in the winter of 1900 and 1901. Superposed surfaces also were to have been constructed for the full-size machine (Langley Memoir, p.231), but I believe they never actually were constructed. The No.5 and No.6 models were flown using superposed wings. Zahm may have been confused by this reference to the tests of the No.5 and No.6, which appears in the chapter describing the quarter-size model.

Zahm's statement that certain 'competent judges' concluded from the flight of the quarter-size model that the full-scale machine was competent to fly is interesting in view of the following facts. The Langley model No.5, weighing 26 pounds with a one horse-power engine, and carrying 26 pounds per horse-power, made two flights in 1896 – one of a minute and a half, and the other of one minute and 31 seconds.

The Langley quarter-size model, slightly larger than the No.5, weighed 42.11 pounds and had a motor of 1½ to 2 horse-power and carried 22 to 28 pounds per horse-power. It was tested in 1901 and launched from the small house-boat at a height of about twenty feet. The best it did was to make one flight of five seconds and one of ten (Langley Memoir, p.232). In 1903 the power of the motor was increased to 3.2 horse-power, and the weight to 58 pounds, so that the weight to be carried per horse-power was reduced to 18.12 pounds. This time it was launched from the large houseboat at a height of nearly 40 feet above the water. The flight lasted 27 seconds, and was terminated through lack of motive power (Langley Memoir, p.258). You will note that when the weight was increased less weight could be carried per horse-power, and that the larger model never performed so well as the earlier and smaller one.

Langley was aware that the difficulties increased enormously with increase of size of machine. In the introduction to the 'Greatest Flying Creature', he says:

'From the obvious mathematical law that the area in bodies in general increases as the square of their dimensions, while their weight increases

as the cube, it is an apparently plain inference that the larger the creature or machine the less the relative area of support may be (that is, if
we consider the mathematical relationship, with out reference to the
question whether this diminished support is actually physically sufficient
or not), so that we soon reach a condition where we can not imagine
flight possible.'

In other word the difficulties increased approximately as the square of the
dimensions, so that it would be approximately sixteen times harder to build a
full-size machine that would fly than a quarter-size model of it. Wilbur and I,
when 7 to 11 years old, built small helicopters which lifted themselves into the
air. The best aeronautical engineers of today, with all the accumulation of scientific knowledge of the last thirty years, can not build a large machine of that
same design that can lift the weight of a man.

Zahm in his letter also says that the Ader machine made flights up to 100
meters in 1890–1891. If the flight of 150 feet at Hammondsport was a sustained
free flight, as claimed by Zahm, then surely these Ader flights of twice the
length must have been sustained flights. Therefore, Zahm's statement that
Langley 'developed and built the first man-carrying aeroplane capable of sustained free flight' must have been false, as are so many of his other statements!

The editorial in the October 'US Air Services' was called forth by a state-
ment which appeared in a publication put out by the Bureau of Air
Commerce, US Department of Commerce, and was as follows:
'Contemporary with the Wright Brothers was Samuel Pierpont Langley whose
'Aerodrome', as it was then called, crashed onto the Potomac at Washington
D.C. nine days before the Wright plane flew. The machine was repaired and
flown in 1914 by Glenn H. Curtiss.' This editorial certainly 'got under the skin'
of Vidal. He waited a half hour to get a chance to make apologies to me a few
days ago when I was in Washington, and he has been paying all sorts of attention to Findley ever since!

Colonel Lindbergh has not reported as yet any reply from the Smithsonian
in regard to the list of changes at Hammondsport. I am sending you copies of
all the correspondence since the letters already sent to you.

You will note that the changes enumerated in the list all refer to the tests
before the Curtiss motor was installed.

Sincerely,

Orv

45. Side view of the model Langley *Aerodrome* No.6, 1895–96.

Enclosures:
    Copy letter C.G. Abbot to Orville Wright, Jan. 27, 1934.
    ”   draft letter Abbot to Sec. of War.
    ”   letter Orville Wright to Dr Abbot, February 17, 1934.
    ”   ”   Dr Abbot to Orville Wright, Feb. 19, 1934.
    ”   ”   Orville Wright to Col. Lindbergh, March 1 1934.
    ”   ”   Col. Lindbergh to Orville Wright April 30 1934.
    'Comparison of the Langley Machine of 1903 and the Hammondsport
    Machine of May–June, 1914'.
    Clipping from Washington Post, Oct. 11, 1934.

Attached to the preceding letter is Brewer's typescript copy of the following reply.

7th December 1934

Dear Orv.

My mother used to tell me that if a thing was worth doing at all it was worth doing well. Apparently, your Mother instilled in you the same doctrine, because although your letters are long between, when they do arrive they are wonderfully clear and thorough.

Your letter of the 20th November reached me as I was recovering from a bad cold so I went away to Brighton for a few days and have now returned with some back work to make up but not with time enough to do your letter

46. Langley quarter-scale *Aerodrome* in flight over the Potomac, 8 August 1903.

justice. I therefore propose to leave it over for a little time and then come back to it with my observations.

Yours ever,

(SGD) GRIFF.

After its founding in 1866, the Aeronautical Society of Great Britain published the Annual Reports of the Aeronautical Society of Great Britain *(1867–93), and then* The Aeronautical Journal *from 1897 onwards (also published for many years under the title* Journal of the Royal Aeronautical Society).

Orville Wright
Dayton Ohio
June 24, 1936.

Dear Mr Brewer:

Several weeks ago you asked me to send you a list of the Royal Aeronautical Reports missing from Mr Wright's files.

The Second Annual Report for 1867 is missing.

We have all of the reports from 1868 to 1893 inclusive. Our next report is dated April, 1898. All intervening reports are missing, together with the following – July, 1898; January and October, 1899; January and April, 1900.

Sincerely yours,

Mabel Beck

Orville Wright
Dayton, Ohio
September 19, 1936.

Dear Mr Brewer:

Mr Wright has asked me to thank you for the copies of the early journals of the Royal Aeronautical Society. He is most pleased to have these, and if the three missing journals can be had, he will have a complete file. Mr Wright wants to reimburse you and the Society for any expense you have been put to in this connection. Please let him know what the expense was.

Mr Wright returned last week from Canada. He asks me to tell you he will write you at a later date about the Mingos affair. I think that is entirely off.

Sincerely yours
Mabel Beck
Secretary

Orville Wright
Dayton Ohio
December 1, 1937.

Dear Mr Brewer:

Mr Wright was most happy to receive the copy of the Second Annual Report of the Aeronautical Society of Great Britain; and the fact that it comes from the papers of Major Baden-Powell makes it even more valued. He has appreciated greatly your efforts in securing these missing numbers for his files.

I know you will be interested to learn that Mr Wright has received from the Library of Congress the photostatic copies of Mr Wilbur's letters to Mr Chanute, excepting one. I think you will be particularly interested when you get from Mr Wright an account of his experiences in getting the letters, he already has received, and of his efforts to get the missing one.

Mr Wright is in pretty good health this fall and winter, but he has not been in a literary mood.

Thanking you for the copies of the Journals, and wishing you a Happy Holiday Season, I am.

Sincerely yours,
Mabel Beck
Secretary

On 17 December 1937 – the thirty-fourth anniversary of the Wrights' first flight – the Institute of the Aeronautical Sciences, which Gardner helped to found, inaugurated its annual series of Wright Brothers' Lectures. It was delivered at Columbia University, New York, by B. Melvill Jones of Cambridge University. His subject was 'Flight Experiments in the Boundary Layer', later published in Journal of the Aeronautical Sciences, Vol.5 (3), January 1938. Prior to the lecture Orville Wright, an Honorary Fellow of the Institute of the Aeronautical Sciences, attended a commemorative dinner where a short address on the Wright brothers was given by Dr William Frederick Durand, former Chairman of the National Advisory Committee for Aeronautics. He observed that 17 December 1903 was 'the day on which was demonstrated not only the possibility but the practicability of human flight in a self-powered, man-controlled machine'.

Orville refers to Wilbur Wright's paper 'What Mouillard Did', published in the Aero Club of America Bulletin, Vol.1 (3), April 1912, and later reprinted as one of the appendices to Brewer's Fourth Wilbur Wright Memorial Lecture, 'The Life and Work of Wilbur Wright'. This was published in The Aeronautical Journal, Vol.20, July–September 1916. (Wilbur's paper 'What Clement Ader Did', was published in the Aero Club of America Bulletin in May 1912.)

Based upon his observations of bird-flight, from 1856 Louis-Pierre Mouillard (1834–97) developed in Cairo, Egypt, a series of man-carrying gliders. In Mouillard's later years, Octave Chanute financially assisted Mouillard in the development of a new glider which incorporated hinged sections on the trailing edge of each wing. Augustus Moore Herring (1867–1926) had assisted in the development of Chanute's own biplane glider design of 1896. Otto Lilienthal (1848–96) had flown in Germany a series of mono-plane and biplane gliders which were to influence the glider designs of Percy Pilcher (1866–99) of Glasgow.

Orville refers to papers published in Proceedings of the International Conference on Aerial Navigation, held in Chicago, 1–4 August 1893 (The American Engineer and Railroad Journal, New York, 1894) which had been organised by Chanute and Zahm.

The following typescript copy of a letter from Orville Wright to Major Lester Gardner is held in the Royal Aeronautical Society Library.

February 23, 1938.
Major Lester D. Gardner, Secretary,
Institute of the Aeronautical Sciences,
New York, New York.

Dear Major Gardner:

You letter of January 22nd in regard to Mouillard was laid aside at the time of its receipt until I had time to go into it more fully. I am sorry an answer has been so long delayed.

I know of no better answer to the whole Mouillard affair than Wilbur's article 'What Mouillard Did', published in the Aero Club of America Bulletin, of May, 1912. This article was reprinted in the Journal of the Royal Aeronautical Society for July–September, 1916. I am, however, giving some further particulars not fully covered in Wilbur's article.

Our first acquaintance with Chanute was through correspondence. On the 13th of May, 1900, Wilbur wrote to him, telling him of our proposed experiments in aeronautics. Wilbur described the means which at that time we intended to use for maintaining both the longitudinal and the lateral balance. From Wilbur's letter I quote the following:

'My observation of the flight of buzzards leads me to believe that they regain their lateral balance when partly overturned by a gust of wind, by a torsion of the tips of the wings. If the rear edge of the right wing tip is twisted upward and the left downward the bird becomes an animated windmill and instantly begins to turn, a line from its head to its tail being the axis. It thus regains its level even if thrown on its beams ends, so to speak, as I have frequently seen them. I think the bird also in general retains its lateral equilibrium, partly by presenting its two wings at different angles to the wind, and partly by drawing in one wing, thus reducing its area. I incline to the belief that the first is the more important and usual method. In apparatus I intend to employ I make use of the torsion principle. In appearance it is very similar to the 'double deck' machine with which the experiments of yourself and Mr Herring were conducted in 1896–7. The point on which it differs in principle is that the cross stays which prevent the upper plane from moving forward and backward are removed, and each end of the upper plane is independently moved forward or backward with respect to the lower plane by a suitable lever of other arrangement. By this plan the whole upper plane may be moved forward or backward, to attain longitudinal equilibrium, by moving both hands forward or backward together. Lateral equilibrium is gained by moving one end more than the other or by moving them in opposite direction. If you will make a square cardboard tube two inches in diameter and eight or ten long and choose two sides for your planes you will at once see the torsional effort of moving one end of the upper plane forward and the other backward, and how this effect is attained without sacrificing lateral stiffness.'

In the letter Wilbur discussed at even greater length the methods we intended to use in experimenting. He told Chanute that instead of gliding down hill as Chanute and Lilienthal had done, or being towed by a horse as was Pilcher, we intended to fly our glider as a kite on a rope from the top of a tower 150 feet high. He discussed at considerable length the advantages and disadvantages of such a system, and said, 'In explaining these, my object is to learn to what extent similar plans have been tested and found to be failures, and also to obtain such suggestion as your great knowledge and experience might enable you to give me'.

Mr Chanute answered on the 17th of May 1900. (This was the first direct communication of any kind we had from him.) Mr Chanute said, 'I have your very interesting letter of 13th, and am quite in sympathy with your proposal to experiment; especially as I believe like yourself that no financial profit is to be expected from such investigations for a long while to come. You will find in the "Proceedings of the Conference on Aerial Navigation" a paper on "Flying Devices" by G.C. Taylor, who tested much the same method that you propose, he having used a mast 35ft high. See also in same book of which I enclose a folder, "Learning How to Fly" by Duryea, and "A Program for Safe Experimenting" by Mouillard'.

All of the papers cited by Chanute described methods of experimenting with man-carrying kites anchored to towers, in a manner similar to the plan Wilbur had proposed. The paper by Mouillard proposed experimenting over water, flying as a kite with ropes attached high on the masts of a ship anchored in the water. The subject of lateral balance was not even mentioned in Mouillard's paper. The above quotation from Chanute's letter contains the only mention of Mouillard or of his work in that letter, and in none of Chanute's letters to the Wrights for the next two and one-half years was Mouillard's name so much as mentioned.

Our first acquaintance with Mr Chanute, other than by correspondence, began with his visit to us at Dayton on the 26th of June 1901.

I note in the article of Gabriel Dardaud in 'L'Intransigeant' a reference to a letter from Chanute to Paul Renard in which Chanute is represented as saying 'The Wright brothers added the warping of the wings, idea patented by Mouillard (amongst other ideas) to the United States through my agency in '97.'

If the quotation is correctly given, Mr Chanute in his advanced years must have experienced a fundamental change of mind. In 1901 he gave us and others to understand that our system of lateral control was an entirely original one. Although he was informed as to our system in Wilbur's first letter to him (May 17, 1900), and although he visited our experimental camp in three successive years, and saw our system of control embodied in the gliders of 1901 and 1902 and the motor machine of 1903, he did not so much as intimate that he thought our system of control was similar in idea to the one patented by Mouillard.

It seems strange that Chanute, if he thought Mouillard's work of such importance, should mention his name only four times in his correspondence of more than 200 letters covering a period of ten years, and should fail altogether to discuss his work. Chanute gave just eight lines altogether to Mouillard, one of which lines has been quoted above; five of which were devoted to giving Mouillard's measurements of birds' wings. In these same letters Chanute made much more mention of other experimenters and devotes page on page to a discussion of their work.

On December 30, 1903, thirteen days after our first flight at Kitty Hawk with a motor-plane, Mr Chanute read a paper before Section D of the American Association for the Advancement of Science, in which he made mention of these flights. That he did not at that time think the Wright system of control similar to Mouillard's is evidenced by the following quotation from his address which appeared in Popular Science Monthly, March 1904.

For three years they [the Wright Brothers] experimented with gliding machines, as will be described farther on, and it was only after they had obtained thorough command of their movements in the air that they ventured to add a motor. How they accomplished this must be reserved for them to explain, as they are not yet ready to make known the construction of their machine nor its mode of operation. Too much praise can not be awarded to these gentlemen. Being accomplished mechanics, they designed and built the apparatus, applying thereto <u>a new and effective mode of control of their own.</u> They learned its use at considerable personal risk of accident. They planned and built the motor, having found none in the market deemed suitable. They evolved a novel and

47. Chanute biplane glider, c.1896. `

superior form of propeller; and all this was done with their own hands, without financial help from anybody.

Sincerely yours,
Orville Wright

On 12 September 1938 the Wright Brothers Memorial Wind Tunnel was dedicated at the Massachusetts Institute of Technology before members of the Fifth International Congress for Applied Mechanics.

Orville Wright
Dayton, Ohio
September 26, 1938.

Dear Mr Brewer:

I have received this morning copies of the programs of the dedication of the wind tunnel and the Congress at M.I.T. I am, therefore, returning your copies which you so kindly offered to Mr Wright.

Sincerely yours,
Mabel Beck
Secretary

Typescript copy held in the Royal Aeronautical Society Library of a letter from Orville Wright.

Oswald Ryan was one of appointees to the new Civil Aeronautics Authority, created in 1938. One of the Authority's first acts was to select Gravelly Point as the site for what became in 1941 Washington National airport.

July 8, 1939.
Mr Oswald Ryan,
Civil Aeronautics Authority,
Washington D. C.

My dear Mr Ryan:

Your letter asking whether I would have objection to the naming of the airport at Gravelly Point in honour of Charles M. Manly and whether the naming of the field for Manly might re-open the 'Langley-Manly-Wright' controversy was received. From your letter I am led to suspect that you are not acquainted with the nature of the 'controversy'. There never was a 'Langley-Manly-Wright' controversy. The relations of Dr Langley and Manly with the Wright Brothers were always friendly. The controversy has been between Dr Walcott and Dr Abbot, later Secretaries of the Smithsonian, and myself. This controversy is over the Smithsonian's reports of the tests of the so called Langley machine at Hammondsport in 1914.

In 1914 Dr Walcott permitted Glenn Curtiss and A.F. Zahm (Curtiss' chief witness in law suits), to take the original Langley machine from the workshop of the Smithsonian Institution and to make fundamental aerodynamic alterations in it. With these alterations many attempts were made to fly the machine but not a single sustained flight was accomplished. The 50 h.p. Manly motor was then replaced with a 90–100 h.p. Curtiss motor and some short flights were made. This letter will be confined to the alterations in the machine at Hammondsport while the Manly motor was used.

The collapse of the wings of the Langley machine in the first trial in 1903 was attributed to a fault in the launching device. The supposed fault was remedied before a second trial was made; but the wings collapsed in the second trial just as in the first. The failure in neither trial was due to the launching device, but to the faulty position of the wing guy-posts. Langley had no data giving the location of the center of pressure on cambered surfaces, and so placed the guy-posts as they would have been placed for flat wings. Thus the centre of pressure on his cambered wings was far in the rear of his guy-posts. This produced a backward pull of 170 pounds acting on a radius of 6½ feet on the frail guy-post of the forward wings. As a result the post was bent backward in both trials and the forward wings collapsed. The machine never could have borne its own weight in flight without a correction in the location of the guy-posts.

This fatal defect in the design of the machine was known to Zahm and Curtiss in 1914. At Hammondsport the frail single wooden guy-post was replaced by four posts, each of larger cross-section than the original, and all of these posts were located 28 inches further rearward, to avoid the backward pull which had made success impossible in 1903.

In addition to this vital alteration many other important changes were made, only a few of which I shall mention: Three fundamental changes were made in the design of the wings; (a) The camber was changed from 1–12 to 1–18; (b) the leading edge was shaped entirely different; (c) the aspect ratio was slightly increased. The wing spars, which collapsed in 1903, were greatly reinforced. The wing fabric, untreated in 1903, was varnished in 1914. Langley's split-vane rudder was replaced by a larger and more efficient rudder. A system of control (Wright) not used by Langley was used in 1914. The Langley propellers were modified to get greater thrust in 1914. The Manly engine was changed in these respects: A float feed carburettor replaced the Balzer saturated wood carburetor. A magneto ignition replaced the battery ignition. A modern type radiator replaced the tubular radiator of 1903. A different intake manifold was used.

After all the changes mentioned above, and many more not mentioned, had been made in the Langley machine, not a single sustained flight was accomplished. Many trials were made, but in no one of them could the floats be kept off the water for a period of five seconds. Yet Dr Walcott and other officials of the Smithsonian Institution made statements such as these in Smithsonian publications:

> Owing to a defect in the launching apparatus the two attempts to fly the large machine during Dr Langley's life proved futile, but in June last, without modification, successful flights were made at Hammondsport, N.Y.
>
>   – Rathbun.

> The machine was shipped from Langley Laboratory to the Curtiss Aeroplane Factory to have the plane recanvassed and hydroaeroplane floats attached before launching on Lake Keuka May 28th.
>
>   – Walcott.

> The tests thus far made have shown that the late Secretary Langley had succeeded in building the first aeroplane capable of sustained free flight with a man.
>
>   – Walcott.

Statements similar to the above were repeated year after year in Smithsonian publications so that thousands of intelligent people were misled. The Smithsonian no longer denies any of the changes which I have mentioned above, yet I have been unable to get them to make any correction of their former statements which will give a clear and understandable account of the tests made a Hammondsport in 1914. Some years ago Dr Abbot made what purported to be a correction, which, in the Smithsonian's scientific way of thinking, he seemed to consider sufficient. This was:

> The claims published by the Smithsonian relating to the 1914 experiments at Hammondsport were sweeping. In the Report of the US National Museum for 1914, page 47, we read: 'Owing to a defect in the launching apparatus, the two attempts to fly the large machine during Dr Langley's life proved futile, but in June last, without modification, successful flights were made at Hammondsport, N.Y.' Certainly this was not literally true, but Assistant Secretary Rathbun, who wrote the statement given above, I am certain believed this to be true. There were, however, many differences. (I refer only to the first tests when the original Langley-Manly engine was used.) Mr Wright claims that essential

changes tending to improve the chances of success were made on the basis of knowledge gained subsequent to 1903.

Some of the differences were favourable, some unfavourable, to success. Just what effects, favourable or unfavourable, the sum total of these changes produced can never be precisely known.

All statements so far put out by the Smithsonian Institution would lead one to believe there were no alterations made in the Langley machine at Hammondsport, or a least no important ones. Dr Abbot quoted above says, 'There were, however, many differences'. This entire 'controversy' is over the Smithsonian making inaccurate statements which led the public to believe the Langley machine, without important alterations, was successfully flown in 1914, and then refusing to let the public understand the nature of these 'many differences', so the public can judge for itself whether the Smithsonian's inaccurate statements are misleading.

There was never any other than kindly feeling on our part towards Langley and Manly, and I have no objection to the naming of the airport for Manly, so long as nothing on the airport or in the dedicatory ceremonies or the press releases, etc., concerning it, gives the impression that in later years the Langley machine was successfully flown.

I have extended this letter to considerable length in order that you may clearly understand my attitude.

Sincerely yours,

Orville Wright

Orville Wright
Dayton, Ohio
December 22, 1943.

Captain J. Laurence Pritchard, Secretary,
The Royal Aeronautical Society,
London, W.1, England.

Dear Captain Pritchard:

Please extend to the officers, council and members of The Royal Aeronautical Society my sincere thanks for their message bearing congratulations on the fortieth anniversary of our first flight. It was much appreciated.

Sincerely yours,

Orville Wright

48. Handing-over ceremony of the original 1903 Wright Flyer at the Science Museum, October 1948.

In April 1942, on the instructions of Colonel E.B. Macintosh, Director of the Science Museum, the original 1903 Wright Flyer, which in October 1938 had been stored for fear of war damage in the basement of the museum, was moved to a quarry in the West Country one hundred feet below ground and moved again in February 1943 to another nearby quarry.

In October 1942, with the co-operation of Orville Wright's authorised biographer Fred C. Kelly, the Secretary of the Smithsonian (C.G. Abbot) effectively ended Orville's dispute with the Smithsonian Institution. In a paper entitled 'The 1914 Tests of the Langley Aerodrome' (Smithsonian Miscellaneous Collections, Vol. 103 (8), Washington D.C., Smithsonian Institution, 1942), Abbot publicly acknowledged that, 'It is to be regretted that the Institution published statements repeatedly to the effect that these experiments of 1914 demonstrated that Langley's plane of 1903 without essential modification was the first heavier-than-air machine capable of maintaining sustained human flight...' He concluded that,

If the publication of this paper should clear the way for Dr Wright to bring back to America the Kitty Hawk machine to which all the world awards first place, it will be a source of profound and enduring gratification to his countrymen every-where. Should he decide to deposit the plane in the United States National Museum, it would be given the highest place of honor, which is its due.

Orville Wright died on 30 January 1948. Brewer died on 1 March 1948; his obituary pub-lished in The Engineer, *12 March 1948, noted that he visited the Wrights in Dayton 'no less than thirty times... the last time in 1941... It was due to the instrumentality of Mr Griffith Brewer that the Kitty Hawk was secured for exhibition at the Science Museum, which will, in accordance with Mr Orville Wright's wishes, be shortly returned to America'.*

At a handing-over ceremony in October 1948 at the Science Museum, the American Civil Air Attaché Mr L. Satterthwaite formerly accepted the original 1903 Wright Flyer on behalf of his Government. A replica constructed by the de Havilland Aeronautical Technical School took its place.

On 17 December 1948 – the forty-fifth anniversary of the Wrights' first flight – the original 1903 Wright Flyer was formerly presented to the Smithsonian Institution. It was displayed in the North Hall of the Arts and Industries Building, replacing Lindbergh's Ryan NYP Spirit of St. Louis *in the place of honour.*

Subsequent to the completion of the text of this volume, a file of around fifty letters to and from Griffith Brewer covering the years 1923 to 1929 were returned by the Science

49. The original 1903 Wright Flyer on display in front of Lindbergh's Ryan NYP *Spirit of St. Louis* in the Smithsonian Institution's North Hall of the Arts and Industries Building. From the programme of ceremonies issued at the formal presentation of the aircraft on 17 December 1948.

Museum to the Royal Aeronautical Society Library in February 2003. They had been found in a folder marked 'Property of RAeS' among the papers of the aviation historian C.H. Gibbs-Smith (1909–81), who had been a Research Fellow at the Science Museum.

Most of these letters are between Harry Haskell and Brewer, but there is some correspondence between Katharine Wright Haskell and Brewer dating from January 1927 through to October 1928. Katharine Wright had married Harry Haskell on 20 November 1926, and moved from Dayton to Kansas City. Sadly, after her marriage, Orville Wright refused to have any further dealings with his sister, even returning her letters unopened, and there is little of aeronautical interest in her later correspondence with Brewer. It has been noted that Katharine died on 3 March 1929, Stefansson informing Brewer of her death in a cablegram dated 4 March 1929:

NLT Infallible, London,

Orville reached Kansas City Saturday afternoon. Katharine died Sunday night. Funeral Dayton Wednesday.

Stef.

APPENDICES

50. Side-view of the Wright A at Camp d'Auvours, Le Mans, 1908.

APPENDIX I

Unpublished typescript held in the Royal Aeronautical Society Library.

SOME NOTES ON W. WRIGHT'S AEROPLANE
Taken by Major B. Baden-Powell on Oct 3 to 9 1908
at the Camp d'Auvours, near Le Mans.

The following notes were made chiefly from personal observation, though some of the facts were given by Mr Wright or his associates. Most of the figures are therefore only approximate.

I was present on six different working days, and there were at least 3 or 4 flights on each day.

I twice made an ascent with Mr Wright, but the first attempt only lasted a few seconds, the start being made in a light cross wind. It however gave one some experience of the start and landing. The second flight lasted 4 mins 25 sec.

WILBUR WRIGHT'S AEROPLANE MACHINE.
Le Mans. Oct 1908

The machine in general consists of a framework of spruce poles supporting two superposed main planes with two small superposed foreplanes in front and two parallel vertical rudders behind.

Main Planes

These are both about 40 feet wide in front and about 6 feet from front to rear, the after corners being cut away. The frame of the planes is stoutly made of spruce consisting of an oval frame, about 1½ inches thick to which are attached the longitudinal ribs and the uprights. The ribs consist of an upper and lower batten of ash joined together at intervals by small blocks of wood which are nailed on.

There are 18 upright rods of wood, about 1½ by 2 inches and about 6 feet long. These have metal eye bolts let in to each end, which engage in stout metal hooks fixed to the main frame. Wire pins prevent the eyes from coming unhooked.

Diagonal wire stays run from the top of each rod to the bottom of the next. These are of soft steel (not piano wire) 14 s.w.g. with loops at either end wrapped round with thin metal and soldered. They are not tightly stretched.

The lower plane, on which rests the engine and passengers etc. is supported about 18 inches off the ground on runners, which extend from just below the after edge to about 12 feet in front. The runners are of spruce, and 2½ inches wide and 1½ thick.

The planes are covered with an upper and lower sheet of grey cloth placed diagonally. This is nailed to the frame. The cloth, which is not varnished, is quite slack in dry weather, although said to become tight in damp. It is dirty and oil-spattered.

Fore-Planes

These are each about 14 feet wide and 3 feet front to rear, but the last 3 feet at each end are formed into a ogival, so that the area would be about 35 sq. ft each.

The frame consists of a transverse piece about one-third of the way from the front, a series of longitudinal ribs, and a frame all round the edge. The two planes are connected, about three feet apart, by a number of thin wooden vertical rods, two of which near the centre carry vertical vanes, The planes are practically flat. They are pivoted on a transverse steel rod in the middle. To this is clamped a short arm to which the connecting rod of the lever is attached.

Vertical Rudders

These are supported by two rods about 8 feet behind the main planes, these rods being so connected as to allow of considerable play in a vertical direction, but are held down by a strong spiral spring. If, in landing, the bottom of the rudders strike the ground, they rise against this spring. They are prevented from moving from side to side by wire stays. The rudders are about 6 feet high and 18 inches wide, and are covered (slackly) with cloth. The rudders are fixed about two feet apart by several small wooden rods, one at the top and one at the bottom being pivoted to the above mentioned rods. Wires from the ends of the lower cross-rod are fastened to the ends of a similar cross-rod pivoted to the frame of the lower main plane, which is actuated by the hand lever for steering.

Steering Devices

There are three steering devices, controlled by two levers on the right and left of the driver.

1. Front Control. The lever, held in the left hand, is pivoted at the bottom to the frame, and about six inches up is connected to a long rod, the far end of which is attached to the arm, already referred to, on the transverse steel tube which supports the foreplanes. When this lever is pushed forward the front planes are consequently depressed. The connecting rod passes through a slot in the frame and is held tightly in it by a plate of metal, the friction of which prevents the rod from shifting.

2. Horizontal steering is effected by two means, by the right-hand lever. This lever has an ingenious double action. The lower end is fixed to a longitudinal steel tube mounted in bearings, when the lever is pushed towards or from the operator this tube is caused to turn. At its after end it carries a small upright arm which turns the same as the lever. To the end of this short arm are attached the wires which, passing round pulleys cause the main planes to be 'warped', These pulleys are placed at the top and bottom of the third upright connecting poles from each end (of the rear row of uprights). In order to prevent the wires breaking from continual bending round the pulleys, short pieces of chain are inserted in the wires at those places.

3. The other action of the right-hand lever is that when pushed forward or back it causes the pivoted cross-piece (before referred to) to turn and move the vertical rudders to one side or other.

The Motor

The engine has four vertical water-cooled cylinders. These are bolted to a solid-looking gear case which rests on the lower plane. It has automatic inlet valves, and the exhaust, in addition to valves, is conducted through a series of holes in the cylinder direct into the air. The motor developed 30 horse-power during long trials in America, but, Mr Wright says, since being set up in France it has not developed more than 22 to 24 h.p. It makes about 1300 revs per min.

The engine complete weighs about 90 kilos (200lbs) or 78 without coil, plugs, &c. The ignition is high-tension magneto (though Wright prefers low tension). This weighs 20 kilos.

The petrol tank at first used was a vertical cylinder, but since then a larger tank perhaps a foot in diameter, with conical ends, has been fitted horizontally. This is said to contain enough petrol for three hours' run. The radiator consists of four vertical sets of six flattened tubes, only about an eighth of an inch thick, about six feet high, with two small cylindrical tanks at the top. These sets of tubes are arranged parallel about an inch apart.

In practice a string is run across in front of where the passengers sit, which on being pulled (or accidentally struck) cuts off the ignition. This is a good precaution in case of accident.

Propulsion

The engine shaft terminates in 2 small sprocket wheels with 8 cogs. From this chains connect with sprocket wheels on the propeller shafts, which have 32 cogs, so that the reduction is 1:4. The chains are enclosed in tubes for most of their length.

The propellers are supported on a diamond-shaped frame of steel tubes, the shaft running across the diagonal. This frame is only lightly attached to the upper and lower plane frames but is stayed with wires to keep rigid. The propeller shafts are about four feet long, the sprocket wheels being at the front end and the propellers at the after end. There are plain thrusts bearings, without balls, well lubricated before each start.

Mr Wright prefers not to give any facts relating to the propellers, but they appear to be of wood, about 9 feet in diameter and of considerable pitch. These are new ones, only just fitted on. They are said to be wider and slightly longer than the old ones. They have a considerable curve in the blade. The boss is about 5 inches long and about 2 inches thick, the blades are about a foot across at the tips. The stationery [sic] thrust is said to be 80 kilos for the two screws.

Accessories

In order to move the machine about on the ground, two heavy wheels on frames are employed. These are affixed under the lower plane outside the runners, are tied on with bits of rope, and removed before a flight.

Starting Device

The pylon, or derrick, consists of four wooden poles, 25 feet high, with a large pulley near the top. The rope tackle draws up a weight consisting of (usually) 6 iron discs weighting 100 kilos each, and one of 200 kilos. (800 kilos in all.)

The rope, after leaving the block at the base of the derrick runs round a pulley fixed to the far end of the track and is attached to a second rope which is hauled on by a lot of men or by a motor car. When the weight is thus raised to the top of the derrick, the rope after going round the pulley fixed to the track, is attached to a hook on the end of a wooden rod attached to the machine under the centre of the lower main plane.

The track consists of some seven beams of wood with an iron band on the top, placed end to end. These beams are set upright on solid wooden legs, which are kept in position by pegs driven into the ground. Each section of track is about 15 feet long, so that the whole is about 100 feet long.

The machine is held against the pull of the weights by a loop of wire fixed to the near end of the track, which engages a small hinged lever just below the operator's seat.

When the machine is to be placed on the track, a thick piece of wood like a railway sleeper is placed across under the runners, which has small wheels about 2 feet [in diameter] on a bar fixed longitudinally across its centre to run on the track. Another still smaller roller is fixed under a cross bar of the main frame to support the weight in front. The sleeper is left on the ground when the machine rises.

Manipulation

The methods of preparing the apparatus for flight appear somewhat crude and clumsy.

The machine with its wheels attached is drawn from its shed to the track. Here the wheels are detached and the machine caused to rest on the cross-bar on the track. A small trestle is placed under one end of the lower plane to keep the whole upright. The retaining wire is attached to the machine. Then the weight is drawn up, and the starting rope hooked to the hook.

(The track is laid so as to face the wind. If the wind changes in direction, as was the case in my first ascent, a false start is very likely to result.)

All being ready, two men get on to the propellers, and counting 'one, two, three', start the engine. When the motor is seen to be running satisfactorily, the passengers take their seats, coats buttoned up and caps well adjusted. (In one case the passenger's cap flew off during the trip and was caught in the wire stays behind. Had it fallen on the transmission chain it might have led to an awkward incident.)

Then the driver opens the catch which releases the retaining wire, and the machine rapidly rushes along the track.

The foreplane is inclined slightly downward until about halfway along the track, when it is tilted upward, and the machine, hardly rising, skims through the air and gradually mounts. There are often slight undulations in the course at starting but nothing great.

Should the wind be blowing down the track, in the same direction as the machine is going, at a rate greater than 6 feet per second, Wright considers it impossible to rise.

The rate of ascent is about 3ft per second, or say 1 in 15. The speed of travel is usually about 60 to 63 kilometres an hour, the fastest being 70 kilom. I timed one short bit and made it 60 yards in 3½ seconds.

The machine travels very steadily, often going along for long distances within two or three feet of the ground so steadily that one could easily imagine it was running on wheels.

In turning corners the machine inclines over to a considerable angle. Wright says 25° is about the maximum.

It takes a very wide sweep to get round, the radius of curve being fully 200 yards, but it is possible that a much sharper turn could be made if necessary.

If the engine stopped when at a height, Wright says the machine would glide down at an angle of 1 in 8.

In landing as a rule the machine is brought down very low, and after skimming along just above the ground the ignition is cut off, and the machine lands on its skids, and slides for some distance on the ground. I measured one track, from the point where the runners first touched to the point of stoppage and found it 30 yards.

As regards weight lifted, one of Mr Wright's passengers weighed 108 kilos (nearly 240lbs).

Appendix II

Unpublished typescript — dated May 1914 — held in the Royal Aeronautical Society Library.

The Advantage of the Wrights' Combined Control of Warp and Rudder
By
Griffith Brewer

As far back as the year 1902, the Wrights employed a combined control of warp and rudder, by arranging a mechanical connection between the warping wires and the rudder wires. This arrangement enabled the lateral balance of the machine to be maintained, by the simple operation of a single mechanical part. In the original gliders used by the Wrights at Kitty Hawk, and in the first power machines which they built and flew, the warping wires and the rudder wires were connected together, in such a manner that it was impossible to move the rudder without warping, or to warp the wings without ruddering. This arbitrary connection of these two mechanisms, without option on the part of the pilot to vary the proportion between the warping movement and the rudder movement, necessitated permitting the machine to fly with the lower wing slightly in advance of the upper wing when rounding a curve. In other words, to sideslip to some extent. It was in order to minimise this side slipping that the later Wright control mechanism permits of a subsidiary movement, which enables the pilot to add to or reduce the amount of rudder at will. In actual flying it is usual to only use this subsidiary control when making a turn, when by the additional movement more rudder is applied at the commencement of the turn.

The combined operation of rudder and warp is still in use today on all Wright machines, and I will now consider whether this mechanical connection of rudder and warp is advantageous, and if so, why it is used exclusively by the Wrights.

It is a fundamental law of aviation that an increase in the angle of incidence of a wing at ordinary efficient angles carries with it an increase of drag or head resistance. Consequently when the angle of incidence of the wing on one side of the machine is increased, and the angle of incidence of the wing on the other side is decreased, a turning force is set up which will not only turn the aspect of the machine towards the side of the machine where the wing has most resistance, but which will stultify the very object of warping by increasing the lift of the wing having the least angle, owing to its increase in speed due to the twisting of the machine. It is therefore necessary to counteract this tendency to twist the machine by means of a turning force in the opposite direction, and the amount of this counter-turning force should be as nearly as possible equal to the turning force set up by the wing warping. Obviously, if a mechanism can be given to the pilot, which automatically cures the trouble as it is created, it is one less thing for him to attend to.

Simplicity is the key-note of safety in flying, and the Wrights have never lost sight of this fact. The mechanisms they employ appear to be of kindergarten character, in the same way that their language in describing complicated phenomena has that lucid and clear quality which robs the subject of its mystery. Why they should use two levers if one lever would do they could not see, and they have had no cause since to think otherwise. And all their pupils, who are now numbered in hundreds, prefer the simple use of one lever moved by the hand, to the simultaneous use of a hand lever and a foot lever, which pair of mechanisms, when independently operated, even with the highest skill, can never synchronise correctly. Why, then, if the single lever has these advantages, should those who first learnt to fly and who followed in the Wright's footsteps, have used two levers where one would do?

This brings me to a subject on which many may take issue. I beg them, however before they take up the foils, to bear with me until the end, because I have no wish to use this book for party purposes, but I hope to give information, which will be of value to all who have the interests of aviation truly at heart.

Many of my readers will recognise that I am coming to the subject of the Wright Patent which dates back to 1903, and which has been regarded in some quarters, I regret to say, as a stumbling block to the free advance of aviation. It is not for me to judge whether the Wrights were justified, when, after spending several years of their lives in study and experiments, and risking their lives and their money on a subject discredited by the scientists of the day, they sought to obtain the only reward provided by the laws of nations, by taking out patents in the attempt to obtain a short term of monopoly for the invention they had made. The question of whether they were acting fairly in taking out patents in the same way as all other inventors take out patents in order to recoup themselves for their work, may be left to posterity to decide; but let posterity in deciding that question know, that if the Wrights thought their work entitled them to some reward, they seem to have been alone in this respect, for up to my writing (May 1914) so far as England is concerned, only one aeroplane maker has applied for a licence to work under a patent, and none have been refused. Yet manufacturers of aeroplanes would not have come into existence had it not been for the Wrights' invention. Why are they making and using such machines if they have obtained no licence and if the machines they build and use are the outcome of the Wright Brothers' work?

Let me hasten to explain to the lay reader that it does not follow that the industry, which undoubtedly has come into being out of the efforts of the Wrights, should pay tribute to them because they were the first to show how the thing could be done. The Patent Law has fenced the rights of the public round with a stout fence which though plastered all over with placards advertising the award obtainable by inventors is sufficiently high and thorny to shut out all but the most astute from obtaining the prizes advertised. The Wrights like other inventors, have found that it is one thing to collect royalty, for the reason that manufacturers gauge the ambit of the patentee's claims, and if they can satisfy themselves that the same thing or a suitable equivalent may be done without infringement, they naturally prefer as businessmen to manufacture freely, without adding royalties to their other manufacturing expenses. In such a course no one can blame them.

Now to come back to the double control. Why did the manufacturers with one consent all use two levers where one alone would serve the purpose better?

My reply to that question is that some experts believe that the use of one mechanical movement for the double purpose comes within the Wright patents; whereas, by employing one lever to work the warp and a separate foot yoke to work the rudder; the claims of the patent were avoided. Whether this wide-spread belief is justified or not, the result is extremely disadvantageous to aviation, because the best is not being obtained out of the new art. British manufacturers, for whom this chapter is mainly written, would do well to consider the advisability of changing to the combined system. Certainly the change would be extremely hard at the present time, just as the change from yards and pounds would be to metres and to kilogrammes; but the later this change is postponed, the harder it will be, and in the meantime Aviation progresses under a disadvantage.

I believe I may explain without indiscretion, the British government's attitude in respect to aeronautical inventions used in service machines. I am aware there is a clause in Government contracts, under which the contractor indemnifies the government against loss incurred by the unauthorized use of Patented Inventions. On a subject like Aviation, where men's lives are at stake, and the very safety of the nation depends on the excellence of the machines obtained for service purposes, this clause may for all practical purposes be disregarded by the contractor manufacturing for the government. The Army Council and the Admiralty are willing to accept the risk of actions for infringement themselves, because it is essential to efficiency for them to secure the best apparatus and the best methods of manufacture, and if in doing this they come up against a Patent, they are willing to pay for it in the public interest. The contractor to the government will find, that when he is sued for infringement of a Patent in respect to aviation apparatus which he is making to a government order, the government will take the burden of the action off his shoulders.

The best course therefore for the aeroplane manufacturer who is tendering to a Government department, is to design freely to the best of his ability, and not to let the existence of any patent tempt him to put in a substitute which will serve the purpose, but which may not be as good as some other portion of mechanism he would prefer to adopt but for the patent.

So far as Government orders are concerned, therefore, my advice as a Patent Agent to manufacturers is, not to worry about infringement, but to supply the best without fear. If manufacturers realise the fact that warping gives greater efficiency than ailerons, adopt warping on government machines. When they have learnt that combined warp and rudder control is more rational, adopt it and leave the Government to solve the Patent problem. When they learn that by lying the fabric diagonally on the wings, cross staying is no longer necessary and the wings are stronger, adopt that system by all means. In fact do everything you know which will conduce to efficiency of the machines and the safety of the men who risk their lives in the air for the benefit of our nation.

The above advice is based on experience and on observation. The first of these, viz: instances of Government protection, I cannot particularise; the second, viz: the faculty of observation, is open to all to repeat. If you examine the Army machine BE2 you will observe the designer was not hampered by any obligation to avoid existing Patents. The result is that apart from conforming to the prejudice of the present pilots by adopting the two lever control and so avoiding the mechanically combined rudder and warp, and also reducing the number of struts in order to reduce head resistance, the government machine

BE2 is the same as the Wright machine with the tail at the back. This adoption is to be commended and speaks well for the good sense of those responsible for the design. The BE2 is an excellent machine which has done some of the finest flying, but for the sake of structural strength I should like to have seen the number of struts restored to the number in the original Wright design.

Before leaving the subject of the Wright British Patent, I would like to congratulate many manufacturers on the sensible attitude they have adopted, and on the fact of their not having allowed any misconceptions to hamper their work or progress. It is always best and cheapest in the end to adopt the best methods, than to adopt an inferior method under a false hope of ultimate security and economy.

Appendix III

In Chapter 4 reference is made to the 'First Heavier-than-Air Flying Machine: Hearing before Sub-Committee No. 8, Committee on Military Affairs, House of Representatives, Seventieth Congress – First Session April 27 1928'. A copy of the transcript of the Hearing is held in the Royal Aeronautical Society Library. The hearing concerned the Wrights' objections to the Smithsonian Institution's support of the work of S.P. Langley, and Orville Wright's consequent decision to send the original Wright Flyer to the Science Museum in London. Statements were taken from, inter alia, Hon. Roy G. Fitzgerald (member of the House of Representatives for Ohio) and C.G. Abbot (the then Secretary of the Smithsonian Institution). Orville Wright's statement to the hearing was first published (with some clarifications) in the journal US Air Services, *Vol. 13, March 1928, and is copied below.*

WHY THE 1903 WRIGHT AIRPLANE IS SENT TO A BRITISH MUSEUM.

By Orville Wright

I have sent our original 1903 machine to the British National Museum because of the hostile and unfair attitude shown towards us by the officials of the Smithsonian Institution.

While Professor Langley was Secretary of the Smithsonian all relations between that Institution and ourselves were friendly. At that time Wilbur and I were universally given credit not only for having made the first flight, but for having produced the first machine capable of flight, and for the scientific research from which this first machine sprang. Our 1903 machine was based entirely on our own scientific table and none other. Langley's published work in aerodynamics consisted of measurements of air pressures on flat surfaces only. By an entirely different method we had made measurements of a great number of cambered surfaces, as well as of flat surfaces. Our measurements of flat surfaces did not agree with those made by Professor Langley. Although we were not able to use any of Professor Langley's measurements, because we had found them far from accurate, yet on every occasion where opportunity was offered we expressed our sincere appreciation for the inspiration and confidence Professor Langley's standing in the scientific world had given us when we were starting.

After Professor Langley's death the attitude of the Smithsonian began to change. The Institution began a subtle campaign to take from us much of the credit then universally accorded to us and to bring this credit to its former Secretary, Professor Langley. Through some clever and absolutely false statements it succeeded in doing this with people who were not acquainted with the facts.

To illustrate the kind of thing to which I object in the attitude of the Smithsonian, I will cite out of many a few specific cases:

It misrepresented in the annual report of the Secretary for the year 1910 (p.23) the statement made by my brother Wilbur at the time of the presentation of the Langley medal to us by inserting a quotation not used by him on that occasion, but used in a different connection at another time. The improper use of this quotation created a false impression over the world that we had acknowledged indebtedness to Langley's scientific work; that it was Langley's scientific work and our mechanical ingenuity that produced the first flying machine. This was not true. In a private letter to Octave Chanute at the time of Professor Langley's death we had used the words in acknowledging an indebtedness to Langley for the inspiration he had been to us. We had previously told Mr Chanute of our entire lack of confidence in Langley's scientific work in aerodynamics.

Our original 1903 machine was offered in 1910 to the Smithsonian for exhibition in the National Museum. The officials did not want it, but preferred a much later model of less historic interest.

After the United States Circuit Court of Appeals had giving a decision pronouncing Glenn H. Curtiss an infringer of the Wright invention and recognizing the Wrights as 'pioneers' in the practical art of flying with heavier-than-air machines, Curtiss was permitted to take the original Langley machine from the Smithsonian to make tests in an attempt to invalidate this title of 'pioneer', for purposes of another law suit. The Smithsonian appointed as its official representative at these tests the man who had been Curtiss's technical expert in the former suits and who was to serve again in that capacity in a new one. It paid Curtiss $2,000 towards the expense of the tests.

It published false and misleading reports of Curtiss's tests of the machine at Hammondsport, leading people to believe that the original Langley machine, which had failed to fly in 1903, had been flown successfully at Hammondsport in 1914, without material change. (See report of the National Museum, 1914, pp.46, 47. Smithsonian report, 1914, pp.4, 9, 217–222.) These reports were published in spite of the fact that many changes, several of them of fundamental importance, had been made at Hammondsport; among which were the following: Wings of different camber, different area, different aspect; trussing of a different type, placed in a different location; Langley's fix keel omitted; motor changed by substituting different carburetor, different manifold and different ignition; propeller blades altered; hydroplane floats added; wing spars, which collapsed in 1903, reinforced; tail rudder made operable about a vertical axis, and connected to a regular Curtiss steering post; small vane rudder replaced by a larger rudder of different design.

This machine restored back to its original form which with much new material, the old having been mutilated or destroyed at Hammondsport, was placed in the National Museum with a false label, saying that it was the first man-carrying airplane in the history of the world capable of sustained free flight, and that it had been successfully flown at Hammondsport, June 2, 1914.

Following the controversy on this subject, three years ago the old label was removed and a new one still containing false and misleading statements was put in its stead.

In spite of this long continued campaign of detraction, for years I kept silent, with the thought that anyone investigating would find the facts and would expose them. I had thought that truth must eventually prevail, but I have found that silent truth cannot withstand error aided by continued propaganda. I have endeavoured to have these matters investigated within the Smithsonian itself. I wrote to the Chancellor of the Institution asking for an investigation of the acts of its Secretary in this matter, and received an answer that while the Chancellor nominally was the head of the board of the Smithsonian Institution, his other duties were such as to make it impossible for him to give any real attention to the questions which have to be settled by the Secretary. I have publicly expressed the wish that some national scientific society or other disinterested body make an impartial investigation of my charges against the Smithsonian. To this there has been no response.

In sending our original 1903 machine to the Science Museum, London, I do so with the belief it will be impartially judged and will receive whatever credit it is entitled to. I regret more than any one else that this course was necessary.

Appendix IV

The notes sent by Orville Wright to the Science Museum, Kensington, and copied to Griffith Brewer, in 1928.

DIRECTIONS FOR ASSEMBLING 1903 WRIGHT AEROPLANE

The terms 'right' and 'left' are used as they would be used by one sitting in the machine facing forward.

The forward row of wing struts are numbered from 1 to 9, starting from the right-hand side. The rear struts are numbered from 11 to 19, also from right to left. No.11 strut is behind No.1; No.12 behind No.2, etc. Not all of the wing hinge hooks bear tags, but their numbers are known from the locations. 'Upper' on the tags indicates parts on the upper surface corresponding with the numbered parts on the lower. Example: the first hinge on the forward right-hand corner of the lower plane is number 1. The hinge above it on the upper surface would be indicated by 'upper' No.1.

When more than one wire goes on a hook the diagonal lateral wires (soldered at their centers) usually go on the hook first.

Usually when a tag is tied through a hole and a tag bearing the same number is tied to a screw or a bolt the screw or bolt should go in the hole.

To prevent confusion do not detach tags until machine is completely assembled.

Lacing Plane Covers

Lace the upper cloth of the lower plane first, with knots inside of surface. Then lace lower cloth of lower surface with knots on bottom side of surface.

Lace lower cloth of upper plane first with knots inside of surface; then lace upper cloth with knots on top of surface.

The covers are laced with two rounds of cord around the wires in the turned edges of the cloth, tied and cut at about an eighth of an inch from knot. (Bent needle and linen cord for lacing accompanies plane.)

Erecting Planes

Stand planes on front edges. Insert struts and truss wires; attach skids, then roll over onto skids. A spreader for inserting struts is enclosed in shipment. This should be used with care to avoid tearing cloth. The wires staying the skids at the front edge of the plane go under the skids. The wires to the cross member between the skids. The wires to the cross member at the centre short upright post go over the top of the skid before fastening to cross member.

Some of the wires to the skids will be found to have abrupt bends near the end. These wires go over the top and fasten on the side of the skids.

The tags attached to the motor revolutions counter, the petrol cut-off valve and the hand lever for operating them will indicate their proper installation. In use the manner of operation was as follows: The hand lever was pushed to the left. In this position the revolutions counter remains out of contact with the motor, the anemometer and stop-watch are not recording, and the petrol cut-off valve can be opened for starting the motor. A loop of light string passes through the loop in the loose end of the string attached to lower end of the lever on the centre strut, through the loop fastened to screw-eye on the front spar and through the wire loop from starting rail to prevent machine from moving with motor running. When in starting the machine is released from wire loop, this light string pulls the lever and puts the anemometer, stop-watch and revolutions counter simultaneously into operation. The purpose of the loop on the forward spar was to take the shock of breaking the light string loop. Upon touching the ground at the end of a flight the operator struck the hand lever pushing it to the right, and thus put all of the recording instruments simultaneously out of operation.

The three new plane struts, by oversight, were not bored at their centres for the small horizontal truss wire. These will have to be drilled same as old struts. This small horizontal wire passes through the center of all the forward struts excepting the two end ones. It should be inserted after all the rest of the machine has been finally assembled. This wire is soldered to the diagonal truss wires between struts No.1 and 2 at their juncture, passes through strut No.2 with one of the small wire ferrules soldered to it on each side of the strut, then makes one tight round about the diagonal wires between struts No.2 and 3, but not soldered to them, then through strut No.3 in the same manner as No.2, and so on until it reaches the diagonal wires between struts 8 and 9 where it is again soldered.

The corresponding rear horizontal truss wire starts at strut No.13 with a ferrule on the end of the wire, passes through the strut, wraps around the diagonal wires between struts 13 and 14, and is soldered to them, and then extends to strut No.17 passing through and fastened to the intermediate struts and cross wires in the same manner as in the forward systems of trussing. This wire is also soldered to the cross wires between struts 15 and 17.

The small grooved pieces of spruce are to be cut to exactly fit between struts 13 and 17 and the diagonal cross wires with the horizontal wire lying in the groove and held in with a few wrappings.

Rubber hose to connect the petrol tank and the motor was not included in the shipment. This tube connected to the petrol tank, ran down the back side of the strut, and was lashed to the strut at its centre and near its bottom; extended across on top the plane to the gasoline adjusting valve; then to the gasoline cut-off valve; then connected the gasoline cut-off valve to the brass tube to the motor.

We are no longer able to get in America tubing exactly like that used in 1903. I am enclosing a short piece of the original hose which was still attached to the gasoline valve when we assembled the machine last year. This was the ordinary tubing used on bicycle tire foot pumps twenty-five years ago. The tubing for automobile tire pumps is much heavier. You still may be able to get tubing like the original in England, if not a substitute will have to be used.

LIST OF ILLUSTRATIONS
BIBLIOGRAPHY
INDEX

LIST OF ILLUSTRATIONS

Photographs courtesy of the Royal Aeronautical Society Library unless indicated otherwise.

1. Orville, Katharine and Wilbur Wright (from A. Hildebrandt, Die Bruder Wright, Berlin: Otto Elsner Verlagsgesellschaft m.b.h. 1909).
2. Orville and Wilbur Wright.
3. The world's first manned, sustained, controlled, powered flight in a heavier-than-air machine with Orville Wright at the controls of the Wright Flyer.
4. Lawrence Hargrave and James Swaine experimenting with four man-lifting kites. Reproduced from Hargrave's original glass lantern slides.
5. The Langley *Aerodrome*.
6. Santos-Dumont 14-*bis* at Bagatelle, the first aeroplane flight in Europe.
7. Wilbur Wright caricature postcard by César Giris, produced by A. Noyer of Paris, *c.*1909.
8. Griffith Brewer and Wilbur Wright after the flight at Camp d' Auvours, 8 October 1908.
9. Wilbur Wright flying the Wright A at Pau, January 1909.
10. Wilbur Wright flying the Wright A at Camp d'Auvours, 18 December 1908.
11. Wilbur Wright examining the engine of the Delage, 1908.
12. The Wright A at Pau, 1909.
13. The Hon. C.S. Rolls and Cecil S. Grace on their Short-Wright biplanes, 28 March 1910.
14. The Wright A at Pau.
15. The presentation of the first Gold Medal of the Aeronautical Society of Great Britain to Wilbur and Orville Wright, 3 May 1909.
16. The visit of Orville and Wilbur Wright to inspect the Short Brothers factory at Shellbeach, 4 May 1909.
17. The Wright Brothers outside Mussel Manor at Shellbeach, 4 May 1909.

18. The Wright A, exhibited at the German Air Exhibition, Berlin, 1932.

19. Charles D. Walcott, Wilbur Wright, Dr Alexander Graham Bell and Orville Wright, 10 February 1910.

20. The Hon. C.S. Rolls at the controls of his Wright biplane.

21. Description of the Wright Model R in the Wright Co.'s brochure 'The Wright Flyer' (Dayton, The Wright Co., 1911).

22. The first German factory for Wright aircraft at Reinickendorf. From an original Flugmaschine Wright-Gesellschaft company brochure, 'Wright-Aeroplan', c.1910.

23. Wilbur and Orville Wright with their student pilots, 1911.

24. Description of the Wright Model B in the company brochure 'The Wright Flyer' (Dayton, The Wright Co., 1911).

25. Close-up view of the engine on the Wright Model B, taken from the brochure 'The Wright Flying School' (New York: Wright Flying Field Inc., 1916).

26. Lazare Weiller and Wilbur Wright at Camp d'Auvours, Le Mans, 1908.

27. Alec Ogilvie, Wilbur Wright and F.G.T. Dawson, June 1911. Loaned by Mrs M.G. Varvill.

28. Alec Ogilvie soaring at Kitty Hawk, 1911.

29. Orville Wright gliding from the hills of Kill Devil. From Griffith Brewer's 'Kill Devil Camp' photograph album.

30. The shed showing the rudder and wing of the 1908 Wright machine. From Griffith Brewer's 'Kill Devil Camp' photograph album.

31. Horace ('Buster'), Orville and Lorin Wright. From Griffith Brewer's 'Kill Devil Camp' photograph album.

32. Description of the Wright Motor in the company brochure 'The Wright Flyer' (Dayton, The Wright Co., 1911).

33. Wilbur Wright inspecting the engine of his Wright A biplane.

34. Glenn Curtiss's reconstruction of Langley's 1903 *Aerodrome* in flight, 1914.

35. Wright Model H. From *Aero Digest*, Vol.67 (1), July 1953.

36. Front cover of brochure for 'The Wright Flying School' (New York: Wright Flying Field Inc., 1916).

37. Riley E. Scott preparing two 18lb bombs to be carried by Captain Thomas Milling in a Wright B at the US Army flying school, Maryland, 11 October 1911.

38. Eugène Lefebvre adjusting his Wright A at Reims, August 1909.

39. A Wright A at Reims, August 1909.

40. Samuel Pierpont Langley.

41. Lord Northcliffe helping to haul the Wright A at Pau, 1909.

42. Loening Air Yacht *Wilbur Wright*. From C.G. Grey (ed.) *All the World's Aircraft* (London, Sampson Low, Marston & Company Ltd, 1923)

BIBLIOGRAPHY

In compiling the introductory notes to the letters included in this volume, reference has been made throughout to the contemporary journals and other aeronautical publications mentioned by the Wrights. In addition, the following secondary sources have also been of assistance.

Aircraft Year Book 1919 (New York, Manufacturers Aircraft Association Inc., 1919)

Angle, G.D. (ed.), *Aerosphere 1939* (New York, Aircraft Publications, 1940)

Barnes, C.H., *Shorts Aircraft since 1900 – Revised edition* (London, Putnam Aeronautical Books, 1989)

Bilstein, R.E., *Orders of Magnitude: a History of the NACA and NASA, 1915–1990* (NASA SP-4406, Washington D.C., National Aeronautics and Space Administration, 1989)

Brewer, G., *Fifty Years of Flying* (London, Air League of the British Empire, 1946)

Casey, L.S., *Curtiss: the Hammondsport Era 1907–1915* (New York, Crown Publishers, Inc., 1981)

Combs, H. & Caidin, M., *Kill Devil Hill: Discovering the Secret of the Wright Brothers* (Englewood, Colorado, TernStyle Press Ltd)

Crouch, T.D., *A Dream of Wings: Americans and the Airplane 1875–1905* (New York, W.W. Norton & Company, 1981)

Crouch, T.D., *The Bishop's Boys: a Life of Wilbur and Orville Wright* (New York, W.W. Norton & Company, 1989)

Driver, H., *The Birth of Military Aviation: Britain, 1903–1914* (Woodbridge, The Boydell Press, 1997)

Gardner, L.D., *Who's Who in American Aeronautics – Second edition* (New York, The Gardner Publishing Co. Inc., 1925)

Gardner, L.D., *Who's Who in American Aeronautics – Third edition* (New York, Aviation Publishing Corporation, 1928)

Gibbs-Smith, C.H., *Aviation – a Historical Survey: from its origins to the end of World War II* (London, HMSO, 1985)

Gibbs-Smith, C.H., *A Directory and Nomenclature of the First Aeroplanes 1809 to 1909* (London, HMSO, 1966)

Gibbs-Smith, C.H., *The Invention of the Aeroplane (1799–1909)* (London, Faber and Faber Limited, 1966)

Gibbs-Smith, C.H., *The Wright Brothers* (London, HMSO, 1987)

Gollin, A., *No Longer an Island: Britain and the Wright Brothers 1902–1909* (London, William Heinemann Ltd, 1984)

Gray, G.W., *Frontiers of Flight: the Story of NACA Research* (New York, Alfred A. Knopf Inc., 1948)

Harris, S., *The First to Fly: America's Pioneer Days* (Blue Ridge Summit, Pennsylvania, TAB/AERO Books, 1991)

Howard, F., *Wilbur and Orville: the Story of the Wright Brothers* (London, Robert Hale Limited, 1988)

Hurren, B.J., *Fellowship of the Air: Jubilee Book of the Royal Aero Club 1901–1951* (London, Illiffe & Sons Ltd, 1951)

Kelly, F.C., *The Wright Brothers* (New York, Harcourt, Brace and Company, 1943)

McFarland, M.V. (ed.), *The Papers of Wilbur and Orville Wright. Volume One: 1899–1905; Volume Two: 1906–1948* (New York, McGraw-Hill Book Company Inc., 1953)

Penrose, H., *British Aviation: the Pioneer Years 1903–1914* (London, Putnam & Company Limited, 1967)

Renstrom, A.G., 'Wright Chronology', *Aero Digest*, Vol.67 (1), July 1953, 152–97.

Renstrom, A.G., *Wilbur & Orville Wright: a Bibliography Commemorating the Hundredth Anniversary of the Birth of Wilbur Wright April 16, 1867* (Washington D.C., Library of Congress, 1968)

Shrader, W.A., *Fifty Years of Flight: a Chronicle of the Aviation Industry in America 1903–1953* (Cleveland, Ohio, Eaton Manufacturing Company, 1953)

Villard, H.S., *Blue Ribbon of the Air: the Gordon Bennett Races* (Washington D.C., Smithsonian Institution Press, 1987)

Walker, L.E. & Wickam, S.E., *From Huffman Prairie to the Moon: the History of Wright-Patterson Air Force Base* (Wright-Patterson AFB, Ohio, The Air Force Logistics Command – Office of History, 1986)

Wright, Bishop Milton, *Diaries 1857–1917* (Dayton, Ohio, Wright State University Libraries, 1999)

Wright Miller, Ivonette, *Wright Reminiscences* (Wright-Patterson AFB, Ohio, The Air Force Museum Foundation Inc., 1978)

INDEX